LEEDS UNITED: TRIALS AND TRIBULATIONS

Phil Rostron

MAINSTREAM
PUBLISHING

EDINBURGH AND LONDON

First published in Great Britain in 2004 by
MAINSTREAM PUBLISHING COMPANY (EDINBURGH) LTD
7 Albany Street
Edinburgh EH1 3UG

ISBN 1 84018 888 X

A catalogue record for this book is available from the British Library

Typeset in Apollo and Hammer
Printed and bound in Great Britain by
Antony Rowe, Chippenham, Wiltshire

For Barghy

ACKNOWLEDGEMENTS

Caroline Rostron and Shirley Whitehead for their painstaking audio-typing skills; Neil Hodgkinson for his unwavering patience; John Woodcock, Rob Waugh, Andrew Vine, Jeremy Cross and David Parkin for their co-operation; Stuart Martel and Paul Dews for their revision; Andy Manning and Steve Riding for their excellence and kindness in the photographic field; Peter Ridsdale, Allan Leighton, Professor John McKenzie, Peter Reid, Adam Pearson, Trevor Birch, Geoffrey Richmond, Dominic Matteo and Peter Lorimer for sparing their time; Jo Rostron, Gary Rostron and Hollie Rostron for understanding that their dad was otherwise engaged.

CONTENTS

FOREWORD

The story of the last three years of Leeds United's history is one of a dramatic fall from grace. Anger, hurt, disillusionment, disbelief, incredulity and a river of tears have all been on open display as the club have plummeted from the euphoria of reaching the Champions League semi-final in 2001 to the heartbreak of relegation from the Premiership in 2004. In that short time, there have been five managers and four chairmen. That is incredible. Top-class players such as Rio Ferdinand, Jonathan Woodgate and Harry Kewell have departed the club and they were joined in the summer of 2004 by the much-loved Alan Smith, who moved to Manchester United. The very fabric of the club has been torn apart by a remarkable series of events and it has now entered a phase of damage-limitation. I have taken a seat on the board and fully intend to play my part in ensuring a period of stability. Goodness knows, that is what Leeds United needs after the bumpiest of rides. Leeds have been relegated before and have bounced back and, however long it takes, I am sure they will once again cross swords with the big boys. Few people have been better placed to tell the harrowing story of this topsy-turvy period in Leeds United's history than *Yorkshire Evening Post* sports editor Phil Rostron, who has lived and breathed every minute of its passage both personally and professionally. For Leeds United fans, this book is a compelling blow-by-blow account of what has happened to their beloved club. For non-Leeds United fans, it is the definitive lesson in how not to run a football club.

Peter Lorimer

INTRODUCTION

My interest in Leeds United began during the Don Revie era, just as it did for many others. I was a great admirer of their exploits and triumphs during this time and was present, as an interested spectator, when a Billy Bremner goal finally settled a titanic three-game FA Cup semi-final in a second replay with Manchester United at Bolton's Burnden Park in 1970.

Then, in the 1980s, Leeds were involved in some fantastic games, seemingly always in one of the cups or the play-offs, with Oldham Athletic, whom I have supported since I was a boy. I was sports editor of the *Daily Star* in London when Leeds won the championship in 1992, and I obtained from Howard Wilkinson, their manager, an extraordinary exclusive based on his techniques. I travelled with Wilkinson to Florence as his guest at UEFA's end-of-season managerial awards ceremony and then, the following season, initiated for the *Daily Star* a prestigious sponsorship of Leeds' European Cup games against Stuttgart and Glasgow Rangers.

So, when I was offered the position of chief sports writer for the Leeds-based *Yorkshire Evening Post* in 1999, covering Leeds United on a daily basis, there wasn't much decision-making to do. It was an enticing scenario. Here was a club definitely on the up, having been deprived of third place in the Premiership the previous season only on goal difference. They would be playing in the UEFA Cup, a championship challenge was a real possibility and their compelling brand of attacking football under the new managerial partnership of

LEEDS UNITED: TRIALS AND TRIBULATIONS

David O'Leary and Eddie Gray already had people up and down the country sitting up and taking notice. When you threw into that mix the fact that the *Yorkshire Evening Post*, with its circulation of 100,000 copies a night, is the Leeds United fans' bible, the scene was set for an exciting odyssey. Come Boxing Day, Leeds, playing to sell-out crowds, had lost just three of their nineteen Premiership matches and had progressed to the fourth round of the UEFA Cup. My early impressions were of a club clearly going places, but with a growing paranoia amongst its ranks. The manager, his coaching staff and many of the players were reluctant to discuss anything of substance and it was left to the chairman, Peter Ridsdale, to carry the media flag. From my perspective, with three pages of club news to produce every day, he became a vital contact and he rarely let me down. He understood, unlike others, how critical was the link between the *Yorkshire Evening Post* and the fans, and he did his best to oblige. I enjoyed our conversations. After a while, he would describe our telephone exchanges as his 'daily game of chess', with me moving in for the next exclusive and he either accommodating the move or putting me in check. But it was usually fun, and Peter's affection and enthusiasm for the club were contagious. We talked of big-money transfers, money-spinning cup runs and sky-high player contracts; of the prospects of a new stadium, of the share price and of new investments. The club was on the crest of a wave, bang on course and always on the telly. Yet, no sooner had the new millennium been ushered in than two events in the space of four months conspired to turn the spotlight on Leeds United for all the wrong reasons. First, in January 2000, the late-night brutal beating of a student in Leeds city centre was shown to have had some of the club's players at or near the scene. Then, in April, when football violence once again reared its ugly head, two of its fans were murdered in the main city square in Istanbul on the eve of the club's UEFA Cup semi-final against Galatasaray. Despite these horrendous occurrences, Leeds secured a place in the Champions League for next season (pending a qualifying match with TSV 1860 Munich) with a third-place finish behind Manchester United and Arsenal and were now, unquestionably, in the big time. That they should go on to reach the semi-final with such a young, inexperienced squad defied all logic and belief, but not only did they do so, they also did it in style, with unlikely victories over such European giants as AC Milan and Lazio.

Surely, then, Leeds were here to stay as a major Premiership and European force for years to come. Certainly, any dissenting voices on that score could not be heard as Leeds packed their side with a host of big-name, big-money signings to load the odds in their favour.

Then the alarm bells started to ring. Despite all their best efforts, Leeds failed by a single point to qualify for a second successive Champions League campaign and the repercussions were so swift, so dramatic and so severe that their fall from glory constitutes one of the most remarkable stories in the history of the Premiership. After covering every match for two seasons, I was promoted to sports editor of the *Yorkshire Evening Post,* now with responsibility for story selection, headline writing and picture projection, and watched incredulously as Leeds lurched from an operating profit of £6.2 million to debts of £104 million; from a Champions League semi-final to relegation; from heroes to villains in the space of three years. How could that happen? The entry and exit of boardroom personnel, managers and players resembled the quick-change artists in the stage wings of some provincial theatre as events at this once-proud club degenerated into pure farce. So who were the villains of this piece? The board? The managers? The players? Prevailing financial climates in the loans market and the transfer market? A combination of these things? This book digs beneath the surface, giving eight of the key individuals at Elland Road during this turbulent period the opportunity to voice their versions of events. To a man, they speak with great candour and no little disappointment about the club's reversal of fortunes. What had begun with such great promise in 1999 became, through a series of adverse circumstances; relegation from the Premiership in 2004 and an uncertain future. The last time they were relegated from the top flight, in 1982, Allan Clarke was the manager, Trevor Cherry was the captain and Arthur Graham and Frank Worthington were joint top scorers. It took eight long years for them to return, as Division Two champions, with Howard Wilkinson at the helm and Gordon Strachan both captain and leading scorer. Within two years, they were champions of England.

So is a similar rebirth a possibility? What I have learned is that with Leeds United you must always expect the unexpected. And what always gives them a chance is that they have arguably the most loyal following in the country.

CHAPTER ONE

WHAT PRICE JIMMY-FLOYD HASSELBAINK?

The burning issue at Leeds United on the hot August day in 1999 that I assumed my role as chief sports writer for the *Yorkshire Evening Post* was the immediate future of iconic striker Jimmy-Floyd Hasselbaink, whose forty-two goals in two seasons at Elland Road had cemented their involvement in European football. Qualification for this facet of the game was critical to a club whose ambitions had become lofty and, having fully played his part, the Dutchman knew his true worth in a buoyant financial market. Hasselbaink, who was brought into the club by George Graham at a bargain-basement £2 million from Portuguese club Boavista, had demanded that his £20,000-a-week wages be doubled and, in the face of a rebuttal, had countered with a transfer request. Many fans who had worshipped at his feet were expressing their displeasure at his stance. David O'Leary, who succeeded Graham as the Leeds United manager, had allowed Hasselbaink to line up as usual in the team picture at the pre-season photocall, which I'd attended. With the formalities over, I interviewed O'Leary in the sanctuary of his office, in the company of his chairman, Peter Ridsdale. O'Leary gave me the following insights:

> You want to know about Jimmy-Floyd Hasselbaink? I'll tell you about Jimmy-Floyd Hasselbaink. When it is realised he is already on the same kind of terms as the Manchester United pair Andy Cole and Dwight Yorke – that they are the reigning champions and he is a similar player – then it is unsurprising

that some people have formed the opinion that he is a greedy sonofabitch. It seems to be the mentality of some foreign players, particularly those of Dutch extraction, that they are entitled to get what they want and sulk when they do not. The player keeps peeling off from the rest of the squad and saying to me, 'Why won't you let me go? I want to leave.' Then he cannot understand it when I say that he will leave the club when we are good and ready, not when he is.

As if to make O'Leary's point for him, the official photocall had taken on comic proportions when Hasselbaink hesitated to join the squad line-up. Then, when the players adopted another formation, he was last by a long way to take his place. The mood in the rest of the squad was markedly different. Their fun and banter showed how well they had moulded and bonded, and belied the impression that O'Leary gave me of his team not being in the running for the League championship. 'I fancy Chelsea to be champions,' he said, 'and they will be closely pressed by Manchester United and Arsenal. If we are within shouting distance of those three we will have every right to feel very pleased.'

Then, there was a bizarre twist. I asked O'Leary if he had any objections to my reporting what he had said in the *Yorkshire Evening Post* and he replied, 'Look, I don't give a damn what you write in the *Yorkshire Evening Post*. It is of no significance to me. I don't care.' I expressed the hope that we could work together in a professional manner and, as he shrugged his shoulders, Ridsdale melted the ice by saying our use of the story would be OK but he would appreciate it if I didn't identify the Manchester United strikers whom O'Leary had cited. O'Leary agreed. He was OK with me mentioning the figures and saying that this would raise his wages to beyond the going rate for the best strikers, but, for some bizarre reason, he reiterated Ridsdale's position of not wanting me to name Yorke and Cole. I went ahead and named them anyway. After all, Manchester United were the champions of the previous season, and not a single football fan in the land would fail to recognise the significance of a comparison with these players. When the story duly appeared with their names in it, the newspaper was informed that I was banned from both the training ground and the stadium. This presented an awkward state of affairs, in that I was 24 hours into a new job, the first match of a new season was four days away and, already, the chairman and the manager had been alienated – all this with the *Yorkshire Evening Post* editor, Neil Hodgkinson, away on business in London.

The newspaper's production editor, Howard Corry, and sports editor, Martin Rose, set up an immediate meeting with Ridsdale at which it was stated that my identifying Cole and Yorke displayed a total disregard for their reasonable request. What had happened, in my view, is that a trap had been set for me. My predecessor at the paper, Don Warters, is a lovely man who, in covering events at Elland Road for 29 years, became known as 'Mr Leeds United'. The story being circulated at Leeds before my arrival was that Don was being replaced by a tabloid hack from London whose brief, at a time when the newspaper was being converted from a broadsheet format to compact, was to spice up coverage of the club. My protests that I was, in fact, from Oldham, and had always had some affection for Leeds United, fell only on deaf ears. I had failed their 'loyalty' test. Fortunately, though, the meeting was a success, and my exclusion was immediately lifted.

Hasselbaink doubled his wages when joining Spanish outfit Atletico Madrid and Leeds received a handsome return on their investment when agreeing a £12 million deal. But the transfer was not allowed to go through quietly, with Hasselbaink's agent, Humphrey Nijman, determined to put his player's point of view across. He told the press at the time:

> Jimmy was willing to stay and sign a new contract, but during the negotiations there were various things which occurred which turned the situation around. It was also never Jimmy's intention to put in a written transfer request. That was the initiative of the club; they more or less demanded it. From the beginning of the negotiations, we had an agreement with Leeds that everything that was said would be kept amongst us. But stories were coming out and that was very disappointing. It made Jimmy's attitude change. It was never about money as many people believe. It was a number of issues which altered the situation. We were very unhappy with the way things went and that's the reason why Jimmy was pretty determined in his decision.

The acrimonious split did not end there. Leeds were soon threatening to haul Hasselbaink back to England over the tardiness of Atletico's release of transfer funds. The Spaniards had promised to pay Leeds an initial sum but, after ten days, the Elland Road club had not received a penny. Curiously, Ridsdale received a fax from Atletico stating the club had sent the first half of the payment three days before the chairman's stance, although no trace of it could be found. Leeds also wanted a bank guarantee for the second instalment, but it appeared Atletico were struggling to pay for the Dutch striker despite agreeing a deal more than two weeks previously. With the closure of the Spanish transfer window looming, Ridsdale warned Atletico that they would be facing a major embarrassment if the money was not paid on time. Leeds still held Hasselbaink's registration and were ready to exercise their legal right by making Hasselbaink return to Elland Road. To make matters worse, Atletico played Hasselbaink in a friendly game against Sporting Lisbon, despite him not being registered. Hasselbaink was also in line to play for Holland in a friendly international and the major concern at Leeds was that, should the player receive a serious injury, Atletico could then pull out of the deal and leave Leeds with a striker who could not play. A furious Ridsdale tried to contact Atletico officials but was hampered by the fact it was a Spanish bank holiday. He told me:

> We still hold his registration and if the payment has not been received by the end of the week we will seriously consider recalling the player. Atletico have more pressure on them than we have over this because they have a transfer window and they want the player's registration. We have done a deal and if a club of their standing cannot deliver the price I would have thought the embarrassment would be far greater for them. The club claim to have transmitted the necessary funds but there is no sign of any money. We also want the bank guarantee.

So why the song and dance? Leeds United were setting out their stall to rekindle the glory days of the Don Revie era, when Jack Charlton, Billy Bremner, Peter Lorimer and company struck fear into the hearts of every opponent and European football at Elland Road was taken for granted. By some considerable margin, the £12 million agreed for

Hasselbaink was a club record, and the incoming funds were absolutely crucial to the new blueprint. The timing of Hasselbaink's departure left O'Leary in the difficult position of having to find a replacement with the new season less than a week away but, despite concentrated efforts to sign a top-quality goal-scorer, both O'Leary and Ridsdale claimed they would not be rushed into parting with big money for the sake of it. O'Leary had been promised the Hasselbaink cash to spend on transfers, with Ridsdale pledging, 'All the money will be made available to David for adding to the squad. It is then up to the manager to tell us who he wants and we will go out and try to get them.' Leeds had already made enquiries about Leicester striker Emile Heskey but the England Under-21 international had only just signed a one-year deal with the Filbert Street club to end speculation about his future. Heskey was to go on to play for Liverpool and England.

It was against this backdrop that Leeds opened their 1999–2000 season with a mind-numbing goalless draw with Derby County in front of a full house of 40,000 at Elland Road – a first taste for me of what life in West Yorkshire may be like. O'Leary concluded that it did not take a rocket scientist to deduce that the number one priority for Leeds was for the £12 million realised by the sale of Hasselbaink to be spent on a replacement striker, and after the post-match press conference I followed the hastily departing manager towards his office in the hope of repairing some of the damage already done on a personal level. As I called after him, he picked up speed and, without a backward glance, slammed the door shut. Four days later, Leeds travelled to Southampton and, courtesy of a virtuoso performance from Michael Bridges, ran out easy 3–0 winners. Bridges, bought in the summer from Sunderland for £5 million, scored a classy hat-trick and had another good-looking goal ruled out in a display which suggested that O'Leary had a ready-made Hasselbaink replacement right under his nose. Subsequent events contrived against the likeable Geordie, though, and a wretched run of injuries ruined a Leeds career that ended early in 2004 with a loan move to Sir Bobby Robson's Newcastle and, in time for the 2004–05 season, a permanent switch to Bolton.

O'Leary was in a black mood and delivered a withering condemnation of his players after a sickening 2–1 defeat at the hands of Liverpool at Elland Road 16 days after the Southampton romp. United were outplayed, outfought and outmanoeuvred by a

Merseyside outfit whose start to the season had been so poor that their manager, Gerard Houllier, was installed on the eve of the match as the bookies' odds-on favourite to be first in the Premiership 'sack race'. O'Leary was not happy:

> It was the single worst performance since I have been here. Sometimes you get one or two players who have an off day and their shortcomings are covered by extra efforts from their colleagues. But not the whole team. I have delivered a few home truths to some of the players. I am trying to be honest with them, but they know anyway. We didn't pass a ball, we were poor at the back and we allowed them to run midfield. And if a team of mine does not pass the ball then it is up the creek. Liverpool set their stalls out and ran the game, with Jamie Redknapp outstanding. They have a lot of good players and we made them look even better than they are.

Then, an observation by O'Leary which was to typify his stance throughout his four years at the helm:

> Some people thought we would just turn up tonight and it would be part of the process of winning the League. The facts are that the whole team was bad and everything about their performance was poor, but it will bring some people both inside and outside of the club down to earth. I have said all along that we will not win the League this season – it will rest between Manchester United, Arsenal and Chelsea – and we will have to wait one, two, maybe three years before we are in a position to make a serious challenge. My team are mostly kids and they are still learning. Some good may come of this in the long run. Until now, we have been playing quite well this season but sometimes it is much harder at home than it is away. What we have got to do is to adopt the attitude that if we compete and are hungry and want to win the battle then the niceties of the game will naturally follow.

In contrast to this, Houllier said, 'We have beaten a contender for the title in Leeds and it takes a good performance to achieve that.'

These comments made important statements about Leeds United and their standing in the English game and also about the man charged with delivering results that would meet the ambitions of the boardroom. Here we had a highly experienced manager in Houllier openly recognising the West Yorkshire outfit as a genuine championship challenger and O'Leary himself steadfastly dismissing such a notion. It was, however, the manner of O'Leary's denial which spoke volumes. 'Look,' he would say on numerous occasions throughout a season which was finally to deliver Champions League football, 'I'm just a naive young manager and my players are only babies.' The level of expectation in the city of Leeds and throughout the game was a big burden for O'Leary to shoulder and he was keen to pour cold water over it at every opportunity. This was never going to be easy for him, though. Having finished 4th, just 12 points behind Premiership champions Manchester United in the 1998–99 season, it was natural for the club's vast army of fans to expect an all-out assault on the honours board this time around.

O'Leary was assisted in this, at least, by a cash injection at the club. While they were still deliberating over the sale of Hasselbaink, Leeds were negotiating their way to another major source of income. United joined the financial elite of the world's football clubs with an £8 million payment from Sky Television, with the money going straight into the transfer pot. The BSkyB deal was fostered when the TV giant was in negotiation with Leeds over coverage of their UEFA Cup matches and Vic Wakeling, managing director of Sky Sports, observed:

> There lies a natural alliance between media companies and sports clubs and we can bring a certain expertise in promotion and marketing of the club and securing worldwide contracts. Leeds do not have television rights of their own and the Premiership contract with IMG runs out in two years' time. We will be working with the club to explore all the avenues to increase revenue which will be manifested, as far as the fans are concerned, in the quality of players out on the pitch. There has been an immediate strengthening of David O'Leary's hands in the transfer market. From our perspective, we will not be interfering in the running of the club save the appointment and

input of a non-executive director on the board. We are here to support and help the club.

Ridsdale, delighted by the deal, said:

> I was very upset during George Graham's time here when he made it plain that he thought we were not one of the big guns, had no ambition or desire to compete and had no intention of heading for the big time. There were other managers in the same category and they will have learned today just how ambitious this club is. I think this is a tremendous development for the club, its shareholders, the manager and the fans and will give us a global presence. It demonstrates to the entire world of football that we wish to be among the Premiership elite and we now have the opportunity to go right to the top. In the short term, it does not change the manager's desire to replace Hasselbaink, but neither does it alter the fact that we must wait until the right man becomes available. The only thing is that this newly acquired wealth will undoubtedly put up the price we're capable of paying for any target.

O'Leary said:

> I have just learned of the deal and the immediate reaction is to wonder what to do with £8 million. I should perhaps invest it in a few diamonds! The diamonds I am after are unfortunately not available, probably until the end of the season. OK, you could buy any striker in the world for that kind of money but I am not going to go out and pay that for one player. It would not be right for this club. I am prepared to simply bide my time.

In keeping with this, O'Leary spent the money – along with the Hasselbaink transfer fee, once it eventually arrived – on Darren Huckerby, Danny Mills, Michael Duberry, Eirik Bakke and Jason Wilcox.

The deal confirming Leeds' position among football's elite was in stark contrast to the club's humble beginnings. Such a rise to the game's pinnacle must have seemed a pipe dream to many people back in 1919, when the club was formed following the demise of Leeds City. Leeds' first professional football club was kicked out of the Football League amid one of the game's first 'bung' scandals. City were accused of making illegal payments to players during the First World War, a period when the Football League ruled that professional players should be paid expenses only. Bosses at the League and the Football Association set up an inquiry team to investigate the issue. When City failed to hand over the club's books and documents to the inquiry team, it was expelled from the Football League. Leeds City's whole squad was sold by auction at the Metropole Hotel for a pittance. Soccer supporters were determined Leeds should have a professional football club and United were formed in the autumn of 1919. The club played at first in the Midland League and at the end of the 1919–20 season was elected to Division Two of the Football League. The club then enjoyed – or possibly endured – a rather undistinguished record. The 1950s were enlivened by the arrival of Major Frank Buckley – a colourful manager said to boost the performances of the various teams he commandeered by giving his players a 'monkey gland' potion to make them fitter – and the emergence of John Charles, who went on to become one of the greatest players of his generation. Real success came in the 1960s and '70s under Don Revie, who joined the club as player–manager in 1961. The side, led by skipper Billy Bremner, became one of the finest in Europe, lifting two Division One championships, two UEFA Cups (formerly the Fairs Cup), the FA Cup and the Football League Cup. The team transformed United into one of football's big clubs and also helped to promote the city of Leeds across Europe. If the 1970s were the glory days, the 1980s were the gory days. Leeds United were relegated in 1982 and did not get back to the top flight until 1990. Major changes on the pitch helped the club lift the First Division title in 1992, while major changes off the pitch were occurring throughout the 1990s. A major restructuring in the mid-'90s left former directors Leslie Silver, Peter Gilman and Bill Fotherby each holding 35,000 influential and, as it turned out, lucrative 'management shares'. When, in the summer of 1996, the club was sold to the London-based media group Caspian for £35 million, those shares earned Silver, Gilman and Fotherby a tidy sum. In 1997, Caspian changed its name to Leeds Sporting. It also bought back the Elland Road stadium from Leeds City Council – the club had been forced to sell it in 1985 to pay off its debts – and drew up plans for a sports and entertainment arena to be built alongside the stadium. This, however, has never materialised.

By 2000, O'Leary's new signings were being joined by a horde of youngsters who had now come through the ranks, in the form of Harry Kewell, Jonathan Woodgate, Stephen McPhail and the all-action midfielder Lee Bowyer, who had realised a record transfer fee for a teenager when brought into Leeds by Howard Wilkinson from Charlton.

Only time would reveal the wisdom of O'Leary's investments and the strength of his new team. What was entirely evident was that if there were one aspect of football club management in which O'Leary badly needed some tuition, it was in his handling of the media. From my own perspective, on three occasions in those early days I sought permission to enter the club's training facility at Thorp Arch, near Wetherby, and turned up at the security gate to be greeted by its steward, Jack 'The Rottweiler' Williamson, with a message that the manager had changed his mind about allowing me entry because of some innocuous passage that I had written that was now presented to me with the offending paragraph(s) highlighted by marker pen. Such was the paranoia pervading Thorp Arch and Elland Road that Jack himself, having agreed to do a profile piece with me for our sister Sunday paper *Yorkshire Sport,* rang my office an hour before our arranged meeting time to say that he was unable to proceed. 'I have taken legal advice,' he said 'and I've been told not to do the interview.'

Legal advice? On a soft profile? I concluded that here was a club with an attitude problem. We all wanted them to do well – let's face it, if a big-city club is doing well then so is its leading newspaper – yet, from within, if an obstacle could be put in your way then it was. Requests for player interviews, for instance, were regularly met with a cavalier rejection. I am eternally grateful in this regard to the admirable striker Michael Bridges, who broke the mould to suggest that we carry out a profile piece at his home just a few miles from the training ground. We spent an hour discussing a wide variety of subjects over tea and biscuits in his sumptuously furnished lounge and when it was time for me to go he waved me off laughing, 'Make sure your final paragraph is, "And he makes a lovely cup of tea!"'

If I was being given the runaround, worse was to follow. Leeds' first game in the 1999–2000 UEFA Cup was against Partizan Belgrade – an away fixture for which a neutral ground had to be found because of the war in Yugoslavia. The choice was the Abe Lenstra Stadium – a tidy, tiny stadium belonging to the Dutch team Heerenveen, who had been making giant strides in their League. The atmosphere at Leeds/Bradford airport on the morning of departure was electric. Media representatives and corporate travellers mingled at the check-in with players and the management team and, with Leeds embarking on a European adventure, eager hacks and radio and television crews went in robust search of the interviews which would let the world know that the club was revelling in the big time. On the aeroplane, a delay in take-off on the grounds that we had missed our air traffic control slot was announced and, while nobody else really cared, the manager appeared distinctly unamused. It was to be the first and last time that the media and corporate guests were to be allowed to travel with the club party, with O'Leary blaming the media scrum for a belated departure, which he claimed disrupted his match preparations. We were greeted at the Dutch stadium by a group of Yugoslav exiles whose most potent insult was a chanted, 'Tony Blair's a homosexual,' and so inconvenienced had O'Leary and his team been that they ran out easy 3–1 winners, with two goals from Bowyer and a rare and much-celebrated goal from captain Lucas Radebe, which went in off his backside.

Premiership wins over Middlesbrough and Newcastle preceded the second leg at Elland Road to give the League table a healthy look from Leeds' point of view and now, in the build-up to the return with the Yugoslavs, O'Leary jumped aboard another hobby horse. He branded the UEFA Cup a 'joke' of a competition, stating his unhappiness with a format which allowed those teams competing in the Champions League who finish third in their group to join the UEFA Cup at the third-round stage. O'Leary described the situation as an 'absolute farce' and said:

> I think Europe and the competition we're in is a joke. We've drawn a team in Partizan who should have been in the Champions League and if we reach the third round we've loads more teams from that competition coming into the UEFA Cup. It sounds to me like UEFA want certain teams to keep winning

these European tournaments. It's like saying to them, 'If you don't do well in the Champions League, there's something you can go and dominate.' I think when you start a season and you're in a competition, you don't fall out of one and into another. It's an absolute joke of the highest order.

UEFA were hardly top of O'Leary's Christmas card list. A fortnight previously, the Irishman had criticised European football's governing body over their handling of the situation regarding the neutral venue for Leeds' encounter with Partizan. After finally deciding the game could not be played in Belgrade, UEFA announced the Dutch venue just a few days before the tie – and brought the game forward by 48 hours. Yet, in view of news imparted just then by Peter Ridsdale, perhaps O'Leary should have been more content with life. Bowyer, whose impressive start to the season had pushed him closer to full international honours, became the last first-team player to agree a long-term deal – this one until 2005 – and Ridsdale declared, 'All the players have now signed long-term contracts and we can look forward to the future with huge optimism.'

Leeds had beaten Tottenham and Newcastle and recorded a splendid away win at Chelsea, and in our interview two days before Christmas 1999, with Leeds on the crest of a wave, there was no doubting Ridsdale's admiration for O'Leary:

> The most important appointment in any football club is the manager and there are plenty of examples of clubs who have got that wrong and are forced to change their manager two or three times in quick succession. Therefore, the disappointment, from our perspective, that George Graham decided to go back to London when he did had to be put behind us, and the appointment of the right manager had to be the most critical decision that I have faced as chairman. We took a bit of time. There was a very short short-list of candidates. It was only ever three and then very quickly down to two and David was the first we approached. He said he did not want the job, so we sought to talk to others including, in particular, Martin O'Neill. We were not able to have that opportunity and so we talked again to David at great length and the real value we had was

that he had the opportunity to demonstrate to us what he could do out of George's shadow. The qualities which shone through very quickly have become even more evident as time has gone on. I think that brilliant managers, whether it be inside or outside of football, have the ability to recognise what motivates different individuals as opposed to a single style. Some people, those I would call the Brian Cloughs of this world, have a single style and his was a fear factor which worked only with some players. But I think in today's game you need to know who and when to kick and who and when to stroke. You remonstrate with them one minute and the next you pick them up. David has that ability in abundance. Sometimes, after a great victory, I go down to the dressing room to congratulate them and I have to wait outside because he is giving them a rollicking about one aspect or other of the game. I will be thinking it has been a fine performance, but David can see the things he wants players to improve upon. He is a perfectionist.

A Boxing Day defeat of Leicester made it 14 wins from 19 Premiership games and when Leeds, looking like they would score with every attack, poleaxed Manchester City 5–2 at Maine Road in the fourth round of the FA Cup in January, everything looked set fair for a hugely successful season for a team which was capturing the imagination of the nation with a brand of attacking football which was pleasing to the eye, exciting and compelling. Two major events in the first four months of the year 2000, however – one of which drew opprobrium from much of the public, while the other, conversely, was largely met with support and compassion from fans and non-fans alike – were to destroy their equilibrium.

CHAPTER TWO

A NIGHT OF SHAME

The destruction of Manchester City signalled a two-week break for the Leeds United players and, on the evening of 11 January 2000, a party atmosphere prevailed in the bars of Boar Lane in Leeds city centre. It was student night at the Majestyk nightclub. Drinks were cheap and young people, fresh from the Christmas and New Year break, made their way towards it. Among them, some young Leeds United stars were enjoying the unexpected few days' grace between games. A match against Manchester United had been cancelled because the Old Trafford outfit had gone to Brazil for the World Club Championships, and with time out from training the players were determined to make the most of their freedom. England international Jonathan Woodgate, a few days short of his 20th birthday, paid for two rooms at the four-star Marriott Hotel in Boar Lane, and invited four old friends from Middlesbrough (who weren't professional footballers) to join him — Paul Clifford, Neale Caveney, James Hewison and Anthony Robinson. From the outset, his group was in high spirits, throwing back pint-glass cocktails of vodka-based Mule and Bacardi Breezers. Their pub crawl started at the Square on the Lane, where they met up with reserve team players Anthony Hackworth, Brian McCrystal and other junior players. Together, they went to lap-dancing club DV8, where Woodgate paid £5 for each of them to get in. Woodgate's group then made their way to Yates's Wine Lodge, where it was karaoke night. Finally, they stopped off at the Observatory, before walking across City Square to the Majestyk, where they were granted free VIP entry. Lee

Bowyer, meanwhile, had stayed in drinking wine with fellow players Michael Bridges and Harry Kewell before heading into town and meeting the other two groups in the nightclub's VIP lounge. Michael Duberry, who had been playing a reserve match in Liverpool, arrived at the Majestyk later on. As the pubs closed, the nightclub filled up. Among the student throng was Sarfraz Najeib, his brother Shazhad and three friends. As Muslims, they did not drink, but the brothers had gone to the student night to listen to music as they had neither a TV nor a stereo in their rented student house in Burley, Leeds. It was in the early hours of Wednesday morning when the Najeibs, who had lectures in the morning, decided to leave. Upstairs in the VIP lounge, Woodgate's friend James Hewison was drunk and looking for trouble. Clubber David Sheridan was to tell a court how Hewison stared aggressively at him before walking over holding an empty bottle by the neck. 'As he got within a few feet, the person he had been speaking to ran over to him and jumped on him from behind and wrestled him to the floor,' he said. 'Jonathan Woodgate then came over and had a word with our group, saying something along the lines of, "It's all right. There will be no trouble."' It wasn't long before Hewison was ejected, and, when word filtered through to Woodgate, he and the others left to find out what was going on. In an unfortunate coincidence, the Najeibs left the club around the same time and were standing outside when they saw Woodgate trying to calm down Hewison. There was contrasting evidence at the subsequent trial as to what happened next, but Majestyk doorman Graeme Lawson told the court the Asian group 'began to take the mickey', which angered Hewison, who confronted them. Within seconds, a scuffle had broken out and Sarfraz, who was knocked to the ground by a blow to the back of his head, attempted to retaliate. The Asians then ran off, chased by Woodgate's group. Bowyer admitted to police he had followed Woodgate down Boar Lane, saying he thought they were going to the same lap-dancing club that some of the group had been to earlier, but he denied being in Mill Hill, where the beating took place, or taking part in the attack. Hewison, who had been among the chasers, did not get very far before he became involved in another incident. As a result, he played no part in the attack on Sarfraz. The Asians fled through City Square, along Boar Lane and turned into Mill Hill, where their car was parked. Sarfraz, who had been lagging behind and whose shoes were slipping on the wet pavement, was tripped and fell forcefully against a wall. Then he was set upon in a ferocious attack in which he was punched and kicked repeatedly about the face, head and body. Even when he fell unconscious, the beating continued. Sarfraz suffered a smashed nose, a fractured cheek and a broken leg. He was also bitten by Clifford on his right cheek. A female witness described how the attacker who bit Sarfraz's face shook it from side to side 'like a dog'. Shazhad, who had tried to defend Sarfraz but was punched to the ground, feared his brother was dead as his bloodied body lay motionless on the pavement. Shazhad said he could see blood on his brother's face and pleaded with the attackers to stop. 'I repeated several times, "Stop, leave him, stop, he's had enough."' The jury disbelieved a witness who told the trial he saw Woodgate jump with both feet on Sarfraz's body. One of the Najeibs' friends dashed into a takeaway at the bottom of Mill Hill and asked staff to call the police. Ali Mercan, owner of the Hot Stuff takeaway, said, 'I heard screaming and went out to the middle of the traffic island, took out my phone and called 999. There was something on the floor, with four or five people around. They were pushing, punching, kicking, I couldn't see what.' Since Mr Mercan and his colleagues provided police with witness statements, they have had to have security cameras fitted at their shops. Another witness, Simon Cook, who also worked at Hot Stuff, said:

> An Asian guy came into the shop and screamed, 'There's a fight, there's a fight – ring the police.' We ran outside and saw a group of three or four Asian lads. One was on the floor getting kicked. Eventually, they all stopped and ran off. It was very, very bad. It was barbaric.

Mr Cook said he and his colleagues helped the youth as he lay on the ground, surrounded by his friends, some of whom were crying. 'There was blood coming out of his mouth and head. He was unconscious and he must have been unconscious when they were kicking him. I thought he was dead.' The assault was over in a matter of minutes and Woodgate, Clifford and Caveney began to make their way back to the club. Each of the accused denied they played any part in the attack: Woodgate saying he had followed his friends up Boar Lane to see what was going on but fell and hurt his ankle. Back at the Majestyk, Bowyer was allowed re-entry but Woodgate and his friends were turned away because of Hewison's earlier behaviour. Eventually, Michael Duberry left the club and drove Woodgate and his friends in his Range Rover back to his home in Woodlesford on the outskirts of the city. Hewison was reportedly sick in the car. Bowyer went back to his home near Wetherby in Brian McCrystal's car, along with Michael Bridges and Anthony Hackworth. It was the prosecution's case that those who went to Duberry's house, where Clifford was given a tracksuit of Duberry's to wear, were involved in an agreement to cover their tracks – which meant Clifford's clothes, for example, were not available for later forensic tests. The jury rejected this claim and cleared Duberry, Woodgate, Clifford and Caveney of conspiracy to pervert the course of justice. Taxis later took Woodgate and his friends back to the Marriott Hotel. In the weeks that followed, the players were arrested and charged. Anthony Hackworth was among them, accused of affray and grievous bodily harm with intent. But the trial was offered no evidence to implicate him in the attack and he was cleared of all charges on the direction of the judge.

Meanwhile, despite constant interruptions to training schedules from solicitors and barristers connected with the trial, which was due to take place at Hull Crown Court, Leeds continued with their twin goals of winning the UEFA Cup and achieving a top-three finish in the League. As much as events in court were rocking the club, there was still a football season to be played, and expectations from fans and the boardroom were high. In mid-February, United were soon to go head-to-head with Manchester United at Old Trafford, and after speaking to both managers I wrote in the *Yorkshire Evening Post*:

> There is little doubt that once the mighty Sir Alex Ferguson decides to vacate the managerial hot seat at Manchester United one name very much in the frame as his successor will be that of Leeds United boss David O'Leary. Judging by the start he has made to his managerial career, O'Leary is promising to be every bit as successful in leadership as he was in an exemplary playing span both at club and at international level. Not that O'Leary will go seeking the Old Trafford job. Not only is he very settled in Yorkshire in both working and domestic

environments, he is acutely aware that the man who takes over from Ferguson is on a hiding to nothing. Acts to follow do not come much tougher than the knighted one and there exists a strong argument that it would be better and more rewarding to stay and build upon the foundations he has laid as a young manager than to move and put himself at the mercy of unwavering demands for success in Manchester. Regardless of what the future might hold, a mutual appreciation society has been formed between Ferguson and O'Leary, and whenever one speaks about the other it is always in nothing less than glowing terms. Says Fergie:

From the day that Leeds beat Manchester United in the final of the FA Youth Cup seven years ago, I have had them marked down as the club we would have to keep looking over our shoulders at to see how quickly they were coming up on the rails. That victory was always going to be the start of something big and it is down to the courage of David O'Leary that success is now coming their way. They have led the Premiership for long periods of this season, they are doing better than some people imagined might be the case in the UEFA Cup and they have done so with an exciting brand of football created with plenty of youngsters in the team. It is all very well having a good crop of youngsters in the youth and reserve teams but one of the most critical tests for a manager is the timing of his introduction to the first-team squad of those teenagers. More than that, it is how he then develops the careers of these individuals within the senior squad. David seems to have the knack of knowing when a youngster is ready to be blooded, reasoning that if they are good enough, they are old enough, but he has been brave in handing them the shirt. Some managers would hesitate to do that, delaying the take-off point for perhaps too long through a fear that failure on the pitch would be a bad reflection on them off it. So it's hats off to David, who will be a big name in football management for many years to come.

O'Leary, in turn, finds Ferguson's achievements 'awesome . . . almost beyond belief'. He says:

> *Manchester United are the best team in the country, indeed the world, and they are where they have every right to be – at the top of the Premiership – with everybody giving what they hope will not be a forlorn chase. One thing I'd never do is get into a pre-match sparring session with Alex, because he's a wise owl who has been there, done it and is a past master at every facet of the game, and I'm young, naive and on a learning curve. But I do believe that we're going the right way. It won't be too long now before we're kicking Manchester United's backsides; maybe next season, maybe the season after that. Our bunch of kids have got everything except the one thing that only time can cultivate – experience. When they have that collectively, Leeds United can be a giant of a club again.*

Like Ferguson, O'Leary adopted from day one in the Leeds job a policy of setting out to win every match home and away. It reaped the rich rewards of fourth spot in the Premiership and a place in this season's UEFA Cup in his first six months and, realistic about his prospects of taking the title from United in only his second season, he maintains:

> *Going into the year 2000 was all about consolidating, with the target being a top-three place which would qualify us for the Champions League. If the championship were to come along then that would be very nice and we wouldn't be embarrassed to take it, but finishing third would represent good progress while another fourth, reinforcing our big-club status, would be no disaster.*

O'Leary thought long and hard about his line-up for the first of the season's clashes with Manchester United at Old Trafford back in August and decided that throwing the kitchen sink at them with a bold attacking policy might bring the desired result. With

70 minutes on the clock, and the deadlock still to be broken, it was Leeds who had the more cause to feel aggrieved that they had not plundered a lead, even an unassailable one. They were not the first team, and nor will they be the last, to leave the fortress with regrets about what happened in the later stages of the game, with Dwight Yorke cashing in on momentary lapses in defence to bag a brace. There may be the odd defeat down the line, and this was one of them, but O'Leary's penchant for bright, flowing, attacking football has endeared him not only to the Elland Road faithful but to millions of neutral fans up and down the country. 'Even supporters not attached to this club tell me that they have adopted Leeds as their second team,' says O'Leary, 'and that is very satisfying.' Many of those neutrals will be hoping for a Leeds win to give some added pep to the title run-in and O'Leary says, 'If we don't, it will certainly not be for the lack of trying.'

In fact, Leeds were to lose to the only goal of the Manchester United game on 20 February 2000, but in European competition it was just getting better and better. An excellent performance in holding Italian aces Roma to a goalless draw in the fourth round first leg at the Olympic Stadium raised their hopes and they cashed in with a single-goal victory in the return. A 4–2 aggregate defeat of Slavia Prague guaranteed a semi-final showdown with the notorious Turkish outfit Galatasaray, and the moment the draw was made there were instant recollections of previous encounters with British opposition which had brought big trouble. Not for nothing had it become customary for Galatasaray's fanatical supporters to parade 'Welcome to Hell' banners at the airport for all English visitors to see, and it was with much trepidation, on 5 April 2000, that the media pack and corporate travellers boarded the flight to Istanbul.

It had become a habit for me and my fellow reporters on these European trips to enjoy a meal together once our daily work was out of the way, and our first night in Istanbul was no exception. A quartet comprising the *Yorkshire Post*'s Jeremy Cross, the Press Association's Ian Parkes, the Leeds United official website editor Chris Bargh and myself dined at the Han restaurant, not far from Taksim Square, a bustling quarter of the city and a magnet for its youth.

As friends do, we talked and laughed at our table outside in the warm night air in an atmosphere lightened by our celebration of the fact that expected trouble had not materialised and we were able to breathe more easily.

We spoke too soon. Unable to attract the attention of the waiters, I went inside and engaged in conversation with the Han's night manager, Umit Kilic. When I told him that we were journalists, he beckoned me into a back room, saying, 'You had better look at this.' Incredibly, live pictures were being shown on television of an affray in the Square, with ambulances in attendance. And what followed was a night which can never be erased from the memories of anybody who was there. Two stabbings had occurred and, after the mêlée, police said that 13 Turks had been arrested, a number of Leeds fans had been deported from Turkey and 40 British fans had been detained. In one of the worst nights of football violence for years, Christopher Loftus, 37, and Kevin Speight, 40, both from Leeds, were killed and another fan was left seriously ill in hospital with knife wounds. Mr Loftus' brother Darren identified his body in hospital with Leeds chairman Peter Ridsdale at his side. Mr Speight, who was landlord of the Bay Horse pub in the Farsley district of Leeds, died on the operating table. While tributes were pouring in from close friends, UEFA were deliberating whether or not the match should go ahead. Explaining the difficult decision that the match would indeed be played, Ridsdale said:

> We had three options. The first was for the match not to be played, ever, because of a withdrawal by ourselves from the competition. The second was to reschedule the game, which would have led to an impossible situation through heightened tension, and the third was to go ahead and play. It is UEFA's view that the match should go ahead tonight and we accept that. This is a tragedy. One minute I was talking to Galatasaray directors to promote the friendship between the two clubs, and the next minute I received a call telling me a fan had been killed. It is something that will live with me forever.

The match atmosphere was chilling. In stark contrast to the Galatasaray supporters, the mourning of their pals meant that the Leeds fans could barely raise the United 'Marching On Together' anthem. When the United players emerged for their warm-up routine, their recognition of the supporters was lengthy, animated and heartfelt. A woman announced in English over the Tannoy that Galatasaray regretted what had happened in that wretched city square and hoped that the match would be played in a true sporting spirit. In the absence of an official minute's silence, the United faithful conducted their own, arms raised aloft and backs turned to the pitch in a demonstration of their feelings that this match should not have taken place. For what is football compared to death? What is the taking of kicks in relation to the taking of lives? The game went ahead against a backcloth of a home support so fanatical that it was truly frightening in its intensity. Galatasaray won 2–0. The media pack were whisked to the airport and all formalities were dispensed with as our coach drove straight onto the tarmac to within yards of the plane, which was to deliver us from that awful evening. A uniformed man introduced himself to me as the terminal manager, proffered a bouquet and pleaded that we should not leave with a bad overall impression of Galatasaray, Istanbul and Turkey, in spite of what had happened. The Leeds contingent, though, had left to watch a football match and returned two men short. That was a bad overall impression.

In the next day's edition of the *Yorkshire Evening Post,* I wrote:

> An hour before kick-off, Leeds United goalkeepers Nigel Martyn and Paul Robinson, accompanied by their coach Steve Sutton, made their way onto the Ali Sami Yen pitch for warm-up exercises and, right on cue, the heavens opened on a warm Istanbul night. They entered the arena known as The Hell in a crescendo of derision and the rain cascaded down as angels' tears, wept openly and piteously for events of the previous 24 hours. They dried almost as soon as they had fallen and now we wondered what might happen before the completion of an exercise in futility. A UEFA Cup semi-final it may have been. But so what? As the thousands of red and yellow Galatasaray faithful bobbed up and down to their own creation of a wall of sound, the bodies of two Leeds United supporters, callously murdered in a city street so chillingly recently, had turned cold. The cutting down in their prime of Christopher Loftus and Kevin Speight, a world away from home in the pursuit they

loved best, sparked the biggest security operation in the history of this competition and what this entailed was not in the name of football. It was all in the cause of human frailty, misery, hopelessness; our propensity for conflict. Four police vehicles, two at the front and two at the rear, escorted our media bus to the stadium, red and blue lights whirring constantly. The team bus had the same shield and when we arrived at the dilapidated stadium, we may have been entering a war zone. Armoured tanks lined up alongside awesome vehicles bearing water cannons, their occupants grim-faced and primed for any eventuality. Baying mobs uncomfortably close to either side of our coaches chanted, pointed and gestured threateningly, with facial expressions which could not be mistaken for anything but hatred. Eight ranks of guards separated Galatasaray fans from those of Leeds in a grossly exaggerated show of strength. What had they expected? Revenge?

There was little appetite, either, for the second leg at Elland Road a fortnight later. Although Leeds conjured a 2–2 draw, courtesy of a brace from Eirik Bakke, the two-goal deficit from Istanbul presented an insurmountable task, and Leeds were out of the UEFA Cup.

After mid-March 2000, Leeds were to win only two of their last nine Premiership matches, but a final-day goalless draw at West Ham saw them limp into the Champions League qualifying round with a third-place finish just ahead of Liverpool. The 1999–2000 season had been a bad one for Leeds in many ways, but perhaps the team's performance up to the UEFA Cup semi-finals and the prospect of Champions League football were signs that the club's fortunes were about to change for the better.

CHAPTER THREE

HIGH FINANCE

Before their participation in the Champions League could be confirmed, Leeds had to prevail in a two-leg qualifier against the German outfit TSV 1860 Munich. This they achieved with little fuss in August 2000, winning both home and away legs for a 3–1 aggregate victory. The months ahead now promised great rewards. Champions League football would require large amounts of funding if Leeds were to have a good chance of success, but it was a lucrative arena which would hopefully pay dividends. Accordingly, the start of the 2000–01 season saw major changes in the state of Leeds' finances.

Leeds' turnover of £41 million in the half year to 31 December 2000 had been highly impressive, not only because it beat the previous half year's £24.6 million but because it was higher than the full-year figure of £37 million in 1998–99 – the season in which David O'Leary took over from George Graham as Leeds United manager. Everything, then, appeared on the up at Leeds Sporting – gate receipts, TV income, merchandising and commercial income from areas like sponsorship. The only problem was the bottom-line profit, which was going in the opposite direction because of player costs. Operating profits before amortisation of players – the cost of signing them spread over the length of their contracts – were up to a record £6.2 million, compared to £2.3 million previously. However, the shares barely shifted from their 12-month lows, with pre-tax profits falling to £900,000 from £2.5 million. Leeds signed four players in the period – Rio Ferdinand, Olivier Dacourt, Mark Viduka and Dominic Matteo. Amortisation and the thorny issue of spiralling wages meant the club and the company had to run very hard if they were to make progress. Payroll costs climbed 59 per cent to £19 million from £12 million, taking a bite out of operating performance. Bonuses for performance in Europe accounted for £2.4 million, and valued players like Harry Kewell and Nigel Martyn were signed on improved contracts. So was David O'Leary. Because revenues were so buoyant, the company was able to point to an improvement in the key measure of wage costs as a percentage of sales. This was 46.4 per cent against 48.7 per cent previously. According to chairman Peter Ridsdale, only three clubs fall below the 50 per cent benchmark – Leeds, Aston Villa and the inevitable Manchester United. Amortisation was up to £6.1 million from £4 million and player sales raked in just £1.5 million, compared with £5 million in the previous half year. The shares were up 0.75p to 12p apiece – off their 12-month low of 10p but still well adrift of their high of 29.5p. They floated at 18p in 1996. Ridsdale preferred to concentrate on an operating performance driven by the club's success in Europe and the boost to sponsorship given by deals with Nike and Strongbow. Gate receipts in the half rose 26 per cent to £7.7 million from £6.1 million, due mainly to early stage Champions League fixtures. There would be a bigger bonus in the second half with the run to the semi-finals taken into account. Average Premier League attendances were clipped to 38,993 from 39,044. TV income was also driven by involvement in Europe, plus improved terms from BSkyB. It rose to £15.9 million from £7 million. Merchandising was up by £1.4 million to £4.1 million as a new city centre store was opened and fans flocked to buy the new Nike home and away shirts. Commercial income was £13.4 million against £8.8 million. That, however, was as good as it got. The next three years were to see an operating profit of a record £6.2 million plummet to debts of £104 million, and that is spectacular by any standards. So where did it all go? On players, basically. A shop-till-you-drop spending spree between 1999 and 2001 saw the arrivals at Elland Road of Eirik Bakke (£1.75 million), Danny Mills (£4 million), Michael Duberry (£4.5 million), Michael Bridges (£5 million), Jason Wilcox (£3 million), Olivier Dacourt (£7.2 million), Mark Viduka (£6 million), Dominic Matteo (£4.25 million), Rio Ferdinand (£18 million), Robbie Keane (£11 million), Seth Johnson (£7 million) and Robbie Fowler (£11 million). That little lot comes to a staggering total of £82.7 million. How on earth do you fund that? The Leeds answer was to find credit facilities. The club bank, HSBC, was already facilitating an £11 million debt when it signalled its willingness to offer overdraft facilities beyond that, though with conditions concerning the repayment period. Holding such grand-scale ambitions, the club was forced to look elsewhere for top-up funds and found its provider in the former Manchester City footballer Ray Ranson.

In the days when footballers earned wages which made them no more than comfortable, it was not unusual for them to indulge in activities which would bring in a second income. Ranson's sideline, while he was still playing, was running his own insurance business. Having sold it when he stopped playing, he linked up with a City-based finance house and began specialising in sport and its insurance needs. Then, in 1999, Ranson took his funding ideas to Ridsdale, who was quick to respond when the door was closed on another finance option he had been exploring.

There was a determination to reduce the club's overdraft and Ranson's *modus operandi* was to operate on sale and leaseback deals in which, when Leeds wanted to buy a player, Ranson would find a financial institution that would advance the club precisely the sum of the transfer. This involved Leeds having to pay back the money, with interest, over the course of the player's contract and could reasonably be deemed as having its parallel in the kind of short-term loan that nearly every family in Britain has taken out for cars, holidays and house extensions and improvements. It will come as no surprise to those who have taken out such a loan that the proviso here was that, if Leeds did not maintain its repayments, then the lender could force it to sell the player and hand over the proceeds. And if the sale didn't cover the debt, the bank was entitled to claim the difference from the club. The entire deal was insured with German-based Gerling, whose risk it was that, if the club were to go bankrupt, they would cover the lender's loss. These loans were short-term and carried a higher interest rate than those of the banks, which not only meant that the quarterly payments were substantial, but also that the extra insurance was expensive and had to be paid up front. In the late summer and autumn of 1999, Ranson successfully arranged separate financial packages of this kind to cover the purchases of Bakke, Mills, Duberry and Bridges. The club's run to the semi-final of the UEFA Cup, with its income of £6.9 million, whetted appetites and the new target became the cash-rich Champions League. Come in, then, Matteo, Dacourt and Viduka. Come in, too, for a king's ransom, Rio Ferdinand, because Leeds had now qualified for the second phase of the Champions League and the money would come rolling in. The signing of Ferdinand in November 2000 captured the imagination of the football world, and I wrote at the time:

In the best of marriage traditions, this one featuring Leeds United and Rio Ferdinand, the central character kept us all waiting. The conference confirming the joining together was scheduled for 2 p.m. sharp, two hours before kick-off in a Premiership match against Arsenal in which Ferdinand had been unable to make his United debut because of the player registration deadline. At 2.12 precisely, the onlookers craned their necks for a first glimpse of the world's most expensive defender as he walked into the United Pavilion surrounded by his family, his agent and United's directors. The 22 year old took centre stage as United chairman Peter Ridsdale, to his left, announced:

This is a very special day for Leeds United. I also think it's a special day for English football. We are often criticised in this country for not supporting English talent, but I think Leeds United have done more than most before today to demonstrate that, if possible, we will go on to support players in the British Isles, and I include Ireland in that. I noticed the odd individual criticising us for paying so much money for an English footballer. Well I have to tell you that we think we have got a bargain. As far as we're concerned, this underlines the ambition of this football club and the commitment of the board in their support of the manager and I believe that in the next couple of years people will reflect on this day as acknowledgement that Leeds United have arrived. People all over Europe as well as the Premiership will take note that we are here to stay, that we are hungry for titles and silverware.

43

Then, for the first time, the man who has rewritten transfer history, told us his feelings:

First of all, I am pleased to be joining such an ambitious club. I must admit it came as a bit of a surprise to me, because all along West Ham said that they did not want me to go. In the end, it was a wrench to leave them and I appreciate what they have done for me. I owe them a lot. But this is a new chapter. European football is what I need and what I want and Leeds United can offer me that. This is a big step forward for me. Mr Ridsdale impressed me beyond belief when he came to see me. He made it easy for me. The money does not concern me. I am here to play football and it's a good deal for both parties. The manager's former playing role was another big factor for me. He was a world class centre-half and has a lot to offer me. But I don't care what position I play in, as long as I am in the first 11 and out there on the pitch.

When Ferdinand was asked whether he thought any player was worth £18 million, Ridsdale jumped in and said:

I'll answer that question. A lot has been made over the last few days about the price tag. It is nothing to do with Rio. He's a quality footballer. Leeds United have decided, with West Ham, what the price needs to be. It's a little like asking if pop stars should earn what they do and should footballers earn what they do in a week. We are in a natural market place and what that market means is that if there is a rare commodity, and Rio is a special commodity, then there is a price to pay. We have decided that price is acceptable to Leeds United and we are delighted to have him with us. The income stream at this football club is decided by how well we do on the park. How well we do depends on the players we have got. And if you want the best players available, you have to pay the price at any moment in time. Frankly, if the transfer system were to disappear overnight, and I do not believe it will – it will be amended, but it won't disappear – you could imagine all sorts of clubs all over Europe who might just want players as trophies just to park them so other people can't have them. Under that scenario we would be competing in a very difficult market place. Today, we are sitting here with Rio Ferdinand as a registered Leeds United player.

Back to Rio who, surely, must have canvassed some Leeds players before committing himself to the move?:

Yes, I did. I know a few of the lads from the Under-21s and the senior England side and they had nothing but complimentary things to say about the club. They are all happy and it seemed to me that they are all in it together. They win together and they lose together. That had a big effect on me. There are a lot of other teams out there and when you speak to some of their players you feel that there is nothing like the same togetherness as is the case at Leeds and, indeed, was at West Ham. It was another big factor that I wasn't coming to a place where I would be a complete stranger. I also spoke to people outside of both Leeds and West Ham who have my best interests at heart.

Come in, then, Number 29. The 15 shirt is vacant at Leeds and most observers felt sure he would go for that – the same number he wore at West Ham. 'Definitely not,' said Rio. 'This is a new beginning for me.' The vows had been taken.

Ferdinand arrived to a hero's welcome as Leeds paraded their record-breaking signing at Elland Road before they went on to a single-goal victory over big rivals Arsenal in the Premiership. The world's costliest defender responded to the unbroken applause and chants of 'Rio' by holding aloft his chosen Number 29 shirt. 'Where's your Rio gone?' sang the Southampton fans against West Ham the previous day and the 22 year old watched from the stands against the Gunners as United's defence, anchored by captain Lucas Radebe and Jonathan

Woodgate, put up a sterling performance to keep Arsenal's rampaging forwards at bay. And that was a massive contribution to a fine victory which delighted manager David O'Leary. 'We needed three points to give us a lift,' he said. 'Last season we were not beating the big teams; now we've added Arsenal to Liverpool. Let's hope we start climbing the table now.' O'Leary praised man-of-the-match Alan Smith, by saying:

> They don't come better than Martin Keown and Tony Adams, but they will travel home knowing they have been up against Alan Smith. He hustles people and harries them and has a great attitude. Alan's a fantastic lad. He respects people off the pitch, but he has no respect for them on it.

O'Leary would shed no light on his team selection plans now that Ferdinand was available to play, starting at Leicester:

> People can keep wondering. It's a nice choice for me to have. We want a bigger squad. I'm trying to build a young, talented squad, particularly with players from the British Isles. It would be nice to have some more over the next few weeks, but we are being patient, trying to bring in the ones we want. I try to do business quietly because we are being used by agents and, as a manager, I don't like that.

The capture of Ferdinand almost certainly meant that O'Leary would play him in a back three with Radebe and Woodgate. And, once Harry Kewell was fit, the manager was likely to adopt a 3–4–1–2 system, with the Aussie roaming free behind the Smith-Viduka strike pairing.

In my year-end review I wrote:

> The year 2000 may have begun with dizzying highs – Leeds United peering down at the rest of the Premiership from their lofty perch at the top – but it ended at the other end of the spectrum. The 12th place in which they were languishing was the lowest they had occupied under the managerial reins of O'Leary, the result of a failure to win no fewer than 12 of their 19 matches. It was a turnaround in fortunes which, contrary to

the scratching of heads and the struggle for a handle on matters within the club, had a simple explanation. The prolific buying and selling of players had disrupted Leeds' cohesion as a team. Whereas United were first carried forward on a youthful tide of exuberance into an early summer of blue-sky bliss, they had now been pitched into a bleak midwinter abyss through an abandonment of homespun family values in favour of dances with strangers. In footballing terms, the family that plays together stays together, with an all-for one, one-for-all mindset that is difficult for opponents to breach. Yet a shipping out of such brethren as David Hopkin, Alf Haaland, Martin Hiden, Robert Molenaar, Matthew Jones and, latterly, Darren Huckerby in favour of flashy signings like Olivier Dacourt, Mark Viduka, Rio Ferdinand and Robbie Keane had broken the mould. The new arrivals were being embraced and welcomed into the family tradition, but it would take time, patience and understanding before they were able to go forward as a unit. One by one, opposing teams had used this readjustment period to their advantage. It didn't take an Einstein to figure out that United's soft underbelly was to be found in a depleted and constantly changing midfield and, in turn, Manchester City, Ipswich, Manchester United, West Ham, Leicester, Southampton, Aston Villa and Newcastle loaded up their engine rooms and burned the team off. Even struggling First Division outfit Tranmere had sussed out that one, and they inflicted a painfully embarrassing Worthington Cup defeat which hurt O'Leary as much as any setback he had endured in his stewardship. Much-maligned as it is, this Cup nevertheless offers a route to Europe and the cutting off of that supply line reduced the options. O'Leary will have piled as much pressure on himself as any amount of pressure from outside influences to ensure the continuity of European football at Elland Road. He is enjoying the Champions League with the same passion felt by everybody connected in any way with Leeds United, but winning the European Cup to join the party next season is a possibility that exists only in dreamland at the moment. The more achievable route, certainly with everybody beating everybody else, is, as last season, finishing third in the

Premiership. The paucity of points in the pot in the first half of the campaign demands a storming sequence of victories, though, and the sooner they embark upon that the better. That they will start stringing it all together is a banker bet for chairman Peter Ridsdale, for whom prospects for the year 2001 are to be greatly savoured. He says:

> *The millennium year was certainly a mixed bag, with events on the field providing much more comfort than those off it. We could all have done without the January arrests of some of our players and the appalling tragedies in Istanbul in April. These two events will go down in the unpalatable section of the club's history. There were waves of euphoria on the football side, with our last-day qualification for the Champions League at West Ham, Harry Kewell's spectacular goal at Sheffield Wednesday and Alan Smith's goals against 1860 Munich and Lazio uppermost in my recollections. I feel there is much to look forward to next year. For people to be talking about a crisis just because we have suffered a few defeats in a transitional period on the field is nonsense. It's only a couple of weeks since we outplayed Sunderland, who are third in the League, and won a tremendous victory over them. And, as Southampton showed when beating Spurs this week, each team is capable of beating the others. We have beaten Arsenal and Liverpool and I am convinced that when this team settles down it will be nothing short of top class. I am not saying that we are guaranteed to finish in the top three this season, but what I would urge against is discounting that.*

Paramount to Ridsdale's pursuit of success at the top level, of course, was the ongoing issue of balancing United's accounts. With the club's bank debt now at an all-time high, and with hefty quarterly payments being made through Ray Ranson's Guernsey-based company, Registered European Football Finance (REFF), the club approached Ranson with a new proposal to cut down their costs. Now they suggested that they should pay off only half the original player costs by stages over the contract period and pay the remaining 50 per cent in a lump sum at the end. With player values rising, there seemed to be no reason for either lender or club to worry about security and the deal was done. Leeds were to turn, now, to Stephen Schechter who, when working for the merchant bank Schroders, raised £55 million for Newcastle United. Several other English clubs employed him to raise cash for them, and early in 2001, now working for another bank, Lazard's, he had a tip-off that Leeds wanted something similar. In fact, Leeds asked Schechter to find them £50 million, and the former Wall Street man had no shortage of offers in London and New York from lenders wooed by his argument that Leeds is the biggest city in England with only one professional club and has an enormous and extremely loyal fan base. The proposed loan would be over 25 years and once-a-year repayments were guaranteed through a special 'locked box' account. Every summer, when Leeds put season tickets and corporate hospitality boxes up for sale, all the revenue would be paid into the locked box, so that a substantial sum had built up by 1 September. On that date, the lenders would withdraw the payments due to them from the locked box and only then was the club entitled to the residue. Deals amounting to £60 million, the biggest loan ever raised by an English football club, were made with M&G of London and two American institutions, Metlife and Teachers.

These financial wranglings, then, were taking place behind the scenes of Leeds' Champions League and domestic campaigns. They were, perhaps, the first symptoms of a period of turmoil for the club which has yet to be fully resolved, and the background against which the club's two major challenges of 2000–01 were played out. Of these challenges, one was set to result in glory and pride, while the other involved the conclusion of one of the 'unpalatable sections of the club's history'.

CHAPTER FOUR

HIGHS AND LOWS – THE CHAMPIONS LEAGUE AND HULL CROWN COURT

Leeds' performances in Europe from August 2000 to May 2001 were remarkable and unforgettable. I was privileged to attend all 18 Champions League games and, like the many thousands of Leeds fans who dedicated themselves to enjoying their club's involvement from the first moment to the last, I was quickly consumed by the intoxicating effects.

United got off to a bad start, losing comprehensively 4–0 at Barcelona's Nou Camp but, six days later, the club's prospects dramatically improved. Passion, not fashion, dominated the Elland Road catwalk as the fancy Dans of AC Milan came to play in an unrelenting torrent of end-to-end football. The elegance of their designer players was swept aside by the good old-fashioned Yorkshire features of a heavy pitch, heaving tackles and an even weightier commitment. In the end, it took a goalkeeping error of farcical proportions to separate the sides, but there was no doubting that the priceless three-point booty went to the team with the healthiest appetite for battle.

Next up were Besiktas at Elland Road, where power-play of the greatest ferocity, intensity and explosive dynamism propelled Leeds United to a European night to rank among their greatest. They simply swept aside a token Turkish challenge with a display which planted them firmly on top of Group H at the halfway stage, the 6–0 scoreline sending reverberations around the continent.

Then, when a return game of mind-numbing tedium on the banks of the Bosphorus stuttered and staggered to its blessed end, there was considerable cause for celebration in the United camp following the goalless draw. The precious point saw them put one foot in the Champions League second phase, and if quality was sacrificed for stubbornness on so important an occasion then the end fully justified the means.

In late October, like tightrope walkers completing a perilous journey, Leeds United's thrill-a-minute stars were just one small step from a glorious feat when, to a chorus of anguished cries, they slipped in a 1–1 draw with Barcelona. After enjoying the luxury of a fifth-minute lead, stoppage time was deemed to be four minutes when two seemed more appropriate and a reinvigorated Barcelona lifted themselves for a mighty last effort which yielded an equaliser. Now Leeds had to take a point from the final Group H fixture against AC Milan in the San Siro on 8 November to guarantee further interest in European football's premier competition.

Bellissimo! Leeds marched into the second phase with a resolute, focused and wholly determined performance against Milan. O'Leary's tigers of the trenches dug deep for a 1–1 draw and the point they needed.

As in the first phase, their opening fixture pitted them in at the deep end, and European champions Real Madrid left an indelible mark on Elland Road, their rich tradition evident in an unswerving self-belief and a shimmering class that were joys to behold in a 2–0 victory to the Spanish team.

And so to Lazio where, laughing last and longest, United's impish striker Alan Smith scored a glorious match-winner 10 minutes from time to end a barren spell of 12 goalless games just when his side needed it most. United stood in second spot in Group D behind Real Madrid, who followed up their Elland Road victory with a 4–1 thrashing of Anderlecht. Now United's next two matches were against the Belgians after a short break in Champions League activity.

In mid-February, after a 2–1 defeat of Anderlecht at Elland Road, one wondered how on earth Leeds continued to scale the heights against the dream teams of Europe as though they were some minor impediment on a purposeful journey.

Over in Belgium, Leeds became the first English club that season to claim a place in the quarter-finals of the Champions League. Their scintillating 4–1 defeat of Anderlecht was quite stunning both in its creation and its impact. On the face of it, United's task in eking out a result in Belgium was mountainous. Anderlecht had boasted a recent record of 21 consecutive victories and 9 European successes on the trot in their compact, neat and tidy Vanden Stock Stadium. Big names like Manchester United had been simply swept aside on a wave of insuperability, so what chance did Leeds hold of stemming the flow? It was by sheer will, class and ability that their hosts were swept aside and made to look distinctly ordinary.

In the Bernabeu, Real Madrid raced to a 3–2 victory but the European champions were handed this passage into the quarter-finals as group winners by an opportunistic goal thief who should have known better and yet another referee who 'didn't see it'. Raul, envied the world over for his goal-scoring prowess, was this time vilified for his palming of the ball into the United net and, Maradona-style, getting away with it. In mid-March, it was entertainment the United hordes wanted when Lazio came to town and, even with many of the celebrated Leeds names missing, it was served up in five-star style in an enthralling 3–3 draw.

In the quarter-final first leg at Elland Road on 4 April 2001, with cavalier spirit and the inspiration of an outstanding show from captain-for-the-night Rio Ferdinand, Leeds continued on their merry way in a most compelling Champions League extravaganza with a 3–0 defeat of Deportivo La Coruna.

Wars are never won without the odd fierce battle along the way, though, and two weeks later Leeds emerged bloodied but unbowed from the fearful second leg on Spanish soil to claim their place in the semi-finals. They lost 2–0, but their 3–2 aggregate defeat of reigning League champions Deportivo set up a two-leg semi-final clash with another Spanish outfit, Valencia, who had taken care of business against Arsenal. The final in Milan's San Siro stadium on 23 May was now, incredibly, well within the sights of David O'Leary's eurostars. The 14,000-mile odyssey held the promise of a real night of glory in Italy in what was shaping up to be one of the most unlikely success stories in the British game since Nottingham Forest won the European Cup in 1979.

In a quite splendid match of technical excellence and compelling drama in the semi-final first leg at Elland Road, they took Valencia, one of European football's most experienced and formidable teams, right to the wire in a goalless draw. So evenly matched were the two factions that they could hardly have been separated in a photo finish, and this first session set up a deeply intriguing second leg in Valencia's Mestalla Stadium a week later.

One way or another, 9 May 2001 was a night destined to end in tears: of sorrow or of joy. And so it was that all those in Leeds United's colours who had derived so much pleasure from their European exploits over the previous nine months cried a river as the impossible dream evaporated in a 3–0 drubbing. The city of Valencia, all tooting horns, firecrackers and euphoria, celebrated well into the early hours, and well it might, after a display which evoked spine-tingling pleasure and simply oozed class. Valencia went on to draw 1–1 with Bayern Munich in the final, with Bayern winning 5–4 on penalties. Leeds were out of the competition but the achievement of reaching the semi-finals, and the way in which it was done, will be remembered by Leeds' fans and football fans in general for years to come.

Regrettably, though, other events were taking place at home which will also be remembered for years to come, and whose concurrency with the Champions League campaign mean that this period of Leeds United's history can never be recalled with unalloyed enjoyment. Leeds' success in Europe was made even more extraordinary, or, depending on one's outlook, more ignoble, by the fact that it was set against the public scandal of four of its players going on trial.

On 29 January 2001, England Under-21 midfielder Lee Bowyer, England defender Jonathan Woodgate and reserve-team striker Tony Hackworth appeared in court charged with causing grievous bodily harm with intent on Sarfraz Najeib. The three footballers all denied the charge. They also denied affray. Woodgate and Michael Duberry, the fourth of the Leeds players appearing, also denied conspiracy to pervert the course of justice. Two other men, Neale Caveney, 21, and Paul Clifford, 21, both of Middlesbrough, denied causing grievous bodily harm (GBH) with intent, affray and conspiracy to pervert the course of justice. The trial of the six men at Hull Crown Court was due to last up to six weeks, with the first week taken up with legal argument in the absence of the jury.

Yorkshire Evening Post editor Neil Hodgkinson was contacted by

Peter Ridsdale during the pre-trial hearing in Hull and asked if he would pop down to Elland Road for a meeting regarding the case. When he arrived at the chairman's office, he was met by Ridsdale, communications director David Walker and – to his surprise – Steve Barker, the solicitor for Lee Bowyer. Hodgkinson recalls:

> The meeting basically centred on Peter telling me that the police were alleging that he had deliberately contacted the YEP ahead of the arrests so that we would print the story and use accompanying pictures, which would have damaged any prosecution evidence surrounding witness identification. I said that was a nonsense as it was the YEP who had contacted Peter in Hong Kong about the news of our exclusive. If Peter had been that Machiavellian in his dealings, I'd have been worried. He asked me if I'd be prepared to go to court the next day and state that fact. Steve Barker then said it would also be helpful if I'd tell the court who had tipped us off. That, of course, I could never do. He said they could always order me to attend. I replied that I would volunteer to attend and comment on the fact that Peter had not been the source of the story. If they ordered me to attend with a hidden agenda I would become a hostile witness.

Hodgkinson travelled to Hull Crown Court with Peter Ridsdale and Adam Pearson, then the club's commercial director, in a car driven by David Walker. He continues:

> When we got to the hotel to link up with other members of the legal defence team, Steve Barker again took me to one side and told me it would be a real help if I revealed the source of our story. I declined and it was never mentioned again. I was first up in front of the judge and I repeated on oath that Peter had not tipped us off. I was then asked by the prosecution on behalf of West Yorkshire police and the judge if I could tell them who had. I declined to answer several times. It was very warm in the court and the fact that you are warned that you could be charged with contempt and ultimately fined or jailed for refusing to name your source, made it even warmer. However, though you could blame Peter for many things in his latter

months at United, I could not blame him for that. Peter followed me into the dock and, after the judge heard his statement, that element of the hearing was dropped.

On 12 February 2001, the court was told that three Leeds United footballers and their friends left Mr Najeib with serious injuries when they chased and attacked him after they had been drinking into the early hours. The violence happened when the teammates and their friends left the Majestyk nightclub in City Square, Leeds, after midnight, the court heard. Among those who chased Sarfraz Najeib, who was studying at Leeds Metropolitan University, were Bowyer and Woodgate, said Nicholas Campbell, QC, prosecuting. Mr Najeib was left injured on the ground in Mill Hill, off Boar Lane, less than half a mile from the nightclub. Mr Campbell told the jury all six defendants in the dock had been enjoying a night out and 'spirits were high'. 'The six young men had enjoyed their evening in the company of other footballers and friends. Most had been drinking heavily and drink played a part in what happened that night.' Mr Campbell said what took place had been further fuelled by the loyalty some felt towards their teammates. He said that there had been trouble inside the Majestyk at around half past midnight early on Wednesday, 12 January 2000, which spread outside. Mr Najeib and his friends were outside the club, but had not been involved in the violence. 'They had not been drinking and it was entirely coincidental they left at the same time as this other group,' said Mr Campbell. 'Suddenly, the students ran off and they were chased by a group of white males. The prosecution say that the first five defendants in the dock took part in that chase.' He said two of the Asian students were injured, one of them seriously. He said the five headed back towards the club and Duberry gave a lift in his car to three of his co-defendants. Mr Campbell said they agreed to do what they could to hinder the police investigation.

Before their trial opened, Mr Justice Poole warned the jury to ignore anything they may have seen, heard or read in the newspapers because it was irrelevant to the trial. Experienced newspaper hands, then, could scarcely believe it when, right in the middle of the jury's delicate deliberations, the *Sunday Mirror* completely ignored the law and published a two-page spread featuring comments on key aspects of the evidence. And if newsrooms up and down the country were shocked, the effect in the Najeib household was shattering. All the family's efforts to cope with the stress of being at the centre of a national news story for over a year were about to have counted for nothing, their hopes of seeing justice done dashed by the *Sunday Mirror's* arrogant disregard for the law. The following day, 9 April, their worst fears were realised. The damage had been done; the judge decided the article could have prejudiced the jury and a multi-million pound trial was abruptly halted, to be reconvened with a new jury at a later date.

The roots of the first trial's collapse led back to a small holiday cottage on the outskirts of Grimsby. A few days earlier, before the jury had retired to consider its verdict, two journalists from the *Sunday Mirror* had met the victim's father, Muhammad Najeib. Mr Najeib had spent most of the previous ten weeks billeted in the cottage along with civil rights campaigner Suresh Grover, who had taken on the role of minder for the duration of the court case. Requests for interviews from the media had been ceaseless but, in the vast majority of cases, fruitless. This time, Mr Najeib had agreed – possibly because he already had an agreement with the *Sunday Mirror's* sister paper, the *Daily Mirror,* which had been arranged through the family's lawyer, Imran Khan. It was to prove a fateful decision. A week later, he had to endure the agony of hearing Mr Justice Poole discharging the jury after the *Sunday Mirror* did exactly what Mr Najeib said they promised was out of the question – publish before the jury had reached its conclusion. The victim's father was horrified by what had happened. He had been a determined and dignified presence throughout the trial, missing barely a moment of the long and sometimes laborious proceedings. His motivation in speaking to the *Sunday Mirror* was a genuine desire for the wider public to know more about the impact of what had happened to his family. The trial judge exonerated him from any blame, stating it was 'perfectly natural' to have personal views and he was not to have known when they would be published. What motivated the *Sunday Mirror* to publish when it did is an entirely more questionable matter. With cruel irony, it billed its two-page splash as 'exclusive'. It was an accurate description – the rest of the media were following an established legal principle not to publish anything which could prejudice the minds of a jury.

The article itself referred to Mr Najeib's belief that the attack on his son, Sarfraz, was racially motivated. For the following reasons, however, this view had been officially ruled out by the prosecution before the trial began. In an early interview, Sarfraz Najeib had told police detectives that when the incident began outside the Majestyk nightclub, he heard someone say, 'Do you want some, Paki?' Sir William Macpherson's official report on the lessons of the Stephen Lawrence case said that if a victim perceived an attack to be racially motivated, the police must treat it as so, so the incident was duly logged in this way in the police records. However, Mr Justice Poole voiced his concerns that a victim's perception of racism did not easily translate into the kind of objective evidence required in a court of law. He said it was 'troubling' that the Macpherson definition meant the incident was publicised as racial 'in the absence of any evidence [that] it was, in fact, racist'. As well as a lack of corroborating evidence, there was confusion over who had actually made the remark. Mr Najeib identified a man in a white shirt as making the comment, which meant it could have been any of the defendants. The judge concluded that Macpherson's 'subjective' definition of racially motivated crime had caused 'nothing but mischief' in this case.

Consequently, Mr Justice Poole had impressed upon the jury that race was not to be an issue in their deliberations. The publication in a mass circulation newspaper of an alternative opinion at a particularly sensitive time – when the jury had retired to consider its verdict – was therefore a very serious matter. Mr Justice Poole ruled that the fact that at least one of eleven jurors had seen the article could have unfairly influenced the outcome of the case.

The fallout of the collapse of such a high-profile and expensive trial was almost immediate. Three days later, Colin Myler, editor of the *Sunday Mirror*, resigned. A month later, it was confirmed that Mirror Group Newspapers, now Trinity Mirror, would be charged by the Attorney General with contempt of court.

There was a chapter of his life that the father of Sarfraz Najeib had kept from his two sons until the attack on Sarfraz. 'I never wanted them to know what had happened to me,' revealed Muhammad Najeib. 'I wanted them to have a normal life and didn't want it to affect them.' For, in an astonishing foreshadowing of his son's fate, Mr Najeib had also been set upon and beaten, 30 years previously. As a sixth-former at Sheffield's Hinde House School, he was attacked by nearly a dozen skinheads. 'Sarfraz was completely shocked when I told him,' said Mr Najeib. 'I feel he is angry, not just at what these people have done but, it could be, at me as well. When I told him what had happened to me, the first thing he said was, "Why didn't you go back to Pakistan?"' The attack on Mr Najeib snr left him in hospital for two days and put an end to his education and dreams of one day following a career in medicine. He had moved from the Kashmir region to England in 1965 when he was 11. He stayed with extended family members in Tinsley, Sheffield, and quickly adapted to his new life. Initially, he went to Parkhouse School, but transferred to Hinde House because he saw more chance of getting O levels. He said, 'I found racism as soon as I got here. I was put in the lowest form. I was told I couldn't do O levels because I wasn't clever enough. I had to persuade the teachers that I wanted to go on to higher education.' He managed to walk away with seven O levels and started studying A level biology, physics and chemistry. But his attack put an end to his education. He failed his A levels and returned to Pakistan where he married his wife Zubaida. Three months later, he returned to Yorkshire as there were better opportunities to provide for a family. Mr Najeib heard about Sarfraz's ordeal the morning after the attack when his wife woke him. His son Shazhad, so traumatised by what had happened, had not been able to bring himself to tell his parents and passed a garbled message to an aunt. Mr Najeib recalled:

> All that was mentioned was a broken leg and that it was a fall. When we got to the hospital, the police were there. We were crying and in a daze. If I hadn't been shown where Sarfraz was, I wouldn't have recognised him. That's how bad he was. He was still bleeding from his nose and mouth. He didn't even know we were there. He was in hospital for eight days.

For Sarfraz's parents, Shazhad and his two sisters, it was the start of months of trauma. Said Mr Najeib:

> Mentally, Shazhad was more damaged because he had seen everything that happened to Sarfraz. I blamed myself. And it reminded me of what had happened to me. I am angry. I want somebody to explain why they did this. When I see them, I just

want to know why – why they have basically destroyed our lives. I want to know how they can live with themselves. What they have done is worse than any animal. It's totally destroyed our happiness, taken it all away from the family. My daughter had graduated, our sons had gone to university – it was perfect until this happened. It's a constant worry. If my children go out we worry about them; if we go out they worry about us. The family has had threats, so any member could be a target.

Their neat semi-detached house in Brinsworth, near Rotherham, which had been the family home for more than 20 years, became little more than a mini-fortress, waiting to be placed on the market. A flurry of threatening letters was sent to the family after the attack on Sarfraz, forcing them to take drastic measures to protect themselves. Four infra-red cameras watched over the front of the property. More were placed at the back and panic alarms were fitted inside. The family became resigned to the fact they would have to sell up. The father said they had suffered psychological damage and Sarfraz, once a carefree student, was a shadow of his former self and no longer wanted to live in this country. 'I think Sarfraz will be permanently scarred. The shape of his face has altered. He is scared of going out now,' said Mr Najeib. 'When he looks in the mirror, he can see his face is not the same. The injuries remind him. Before, he felt British. Now he doesn't know what to feel any more.' Both his sons have suffered nightmares and flashbacks to the attack. Anonymous threats did nothing to help. Leeds Metropolitan University, where the boys studied, received a phone call which included a firebomb threat if anything happened to the Leeds players. Another said, 'You better take this seriously. I am a Leeds United fan and we know that bastard and his Paki friends. Let me tell you this . . . if any player or supporter gets hurt, you will die, do you hear me?' The Najeib family also had to deal with the sinister threat of letters sent to their home. One to Sarfraz, postmarked Sheffield, contained a printed card showing the emblem of the far right-wing organisation White Pride Worldwide, while a letter posted in Bristol warned Sarfraz to drop all the charges or face a severe beating. The family also received several intimidating silent phone calls. Extremists on the other side of the fence made threats against Leeds United, and manager David O'Leary received an anonymous letter saying, 'Bowyer and Woodgate will be dealt with by our court, the pair of bastards.' Against such a background of threats and intimidation, the Najeib family tried to come to terms with what had happened.

On 15 October 2001, Bowyer and Woodgate were back in court, six months after their first trial was dramatically aborted. The Premiership stars, together with two of Woodgate's close friends, faced a second trial in the same dock at Hull Crown Court accused of affray and inflicting grievous bodily harm with intent. The two footballers, together with Clifford and Caveney, all denied the two joint charges. The trial judge, Mr Justice Henriques, told the jury of seven women and five men to ignore any reports they may have seen or heard and to discount racism as a motive for the attack. 'This trial begins now,' he said, before Nicholas Campbell, QC, prosecuting, opened the case against the men. 'Anything that you have heard, seen or read concerning the events you are about to hear of must be put aside,' the judge said. 'When those in the public eye – footballers, politicians or celebrities – face criminal charges, much is written and much is broadcast. But, unhappily, some of it is untrue and in this case there has been inaccurate reporting.' The judge added:

> If you were to act on anything that you have seen, heard or read about this case which you have not heard in this court during the forthcoming trial, you might well be acting on information that was simply wrong. One matter you may have read or seen or heard which is inaccurate is the description of the attack in this case as a racist attack. There is simply no evidence that the attack was racially motivated. The prosecution and the defence and myself are all agreed that there is no evidence and there will be no evidence of any racial motivation.

He told the jury the simple issue they had to determine was 'who did it?'.

Mr Campbell said Sarfraz Najeib ran along Boar Lane behind his brother before they turned into Mill Hill. 'As he ran down Mill Hill, Sarfraz Najeib recalls being tripped from behind and falling against a wall. From that moment on, he recalls nothing, which is perhaps not surprising because during the assault on him he was kicked repeatedly about the face, head and body.' Mr Campbell said he was also punched and eye witnesses believed he quickly became unconscious. 'Certainly, he did nothing to fight back,' he said. After the footballers and their pals left the scene, Mr Campbell claimed that Caveney and Bowyer put their arms around each other in a victory embrace. 'That there was a heavy mix of alcohol, adrenalin and camaraderie operating that night there can be no doubt,' said Mr Campbell. 'In that embrace, the prosecution submit, there is evidence of the strong emotion between two of those responsible for the violence who are now celebrating their victory.'

Woodgate was found guilty of affray but cleared of the more serious charge of grievous bodily harm with intent. He was sentenced to 100 hours' community service. His friend Paul Clifford, who the court heard plunged his teeth into Mr Najeib's face and shook him like a dog, was found guilty of both charges and sentenced to six years in prison. Another friend, Neale Caveney, was cleared of GBH but found guilty of affray and was also given community service, while Bowyer was cleared of both allegations. Michael Duberry endured a nightmare ordeal after deciding to testify against close pal Woodgate. He was acquitted of conspiring to pervert the course of justice in the first trial and became a prosecution witness in the retrial. He revealed he had received death threats.

The *Yorkshire Post*'s John Woodcock wrote:

> In some ways, the most revealing verdict was delivered not in Court 4 at Hull Crown Court, but in a place where young men are judged constantly, often without mercy. Early on during his first trial, Lee Bowyer had left the dock to pursue his trade. Five hours later, he scored the winner in a European Champions League match. His superb goal and flamboyant celebrations were a surreal contrast to events 60 miles away, where the jury had begun absorbing details of his alleged role in a drunken attack on an Asian student – charges of which he was cleared. To a section of the Elland Road crowd that night, it was obvious that the message they took from Bowyer's response on the pitch was business-as-usual defiance. Niceties, such as the pursuit of truth and justice, and whether or not he should even have been playing while standing accused of serious criminal charges,

were not the issue. What mattered was the shirt he wore – them and us – and that he'd been instrumental in United defeating the Belgian champions Anderlecht. More than that, his hero status had been confirmed, despite – for some, because of – what he'd been accused of doing in the city centre a year before. They may not have been able to relate to his talent or the stacks of money it's brought him, but there's a sizeable element that identifies with a laddish night out in which excessive amounts of alcohol lead to violence and broken heads in a dingy side-street around closing-time. It's the same tribalism which has now isolated Michael Duberry. To many of those for whom Bowyer is a superstar, Duberry is now seen to be beyond the pale, whether or not he was directed by his conscience as well as self-preservation in the witness box. Having squealed on his teammate, Jonathan Woodgate, in some eyes he stands convicted of a crime far worse than anything the law could bring against him. For racists among the unthinking mob, a black man shopping a white icon compounds the sin. Sociologist John Williams, who is based at the Centre for Football Research at Leicester University, believes the case has disclosed a great deal about English football, and even more about our society. Williams contends that, for all the game's efforts to reinvent itself as sophisticated and clean-cut, the appearance in the dock of young athletes who have represented their country, reveals something much closer to reality. Even as a second jury was deliberating their colleagues' fate, Leeds players were again living it up in the city's bars. It ended with Robbie Fowler, whom United had bought recently for £11 million, being arrested and later released without charge following an incident involving a photographer. Several of the squad had dressed up as soldiers for the drinking session, irresponsible at the best of times but almost unbelievable given America's recent invasion of Afghanistan, along with the events in a certain Hull courtroom. For those who assume that the brains of indulged, overpaid footballers are in their sponsored boots, here was further ammunition. Williams was right when he said that if the Bowyer-Woodgate case hadn't involved soccer and famous names, it wouldn't be news nowadays:

These kinds of incidents are taken as normal, late-night activity by many young men. The wider significance is that it's not a big leap from the pitch to the terraces and seats in the stand. What connects players to supporters is shared ideas. It's about lads and lads' behaviour. It signifies a much more general problem.

Apart from the defendants being asked for their autographs by the Hull public, one of the unlikelier aspects of the first trial was that Bowyer was going from strength to strength as a footballer in the Champions League, apparently relishing the release from hours of physical restraint in the dock. The question was, though, should he have been playing at all? Williams had his doubts, despite all of the arguments about an accused being innocent until found guilty and the unfairness of a prolonged suspension during the relatively short career of a professional footballer. Leeds made a decision that also seemed to be based on pragmatism and the impact on its balance sheet, and it paid dividends as Bowyer contributed hugely to the club's domestic success and progress in Europe last season. But did glory and finance speak louder than wisdom and sensitivity, especially when Bowyer lined up for a crucial European tie while awaiting a verdict during the aborted first trial? 'It's a difficult judgement but, overall, I don't think it [Bowyer's appearance] has been good for the club,' says Williams. 'There's a danger here that some fans will see this as a reason to celebrate a particular approach to life. It can say that players are, at heart, still like them. I see dangers in that approach.' Williams hoped that Leeds would now display similar support for Duberry. And not just United, but the FA, the Professional Footballers' Association and the game in general. He deserved nothing less, the academic believed:

Irrespective of his motives in changing his story, soccer owes it to him to offer support and direction. He needs to be congratulated publicly. The danger for Duberry is that he will be exiled because he betrayed the 'cause'. Insider-outsider tensions are intensely strong in football clubs.

> *You protect your own, no matter what. In the end,*
> *Duberry was willing to give evidence against his friend.*
> *As a result, it's going to be very hard for him to stay at*
> *Leeds. Duberry now needs to be defended and protected,*
> *but I fear that is going to be difficult.*

Football also had to address other issues, argued Williams. The case had seriously undermined the way the game sees itself. What happened in and around those bars and clubs exposed the myths:

> *Promotional material tells us that it has become a*
> *sophisticated, cerebral sport, that players are thinking of*
> *themselves differently – and are being thought of*
> *differently – to previous generations of footballers. They*
> *are spoken of as athletes and, we are told, have a lifestyle*
> *that is diet-conscious and avoids alcohol. It's a glossy,*
> *cleansed, sanitised view. The actual change is slower. It*
> *takes time to run through other cultural and social*
> *changes. They're happening, but young men like this, for*
> *all kinds of reasons, are not particularly mature. In some*
> *ways, it's hard for them. Because of their status, the*
> *money they earn, and being so much in the public eye, they*
> *feel exposed and don't know who to trust. They have few*
> *social or cultural skills to deal with the situation. It's not*
> *surprising they end up back with mates they can relate to,*
> *and use drink as an escape and to boost their self-*
> *confidence. We have to look much more closely at these*
> *issues. This case is a reminder of the problems and risks*
> *young players face off the pitch. If we want them to fulfil*
> *our expectations and behave more responsibly, we also*
> *have to provide the guidance. It's an opportunity to raise*
> *up and educate young lads for the world beyond football.*

Soccer academies within clubs are seeking to play such a role, and attempt to develop skills that aren't just related to technique and the virtues of a 4–3–3 formation. Surely they also have a moral obligation to the boy-men to whom they pay

fortunes, and who are often worth a fortune in the transfer
market. The Government is looking to go further on the
grounds that the ills of the game, not least the hooliganism it
attracts, are a symptom of something more chronic. In the wake
of the violent events at Euro 2000, it set up a working group
comprising those within football, Sport England, racial
equality campaigners, police and the Home Office. It reported
back with a worthy document presenting new proposals for
tackling football-related disorder. Recommendations included a
leading role in the process for 'decent' fans, an anti-xenophobic
and anti-racist advertising campaign, reform of the England
Members' Club to make it more socially and culturally
representative, and a range of other measures to improve the
overall image of English football. 'We are not prepared to
tolerate our national game being blighted by thuggery and
violence,' said the then Home Office minister, Lord Bassam,
recycling a line that lost credibility long ago. He was directing
it at the yobs who follow club and country. But who are they?
The depth of the problem is such that he could also have been
referring to a gifted young man who had worn the England
shirt – and who betrayed it during a ruinous night out in Leeds.

Events at Hull Crown Court had no sooner been concluded than
bookshops and bookstalls were flooded by a tome entitled *Leeds United
on Trial*. Its author was none other than the club's manager, David
O'Leary, and it was viewed variously as an act of betrayal, exploitation
and disloyalty. In his controversial chronicle of the 2000–01 campaign,
O'Leary admitted that whatever his talented young side achieved on
the pitch was overshadowed by the criminal trials involving three of
its brightest stars. His views on the affair took up around a quarter of
the book, with one reviewer noting:

> There is no escaping the trial, and while O'Leary is unstinting
> in his condemnation of his players' behaviour, one conclusion
> that could be drawn from statements made by O'Leary – his
> description of the way that Woodgate 'valiantly' tried not to let
> the trial affect his performance on the pitch, for example – is
> that in the modern age football always comes first.

65

Leeds United on Trial was lambasted by Mr Najeib's supporters, as shocking pictures emerged of Sarfraz's horrific injuries, taken two days after the assault as he recovered in Leeds General Infirmary. Ruggie Johnson, northern co-ordinator of the National Civil Rights Movement, said, 'It is adding insult to injury in terms of justice for Mr Najeib and his two sons. I find it absolutely outrageous that we are in this position when such a serious assault has taken place.' O'Leary insisted he had not received any money from a Sunday newspaper which printed exclusive extracts of the book prior to its publication. And, in spite of the title, O'Leary maintained his book was not about the two Hull Crown Court trials. After the court case ended, Peter Ridsdale insisted that the club 'had not been on trial'. O'Leary said, 'The book is not about the trial. I didn't get any money from the *News of the World* from their serialisation of what was in the book. I stand by it.' Referring to the timing of its publication, he went on, 'I can't help it. It's not my decision.' Following the trial verdicts, Mr Najeib's father Muhammad launched a furious attack on Leeds United for their decision to allow the two footballers to continue playing in spite of being charged with serious criminal offences. Mr Najeib snr said the club had showed 'no shame or responsibility' in the way they had handled the affair. Mr Johnson, who visited Ridsdale in the initial aftermath of the attack to ask that Woodgate and Bowyer be suspended until the outcome of the court case, said:

> You have to ask the question, who carried out this attack? Who did it? I am 100 per cent behind the family in whatever they seek to do next. I think it absolutely disgraceful that we are looking now at these players possibly wearing an England shirt. I think it is disgraceful they will play for Leeds or anywhere else.

Ridsdale was reluctant to comment about O'Leary's book but said that there was nothing in O'Leary's contract to prevent him from writing one. He was unaware whether or not Mr O'Leary had received payment for the serialisation. Following the trial verdicts, the club said both Woodgate and Bowyer would be made immediately available to O'Leary for selection. Neither was at Elland Road for the next game against Leicester City, where the home crowd was heard chanting

'Bowyer for England' before the match started. Woodgate was doing his community service, while Bowyer was having treatment for an injury, O'Leary said. Earlier, in a newspaper interview, O'Leary hit out at both players, saying they had invited trouble, damaged the reputation of the club and undermined his quest for Premiership glory. He had given Woodgate an ultimatum – move to Leeds from your home in Middlesbrough or face the sack. 'Whatever the court decided, they were guilty in my eyes for failing to exercise control, lacking in responsibility and for failing to behave as professional footballers should,' he said. 'What did they think they were doing, boozed up and running through the streets? Was that not inviting trouble?' He also criticised the Football Association, saying, 'They have handled this disgracefully. I am disgusted with the way Lee has been treated. You are innocent until proven guilty in this country, but they denied Lee the chance to play for his country when he should have been available.'

On the one hand, then, the enigmatic O'Leary swiftly jumped to the defence of a player he felt had been wronged, while on the other, he was quite prepared to wash the club's and its players' dirty linen in public.

CHAPTER FIVE

DAVID O'LEARY – THE ENIGMA

David O'Leary, who declined to be interviewed for this book, was not bad as a footballer, and in almost two decades of life as a centre-half at Arsenal he would have been well accustomed to the machismo that constant battles with bruisers of centre-forwards demand. No quarter given, none asked. Managing a football club and playing for a football club are two different sciences and it is a rare bird which flies to the mountain top in both. Stud marks and groin strains, bloody noses and blackened toenails are a thing of the past when a football person swaps his shirt for a tracksuit and match day Armani clothing and, by and large, the handbag he used in a hundred centre-circle dust-ups can be rendered redundant. O'Leary's trouble at Leeds was that he continued to carry his accoutrement in readiness for swatting away all would-be inquisitors and potential detractors. He always appeared to me as being stricken by paranoia, jumping at shadows and constantly imagining that traps were being set for him, which is understandable if you are managing a club which is struggling, but surely not when your club is on the up? As part of the media pack which attended regular Friday lunchtime conferences at Leeds United's Thorp Arch training ground, along with countless preview interviews and post-match inquests and some very rare one-to-one conversations, I was invariably struck with incredulity at the po-faced, defensive and sometimes aggressive manner in which he would conduct the business at hand. O'Leary did not have to say that he found dealing with the media tiresome and burdening; it showed in his very demeanour.

Granted, O'Leary wasn't in the position he occupied to please the hacks; he was there on a mission to put silverware in the hallowed halls of Elland Road for the first time in years. If only he had taken on board just how wholeheartedly many members of that media pack, particularly the West Yorkshire locals, wanted his quest to succeed. After the debacle concerning O'Leary and myself over the Hasselbaink affair, I embarked on a short-lived morning exercise of trying to reach him on his mobile telephone for the latest updates on club affairs, to no effect. When I put a question to him, his answers often seemed evasive. So what was wrong with the guy? Maybe he had a brief period of self-examination concerning this when, twice, he agreed to talk about the direction he wanted the club to take and revelled in telling me that, one day soon, Leeds would be 'kicking Manchester United's backsides'. But then it was back to the status quo.

On 16 September 2000, an abject home performance saw them lose 2–1 to Ipswich and, in a rare show of displeasure, the Elland Road faithful booed. I made this the subject of the media conference's first question and at the end of the session, with thunder in his eyes, he asked for a private word. With the rest of the hacks streaming out, he made to seize my tape recorder, muttering that he would like to see it switched off. I told him that it was my property and that if it was to be switched off then that would be done by me. He beckoned me to a far corner of the room, put his face close to mine and, in almost whispered tones, we had a mild altercation.

I always believed that O'Leary had a strange perception of what a squad is. Many were the times in European competition – where seven substitutes rather than the usual five are allowed – that he would not fill the bench, claiming a shortage of players. I was not alone in thinking it churlish that these fantastic opportunities for the bubbling-under brigade from the reserves or the youth teams to be given a taste of what it is like to be involved with the first team at that level were spurned. Or was he trying to make a point? I have come across many instances of O'Leary treating people in a way in which he may not have wished to be treated himself, but what of Leeds United stalwart and popular Scotsman Eddie Gray? When, in May 2000, Brian Kidd walked into Elland Road as director of youth development and declared, 'I'm delighted to be taking up such an exciting challenge,' maybe the alarm bells started to ring for Gray, who was then assistant to O'Leary. Kidd, the former number two to Sir Alex Ferguson at Manchester United and ex-manager of Preston North End and Blackburn Rovers, was to be responsible for Leeds' youngsters and the satellite operations which were being set up in association with other clubs. Kidd had been recharging his batteries since he parted company with Blackburn in the autumn and could not resist the approach by Ridsdale and O'Leary. Kidd said:

> I have known David since he was a 16 year old with Arsenal. He was a fine player and is now a manager who is clearly going places in the game. I was deeply impressed with the chairman's ambitions for the club in respect of future development and when I walked into Thorp Arch to have a look round the other day it was like going into a room full of old friends with Eddie Gray, Roy Aitken and David Batty around.

Kidd, who had celebrated his 51st birthday the previous day, went on:

> There will be no empire-building. It will be nice to create a seamless relationship between the youngsters and the first-team squad at a club which has already demonstrated that it is prepared to give youth a chance. Youngsters, whether they are kicking a ball about in the street, or have already found their way into the game, always need idols – my own was Denis Law – and to work in the same environment as the player or players you look up to is something very special. This is going to be a very exciting season for Leeds, with the Champions League and all that, and I can't wait to get my teeth into it.

Nine months later, Kidd was in position as head coach, appointed on the eve of Leeds' visit from Manchester United. In what was viewed as a surprise announcement, O'Leary confirmed that Kidd would be moving up the ladder to become the man in charge of coaching the first team, thereby assuming seniority over Eddie Gray in such matters. The timing of the announcement, it was perceived, would strike a psychological blow ahead of the clash with Manchester United and O'Leary insisted the appointment of Kidd was to help him spread his time easier. Kidd, it was said, would be working with assistant manager Eddie Gray and reserve team coach Roy Aitken. O'Leary explained:

I've made Brian Kidd the new head coach at Leeds, a role which he started today. There isn't a much better coach than him in the country or in Europe. He has fulfilled his task as youth development coach here earlier than I thought, so I felt there was no point in keeping him in that role any longer.

Kidd, meanwhile, said:

I'm delighted to move into my new role at Leeds United. There are some very talented and caring people on the staff. I'm sure the new youth set-up will go from strength to strength – but when the boss invited me to change roles I was happy to oblige.

Chairman Ridsdale, meanwhile, offered his full backing in what was a highly controversial move:

We were going to make this appointment in the summer but felt we needed extra time. It's certainly not a spur of the moment decision and it is something we have talked about for a long while. We have another big game this week with Real Madrid coming up and we felt the timing was right now to announce our decision.

Ridsdale said Kidd's appointment would be a big boost for O'Leary and his squad, explaining, 'Brian will be the senior coach and he will be working with Eddie Gray and Roy Aitken. Brian's track record when he worked alongside Alex Ferguson at Manchester United was second to none and he has my full backing.' Ridsdale was also quick to stress that there would be no change in the management structure, with Gray staying on in the same role. He insisted:

Eddie is assistant manager and nothing has changed as far as he is concerned. The appointment of Brian, coupled with the experience of Roy and Eddie, gives us the best backroom staff in the country. David is finding it increasingly difficult to divide his time and with Brian set to do more of the coaching it will give him more time to view other matches and concentrate on other jobs. David is still the manager and Brian will be reporting to him.

In fact, things did change, with Brian going on to have a high profile and a wide remit at Leeds. In the following season, just before Kidd's return to Old Trafford for the first time in two years, O'Leary was hailing him as one of the best coaches in football:

> He is a fantastic person who has done a fantastic job here and who did an unbelievable job there. I never knew until a couple of days ago that he hadn't been back to Old Trafford since leaving. I thought he went back with Blackburn, so that shocked me. But there is no doubt he's been a real help to me since he came in for that first game against Manchester United. He has been fantastic. He is a great coach. I've got top dollar. It's all very well him being good on the training pitch but I judge a great coach on what help he can give during the 90 minutes of a match and the advice he gives you. On the training ground, I'm the bad guy. I am the one who picks the team, leaves people out, etc. Brian is loved by all the lads. All the players think Brian would have them in his team because of the way he makes them feel. He takes them for the majority of training. He comes and sees me at nine o'clock and I tell him in general what we're going to do. I really let Brian get on with it and just make my points when I have to. It means the lads not hearing me constantly. They think the world of him – what they think of me, I don't know.

Following Kidd's touchline debut as first-team coach, his former boss, Sir Alex Ferguson, was still tipping Leeds for Champions League glory, despite exchanging a bitter war of words with O'Leary. Leeds had already booked their place in the quarter-finals of Europe's premier competition and the mid-week head to head with defending champions Real Madrid was being billed as the Group D decider. Leeds had warmed up with a 1–1 draw with Ferguson's side at Elland Road but bad feeling spilled over following a stamping incident involving Old Trafford goalkeeper Fabien Barthez and Ian Harte. Ferguson admitted immediately after the whistle that Barthez should have been dismissed but Leeds skipper Lucas Radebe stoked up the war of words by claiming referees were scared of Manchester United. Ferguson blasted:

> People who live in glass houses shouldn't throw stones. Ian

Harte is known throughout Europe as a diver and what happened was that he went in on Barthez and flung himself to the ground. People advocating an inquiry by the FA video panel should bear that in mind. Leeds have had more penalties than any other team in the League this season.

O'Leary, savouring the clash at the Bernabeu, was quick to retaliate. 'First of all, I only like to speak about my own players and I always like to stick to that,' he said. 'Maybe it's age. It could be that at the age of 59 his memory is going. He said on Saturday that Barthez should have been sent off. Now he has forgotten that. It smells like some kind of smokescreen, but I don't really know what he is up to. Yet who am I to compete with the great man?' Despite the personal battle between the two managers, Ferguson was still quick to pay tribute to O'Leary and his Elland Road gladiators. Speaking exclusively with the *Yorkshire Evening Post,* Ferguson said:

> What Leeds have achieved in the Champions League this season and what David has done at Elland Road is terrific. They just keep surprising clubs and some of their performances have been amazing. To go and beat AC Milan was the perfect result after losing so heavily in Barcelona and they have carried on like that. Thumpings can happen in European football but the trick is to come back and Leeds have done that. Anderlecht gave us a real roasting in Brussels in the first phase and I fully expected them to beat Leeds. I couldn't believe it when I saw how well Leeds played over there and how easy they made their win look. Their result in Lazio before Christmas was tremendous and they might be a surprise package. They're already in the quarter-finals and they have every chance.

O'Leary had been coming under fire for some of his side's performances in domestic competition, but his Old Trafford counterpart had no doubts that Leeds were on the right track. Said Fergie:

> What Leeds have done is found a way of playing in the Champions League. Their away form is tremendous and any side that can play like that on their travels is a real threat. Eddie

> Gray will have been a big help to David. It must be fantastic having someone like him around because he was there when Leeds were really successful in Europe.

O'Leary was freely admitting he would like to emulate the Ferguson dynasty at Old Trafford and the Manchester United boss believed there were plenty of similarities between the two clubs. 'Leeds have done the same as us in that they have given their young players a chance,' he said. 'David has a core foundation of good youngsters and that is good for the future. It's flattering that David has said we are a role model, but Leeds are doing very well in their own right and it's great to see English clubs doing so well in Europe.'

A good run in the Champions League and a pat on the back from Sir Alex Ferguson may have been moments to cherish for O'Leary, but it was not going to get any better. Despite back-to-back wins over Bradford and Leicester at the end of the 2000–01 campaign, there was to be no Champions League in 2001–02. Leeds missed out on qualification by merely one point, finishing in fourth place behind Liverpool.

This had grave financial implications for the club, as playing in the Champions League had been the very basis on which all sums had been done. Players' wages were spiralling in the 2001–02 season to the degree that, in a single year, costs rose by £12 million and the total club wage bill, mostly incurred by the players, was now £38 million. Going north too, with the speed of a Manchester-bound jet from Heathrow, was the debt. The end-of-season net debt rose from £9 million in 1999 to £21 million in 2000 to £39 million in 2001, the latter without the £60 million loan showing up in the books. A £5 million development of the club's Thorp Arch training ground and a further outlay of £29 million on Robbie Keane, Robbie Fowler and Seth Johnson all added to the pressure on O'Leary.

In December 2001 and January 2002, rivals for Europe Newcastle United inflicted a Premiership double upon Leeds in the space of a month, before Chelsea and Liverpool dismissed them so easily that they were unrecognisable from their earlier performances. Far from competing with Manchester United for the League title, as O'Leary had predicted, Leeds finished fifth in 2001–02, 11 points behind the Reds, and 21 points behind champions Arsenal.

Roll on to the summer of 2002. O'Leary had won a slot as a TV pundit for the World Cup in Japan and South Korea, and was reminiscing in the papers about his own moment of World Cup glory which had been voted into the top 100 memories of the tournament's history. On 25 June 1990, the eyes of the entire footballing world were on O'Leary as he stepped up to take a crucial penalty kick in Italia '90. On his shoulders rested a nation's hopes and dreams, the like of which they had never experienced before. With Romania and the Republic of Ireland tied at four apiece in a tense shoot-out in Genoa, O'Leary had the opportunity to become immortalised in Irish soccer folklore – and he was not about to miss. A place in the quarter-finals of the World Cup, and against hosts Italy, beckoned for Jack Charlton's unfancied, uncompromising side, who had defied all the odds simply to get there. The tension was so unbearable that Charlton concedes he smoked his first cigarette for three years as he watched O'Leary stride towards the penalty area. When the ungainly defender placed the ball on the spot, not once, not twice, but at least half-a-dozen times in his efforts to get it to sit up, every Irish follower in the ground and at home held their breath. 'I'd never taken a penalty, not ever, but I'd always fancied taking one,' confessed O'Leary, who by that stage had been playing for Arsenal for 15 years.

> I think a few people, when they saw me step up to take that fifth penalty, must have been having heart attacks. But I'd always wanted to do it. As I walked up, all I could see was this sea of green, these 20,000 fantastic supporters of ours behind the goal. But they were all still. I'd never seen them so still. Taking that penalty, I felt like a golfer standing over an eight-foot putt to win a Major. It was all in my hands. I never thought I'd get tested like that in a team game.

O'Leary then stepped back, ran up and tucked the ball away into the bottom left-hand corner of the net, raising his arms aloft before being mobbed by his teammates. 'When I scored, that sea of green just erupted,' smiled O'Leary. 'It was a great feeling, to send your country through to the quarter-finals of the World Cup. But my biggest mistake was standing still because I nearly got killed under all those bodies who pounced on me in celebration!' For that brief, glorious moment, the bad blood which existed for three years between 1986 and 1989, with O'Leary cast into the international wilderness by Jack Charlton, was forgotten. 'He was the one who said he was going on holiday and couldn't go on tour, so he was the one that didn't get into the team,' explained Charlton. The decision has left O'Leary bitter to this day. He said:

> In leaving me out for three years, I missed a load of international caps and I thought he was totally wrong, but he will never admit that. It showed what he was like because when I scored that penalty Jack just came over and said 'Well done, I didn't think you'd ever miss.' It was typical Jack.

What Charlton achieved with the Republic in guiding them to the finals of both Italia '90 and USA '94 was emulated by Mick McCarthy in Japan/Korea 2002, for whom it was third-time lucky after play-off heartbreak for France '98 and Euro 2000. Ireland beat Iran over two legs after nobody gave them a prayer of coming through a qualifying group which contained Portugal and Holland. But they emerged as runners-up, unbeaten from the group stages, before taking their place in Japan and South Korea with a 2–1 aggregate triumph over Iran.

O'Leary, when asked whether he felt McCarthy's team was as good as Charlton's in 1990, replied:

> I don't think so. But I'm delighted for Mick because people said, when he took over, 'How are you going to follow Jack?' It just shows how thin the dividing line is between success and failure because he has been involved in two other play-offs and been cruelly beaten. When the draw was made for this competition and I looked at the group they were in, with the Dutch and Portuguese squads, I thought the best they could hope for was a play-off again. In fact, I didn't even think they would get that. But beating Holland was just unbelievable and then to go on and win the play-off was fantastic. Mick deserves a lot of credit because I don't think he has the same quality available to him Jack had, but he's blended together a team that's done well and who want to play for each other. And those fans, with all that green and white, that colour, will bring a great atmosphere to the World Cup – but will Japan be able to cater for 30,000 mad Irishmen?'

The *Yorkshire Post*'s Jeremy Cross wrote:

It has been a disappointing season at Leeds United but for Rio Ferdinand, Robbie Fowler, Nigel Martyn and Danny Mills the World Cup finals offer a chance to put the last nine months behind them and experience what could be the best month of their lives. When David O'Leary watches the tournament unfold from the BBC studios in London, where he is working as an expert summariser, he will feel justifiably proud that a quartet of his own players are representing England's finest. Taking into account the trio of Irish players – Gary Kelly, Ian Harte and Robbie Keane – on duty in the Far East as well, he will also wonder how Leeds' season remained trophy-less. Ferdinand and his England colleagues will have no such thoughts for the time being, however. For the month of June, all four can put country before club and do themselves justice before a worldwide audience in excess of four billion. When the Leeds players touched down in South Korea with the rest of the England squad nine days ago, the quartet will have had their own agendas and targets prior to the big kick-off and the month ahead should prove to be more rewarding for some than others. While this will be Danny Mills' first World Cup, Nigel Martyn knows it is his last, but what will make him feel even more desperate to make an impression is the fact that David Seaman starts as Sven-Goran Eriksson's number one goalkeeper. Martyn has lived in Seaman's shadow for almost the last decade and this has restricted him to just 21 caps at the age of 35. He should have earned more. Never one to show his disappointment, Martyn is a credit to himself, his club and country but yet more disappointment could follow. He is expected to lose his place in the Leeds side to Paul Robinson next season and it could be that he has played his last game for the club. Mills knows his career is at the opposite end of the spectrum. A controversial choice for Eriksson's squad, the defender has a genuine chance of starting against Sweden if the England coach decides to choose a specialist right-back instead of Wes Brown or Owen Hargreaves. Pleasant and articulate off the field, Mills transforms into a Rottweiler on it and this has made him one of the fiercest competitors in the Premiership. Poor discipline for Leeds this season almost cost him his place in Eriksson's squad and his behaviour will be under more scrutiny than ever before at the World Cup, but Mills' pace and strength in the tackle make him hard to beat. Ferdinand is the only Leeds player on England duty to be guaranteed his place in the team against Sweden on 2 June, injuries permitting of course. When Ferdinand travelled with Glenn Hoddle's England squad to France '98 he was a rebellious teenager, watching all four games shoulder-to-shoulder with the rest of the squad's unused substitutes. This time round he arrives in the Far East as the £18 million captain of Leeds, part-time businessman and role model for inner-city youth. 'I learned how to appreciate a World Cup,' said Ferdinand, recalling France '98. 'I knew I wasn't going to play, but it was valuable experience first-hand of how England players conduct themselves. It was good to see and it was good grounding for this one.' Ferdinand is one of the few players to have emerged from Leeds' season with credit. Another is Fowler. Fowler's £11 million transfer from Liverpool to Leeds shocked the Premiership, not to mention Leeds themselves, but the striker's rehabilitation from bit-part player under Gerard Houllier at Anfield to goal-scoring talisman at Elland Road has been to the benefit of Leeds, O'Leary and Eriksson. Injuries, combined with the emergence of Michael Owen, have restricted Fowler to 24 caps but he remains among the best finishers in English football. O'Leary is still pinching himself that Liverpool agreed to sell Fowler for £11 million and the Irishman is attempting to build a championship-winning side with him and Ferdinand at the spine of the team. He still has much to prove at international level, however, and this could be his chance to do so at the age of 27. With Emile Heskey and Owen expected to lead England's attack, Fowler will have to be patient, but there will be every opportunity for him to make an impact.

O'Leary may have been revelling in his World Cup media role but out there in the Far East and in Yorkshire the knives were being sharpened. O'Leary's Leeds full-back Danny Mills claimed that his

World Cup plans were being undermined by 'unprofessional' behaviour back home in England. Mills said he had been the victim of a character assassination, with O'Leary claiming he would slap the player on the transfer list if his disciplinary record did not improve. Mills impressed in England's final warm-up match against Cameroon, but his on-field behaviour was being called into question as the national side put the finishing touches to their World Cup preparations. 'His disciplinary record was abysmal and if I knew Danny would miss ten games again next season through suspension I'd put him on the transfer list now,' insisted O'Leary. 'He let himself, the club, the management and the fans down with his behaviour on the pitch. That is why all eyes will be on him when the competition begins.' But O'Leary added, 'He has a wonderful opportunity to make a name for himself at the World Cup and I hope he realises that this is the big platform on which he can publicly unveil the new Danny Mills.' However, Mills was furious with the criticism and he said:

> The examples of Arsene Wenger and Alex Ferguson, arguably the two best managers in the country, should be noted. It's very rare that they come out and comment on what their players do. Some things should be kept internal. Would anybody be happy if their boss walked into the middle of the office and started having a go at them? Over the years, enough lessons have been learned that whatever you want to say should be kept in the dressing room.

Within days, Lee Bowyer's solicitor was telling O'Leary to forget about trying to persuade the transfer-listed midfielder to stay at Elland Road. Bowyer had declared his intention to quit Leeds, claiming he needed to move on to further his career. His boss was still hopeful of a change of heart, but the midfielder's representative, David Geiss, said, 'He's made his decision and nothing has changed. He certainly doesn't look like signing a new contract.' Liverpool had been linked with a move for the former Charlton favourite, but O'Leary was still keen to keep him on board. He said, 'I want him to stay, but he has to go away and do a lot of thinking. There has been a lot of speculation but there are interesting days ahead.'

More significantly, Peter Ridsdale had already made up his mind to dispense with O'Leary's services but bided his time until the World

Cup was over and his manager had completed his television punditry. On 27 June 2002, the club published a statement on chairman Ridsdale's behalf which read:

> Leeds United plc today announces that David O'Leary, manager of Leeds United Football Club, has left the company by mutual consent. After four successful years, the pressures of some of the off-field incidents have resulted in both the company and Mr O'Leary agreeing that it would be of mutual benefit for a change of manager. It is hoped that an announcement regarding a successor can be announced in the next few weeks. Leeds United would like to place on record its thanks for David's enormous contribution over the last four years.

The *Yorkshire Evening Post*'s Paul Dews observed:

> David O'Leary today became the first casualty of a summer of turbulence at Elland Road. The pressure has been mounting on the United boss since last Christmas and the endless rounds of speculation linking big name players with mega-money moves away from the club finally took its toll when O'Leary was sacked. The latest bout of transfer gossip linked Rio Ferdinand with a £35 million switch to Manchester United and O'Leary shocked club officials when he announced he was powerless to keep his prize asset at the club. The manager even took the unusual step of admitting he would understand if Ferdinand wanted to quit the club in favour of a move to Old Trafford. The Ferdinand saga has been going on against a backdrop of transfer-fuelled speculation with a host of star players thought to be unhappy at Leeds. Lee Bowyer has refused to sign a new contract with the club, while Olivier Dacourt and Gary Kelly were also weighing up their options. Even United favourite David Batty has been considering his future after falling out of favour with the manager. While United chairman Peter Ridsdale has taken a defiant and diplomatic stance over the alleged exodus, O'Leary was quick to voice his thoughts over the players and his comments have angered the board. The United manager was highly critical of full-back Danny Mills prior to the

World Cup campaign, prompting the defender to hit back through the media. The *Yorkshire Evening Post* understands that a parting of the ways has been imminent. Of course, United's failure to qualify for the Champions League last season heaped more pressure on O'Leary. United were top of the Premiership last Christmas and were mounting a serious challenge for honours. But the release of O'Leary's book, *Leeds United on Trial,* coincided with a dreadful run of form and his criticism of players is thought to have opened up a rift within the dressing room. One United player's agent recently told the *Yorkshire Evening Post,* 'All the players are unhappy at Leeds and if they offered voluntary redundancies some of them would take it.' The departure of O'Leary seems certain to heal a few wounds within the United camp as the club looks to appoint a successor.

Ridsdale, meanwhile, insisted, 'It was all down to football.' Ridsdale spoke out as O'Leary took a swipe at his former club and speculation grew about the identity of his successor. The chairman said:

> We felt that, having spent £100 million and for two years running failing to get into the Champions League, it was time to make a change. I understand the shock, but most Leeds supporters have told me that what they want to see is silverware and after a £100 million investment we have failed to achieve that. After four years, given some of the pressure off the field, perhaps it was time to freshen up and make a change. It was fair to everyone to make a fresh start.

As the heat started to rise, O'Leary made barbed comments about an unnamed 'spin doctor' at Elland Road as he prepared to head off on holiday. And he warned that if he felt his name was being blackened by the Leeds hierarchy then he would come out fighting. He said:

> As long as the club stick to the reasons I'll keep my silence and go peacefully. But if I see some spin to suit the image of the club then I will have something to say. They have a great spin doctor at the club. I've heard that the sacking could have had something to do with the players and that amazes me. I've spent

£60 million and I don't think that was squandered. What concerns me is the spin put on it. I got the sack for reasons I can accept but where I will come out in anger is if spin is put on it that is wrong. There is one person at the club who is particularly good at spinning.

O'Leary said he believed that Leeds had already signed their next manager, though Ridsdale insisted that no deal had been done, despite reports naming Celtic boss Martin O'Neill as the hot favourite for the job. Said O'Leary, 'I think I have done a good job. I went in and he (Ridsdale) said I was sacked – simple as that. He said nothing else, just that. I think I know who has got the job. It's already in place.' The chairman said:

> There is no successor nominated or indeed approached and we have to decide who we believe is the best manager to take us to the next stage. I haven't approached anybody. At the moment, we have a shortlist which has been added to because a number of people have let it be known they would like to be considered. I've been pleasantly surprised by the interest expressed by some quality managers.

Dominic Matteo insisted the players must shoulder the blame for O'Leary's departure. Matteo believed Leeds underachieved last season and that their failure to qualify for the Champions League for a second successive season was the final nail in O'Leary's coffin. Said Matteo:

> At the end of the day, it is down to us, the players, to get the results on the field and we certainly underachieved last season. Results were very bad for us and we know that it was not good enough. If those results have ultimately cost David his job, then on behalf of the players all I can do is apologise to him. We are now waiting to see who takes over and it will be a huge change for all of us, but to be honest my thoughts at the moment are with David and his family. I went in to sign a new contract with the chairman and an hour later I found out that the manager had gone. I am gutted for David O'Leary. He brought me to the club and I feel that I have improved personally under him. He

must have done something right in the past because my football has improved greatly under him and I am sure a lot of the other players will say the same.

Danny Mills observed, 'The news came as a complete surprise to me, as it has to most people. Like the rest of the lads, I had absolutely no inclination that his departure was on the cards.' Rio Ferdinand was O'Leary's biggest gamble when he splashed a club record £18 million on the central defender, and Ferdinand was being made a scapegoat in some quarters, with his projected move to Manchester United being cited as one of the reasons behind O'Leary's departure. But Ferdinand hit back at claims that he was responsible for the axing and was quick to defend his former boss. 'What has gone on has been done behind closed doors and has nothing to do with me,' he insisted. 'I owe David O'Leary a lot of thanks. He had the bottle to sign me for a big fee when people were questioning whether I was worth it.' Ridsdale refuted claims from O'Leary that his sacking was due to the Irishman's opposition to the sale of Ferdinand:

> I have no intention of selling him. He has a clause in his contract that says he can't go to another Premiership club. We've had no offers for him and if I've got anything to do with it he'll see out his contract. We've told Rio we do not want to sell him and the parting of the ways with David O'Leary had nothing to do with Rio. We are not selling Rio Ferdinand to Manchester United.

Elsewhere, there were mixed reactions to O'Leary's departure. 'You can't feel sorry for David O'Leary because Leeds United have given his family security,' said former Leeds star Allan Clarke. Leeds legend Norman Hunter observed, 'It's amazing. One minute we're all talking about Rio going to Manchester United then the next minute, the manager goes.' Ray Fell, the Leeds Supporters Club chairman, said, 'There was no indication whatsoever of anything like this. Most Leeds fans, like me, will be very surprised.' Former United player Mel Sterland said, 'It's a massive job, but Martin O'Neill is already managing a big club and he could probably do it,' while former goal machine Lee Chapman said, 'The players will understand it and they

will know they are under pressure to impress the new manager.'
Former player Gordon McQueen commented, 'It's not David that has
let Leeds United down, it's the players who have simply underachieved
massively. David spent a lot of money but they just haven't produced
as they should have done last season.'

Jeremy Cross saw it like this:

> David O'Leary left Leeds United with no choice but to sack him
> after losing the respect of his players and that of a significant
> section of the club's supporters. His reign as manager was
> ultimately undermined by flaws and failings that resulted in the
> Leeds team underachieving when it mattered most. Like the side
> itself, O'Leary flattered to deceive despite inheriting a talented
> young side and a chairman and board who were prepared to back
> him with £95 million to spend on strengthening his squad
> without undue pressure to return the compliment and win some
> silverware. Ironically, O'Leary was true to his mantra of being a
> 'young manager who has done nothing yet' and in time will
> realise that he has nobody to blame for his expensive failings but
> himself. The soft and seemingly eloquent Irish brogue that made
> him popular with housewives and grandmothers became
> transparent to those within the game when the pressure on him
> to deliver increased. In O'Leary's world, the side's failings never
> seemed to be his fault. Nothing ever was. Excuses from him were
> plentiful but in time became tedious and predictable. Successful
> campaigns in Europe, including reaching the semi-finals of both
> the UEFA Cup and Champions League, offered genuine hope that
> Leeds were on the threshold of a winning period, but O'Leary
> proved incapable of building on the foundations. The
> circumstances generated by the court case involving Lee Bowyer
> and Jonathan Woodgate were out of his control but nevertheless
> proved to be the beginning of the end. Standing by the two
> players and criticising the Football Association for not selecting
> them for England was admirable and expected. Then came his
> biggest mistake. Following the culmination of the trial at Hull
> Crown Court, O'Leary, in his wisdom, released a book entitled
> *Leeds United on Trial* in which he proceeded to contradict his
> earlier support for both Woodgate and Bowyer. In that one

moment, O'Leary sacrificed the respect, desire and determination of his dressing room. It was the beginning of the end but O'Leary continued to fall on his own sword by writing an outspoken column in a national Sunday newspaper that only served to antagonise the Leeds plc. Their patience in a manager who was paid £1.6 million a year had finally run out and the board must be applauded for making a brave but correct decision.

O'Leary pushed himself towards the exit door with his lack of success at Leeds United but it was player power that ultimately forced him through it as the club sacked him. The reasons for Leeds to keep him in office for a fifth term as manager were outweighed by views pointing towards the opposite. The most convincing one was that the players had lost their faith and confidence in the Irishman. The final shove came when Leeds' chairman Peter Ridsdale consulted several senior members of the squad and learned that they had become disillusioned with their manager. O'Leary claimed that he knew who his successor would be and was speaking to his solicitor, Michael Kennedy, to negotiate a compensation package from the club. It seems almost poetic that O'Leary is costing the club money to the very end, considering he has spent more than £90 million since taking over from George Graham in October 1998 without being able to win a trophy. This lack of success, his behaviour following the high-profile trial of Lee Bowyer and Jonathan Woodgate at Hull Crown Court and the gradual changing attitude towards him of his squad, convinced Leeds to cut their losses and terminate his £1.6 million a year contract. O'Leary, who reacted to the news by going shopping for some new holiday clothes ahead of his trip to Sardinia, spoke to waiting reporters outside his home in Harrogate. He said, 'All I know is I went to see Peter Ridsdale at 11 a.m. yesterday morning and I was told I was sacked. Nothing should surprise you in football. I have tried to give the club all my best. In the circumstances I think we have done a good job.' He went on to offer the club – and new manager – his best wishes, adding:

I think I know who it is. I want to thank the supporters and the people around here who have all been wonderful.

> *Of course I am disappointed, but then that is football. People talk about spending £60 million (net) but that is nothing in football these days. I'm sorry I've been such a long time but I've been shopping for some jeans for my holiday.*

O'Leary looked to have the potential to reward Leeds' faith in him when blooding promising youngsters such as Woodgate, Stephen McPhail, Alan Smith and Paul Robinson. Inspired by O'Leary's bold selection and Eddie Gray's coaching, Leeds became a challenging force in domestic and European football, reaching successive UEFA Cup and Champions League semi-finals as well as securing fourth, third and fourth-place finishes in the Premiership. Despite this success, Leeds were still without a trophy and the pressure on O'Leary to deliver increased. Despite leading the Premiership on New Year's Day 2002, his side capitulated to finish fifth. Scraping into next season's UEFA Cup failed to impress the club's board, considering Leeds had budgeted for a return to the riches of the Champions League. Despite taking into account the difficult circumstances the court case generated and the subsequent hate mail O'Leary and his family received, the bottom line is that Ridsdale lost patience with an underachieving manager who, in footballing terms, had quite simply run out of excuses.

The day after Terry Venables signed a two-year contract to replace him, O'Leary said he believed his successor could win a trophy with the squad he left behind at Elland Road. He said:

> Terry has been left with a top-four team and some very talented young players. With a bit of luck and no off-field problems, he will not be far away from winning something at the end of the season. The squad is there and they have proved their ability by what they have done in the Premiership and in Europe over the last four years. Terry has to turn it into trophies, and without the problems of recent years, he can deliver them. He is a very experienced coach and manager. I hope he can keep the players he needs for silverware.

O'Leary, overlooked by Sunderland when they replaced Peter Reid with Howard Wilkinson, was to find himself in the eye of a storm over allegations from Aston Villa chairman Doug Ellis that the Irishman had been touting for the Villa Park post then held by Graham Taylor. Ellis insisted that close connections of O'Leary had been urging him to sack Taylor to make way for him and O'Leary countered:

> Agents who do not represent me are hawking my name around clubs. Since I left Leeds in the summer I have been linked with a number of jobs that I have absolutely no interest in. Graham Taylor is fully aware of the situation. I have made a point of talking to him personally to explain what is going on. This is one of the reasons why I have deliberately steered clear of going to games this season. I did not want anybody spotting me in the crowd and coming to the wrong conclusion that my presence was putting pressure on managers.

O'Leary has convinced himself that he did a good job in his four years at Leeds and rails against suggestions that he lost the dressing room. After actually joining Aston Villa as manager following a year out of the game, he hit out at the 'smear campaign' that followed his sacking at Leeds, maintaining that he believed he was proving at Aston Villa that it was unjust to brand him 'a cheque book manager'. O'Leary spoke about what he felt was a campaign to discredit him after he was dismissed by Leeds, admitting that one of the main reasons for taking charge of Villa was to prove he could be a success without relying on large sums of money to spend in the transfer market. O'Leary didn't spend much in acquiring the services of Thomas Sorensen, Gavin McCann and Nolberto Solano and a very conservative sum was put aside for new blood in the summer of 2004 despite shedding the club of ten players. O'Leary said:

> Am I frustrated by the lack of funds? No, I'm not. Honestly. I'm absolutely delighted. I took this job for the reason of not having money to spend. I had my own personal agenda to shut a few people up. I did a job at Leeds. I thought I did a really good job. Every year of the five I was there we qualified for Europe, which was big money for the club. Commercially, a deal with Nike and

other sponsorship deals made the club a lot of money. I didn't sign the players with the monies involved because, quite rightly, someone else who was better qualified dictated the finances of the club. The part where you are disgusted is where they try to smear you afterwards – when I was sacked at Leeds. There was the smear of 'You've lost the dressing room' which was given a spin and they tried to smear me in other ways. I spent what I was allowed to spend and I was governed by that. It was important to come here to Villa because there was the spin and smear put around of 'You're a cheque book manager' so this was the right club for me to come to. When people put that spin out, some people will believe it, so it was important to come here and do well – not to show people at Leeds but to show people who believe the spin. It was the right club for me to show people that I can work the other way with little money. Just imagine if I had come here and we'd have been doing like we have and I had brought in really good players. It would have been, 'Yes, but he was able to spend money'. So it was good for me to come here with little money to spend. I had my own agenda here on that one – to shut a few people up. Lots of people knew that I did a good job at Leeds. I could have gone back into football very quickly after being sacked there. But I thought this job was right for showing a few people what I could do. I was delighted not to have money here. I didn't need to prove anything to myself but you still had to answer a few people, not by words but by actions. I hear people say Villa is a top six club. Why? Just because it's got a fantastic stadium and it's an old name? I am proud to be here. It's got a fantastic old traditional name. The club finished in 16th place last season so the ground and the name doesn't give you any rights in terms of being successful. But I'm going to try, hopefully. Who knows how long I'll be here? But someone has got to try to put it right and put a real quality team on the pitch to go with the quality stadium and the quality name.

Then came a tune familiar to all Elland Road-watchers, with O'Leary warning that Aston Villa would be unable to repeat their 2003–04 battle against the odds for a European spot next season unless new blood was added to the squad. O'Leary said:

In the summer, we will have 14 players, including two goalkeepers. There is no getting away from it — bodies need to be brought in here. It is the type of bodies that you bring into the club which will decide the kind of ambitions that the club have. I know I can't have an absolute abundance of players but I do know we cannot operate on as small a squad as we have.

In April 2004, O'Leary admitted to being 'a bit of an arsehole' during his final year in charge of Leeds United. He said:

I thought I had changed a bit and had too much to say. I was put up by the club to say too many things and now I think I just want to be myself again. I was told to do this and that at Leeds and became too opinionated about things that had no relevance to myself. I had changed and I suppose the court case changed me a bit. There was a siege mentality. Now I just want to be the person I was during my first three years at Leeds. I have no complaints if someone wants a change, but just do it right. Just say, 'Thanks, but we are sacking you', pay me off and wish me all the best. But to try and blacken your name as well isn't right. It was dirty. You hear Leeds spent £90 million under me but you never hear that they recouped £60 million and qualified for Europe four years running. I also left them with good players, not people at the end of their careers. The smearing came as low as people saying that when I left Leeds we were on a bad run. We won seven of my last ten games in charge and only lost once; people forget that. Then the smear came out about how I had lost the dressing room and it's amazing how stuff like that can stick. But it's amazing that all the players rang me to say goodbye. I had to endure a smear campaign when I left Leeds and the way Leeds tried to do it was sad.

CHAPTER SIX

TERRY VENABLES – A MARRIAGE MADE IN HELL

It was early July 2002, and Peter Ridsdale whistled happily as he mowed the lawns at his Cumbria home. The Leeds United chairman had pulled off the massive coup of installing world-renowned coach Terry Venables in the Elland Road hot seat. And the ink was still not dry on the contract when he called me at home to reveal, 'I've got him!' I was privileged to have been the only journalist in Britain to have been informed every step of the way as Ridsdale's hunt for a successor to the sacked David O'Leary took myriad twists and turns. That is why the *Yorkshire Evening Post* was able to exclusively reveal Venables as the new man, leaving the rest of the media pack floundering. Ridsdale said:

> If you wanted to draw up a comparison with the signing of Terry then the best would be Bobby Robson. He went to Newcastle as an ex-England manager and look what he's done. He has transformed the club. I am not prepared to divulge their names, but you would not believe the quality of the people who wanted to manage Leeds United. I firmly believe we have got the very best. You could not possibly go through the entire Venables *curriculum vitae* both as a player and a manager without arriving at the conclusion that he is supremely well qualified. Managing Leeds United is a big job. A huge job. It is therefore not surprising that when the position became vacant there were, over a period of days, many names in the frame. The

one name which jumped out was Terry Venables. You talk to anybody in the game – the players, the managers, the coaches – and they are almost unanimous in their verdict that Terry is the best coach and manager in the game. Players respect him; coaches admire him. I had lunch with him in Spain on Saturday and within ten minutes – so infectious is his enthusiasm – he has you believing you can play for England. Imagine how that must make a player puff out his chest. For tangible evidence of his qualities you only have to look at the incredible rescue act he performed at Middlesbrough the season before last. Barring a miracle, they were down and out of the Premiership with not even a hope of survival. They couldn't get a result to save their lives but in walked Terry and from the moment he made his entrance things changed for the better. I suspect he told them they were good players who had not become bad players overnight and restored their confidence to the degree that they were able to dig deep enough to retain their Premiership status. It takes a special man to be able to do that – and Terry is special. Anybody who watched his World Cup punditry had to be impressed by his tactical awareness and reading of the game. We talked over lunch about all our players and the players he wants to bring in as and when required. Rio Ferdinand was obviously one of those we discussed. Of course, Terry would like him at Elland Road; he is a player who is contracted to us and, as far as I am concerned, that is the way it will stay. Terry is aware of the situation with Lee Bowyer; the door is still open to Lee to sign a new contract and commit himself to Leeds United. Terry has demonstrated his commitment by signing a two-year deal, agreeing to forego his television work and embarking straight away on a house search in Yorkshire. He is genuinely thrilled by the prospect of taking on and beating the big guns, and I'll tell you this: I am glad he will be sitting in our dugout and not the opposition's.

Stirring stuff from a chairman who was still wrestling with his conscience over the removal of David O'Leary and who had to get the appointment of his successor bang on. The capture of Venables was a personal triumph for Ridsdale, who landed his prize-catch seven days after his massive manhunt was launched. The former England manager's agreement to a two-year deal brought to an end a nightmare week in the life of Ridsdale, consisting of endless telephone calls, energy-sapping travel, detailed legal documentation, nerve-jangling uncertainty and countless hours of lost sleep. It was no secret that the number one target was Celtic's Martin O'Neill. But it was always the case that if O'Neill decided to see out his contract north of the border, United would zoom in on Venables. Football, with its complex rules, miles of red tape and code of etiquette is unique as an industry in that it is forbidden to approach a desired employee who works for somebody else. In other branches of commerce, if you want to pinch another company's manager you take him to lunch, woo him, offer a better package and ask him to join you as soon as possible. That is a complete no-no in football. It is known as an illegal approach. Ridsdale, therefore, had to be very careful about what he said and did over the past few days. It will not have escaped the attention of thousands of fans gripped by the saga of United's successor to O'Leary that the words coming out of both Leeds and Glasgow may have been plentiful, but that their content had been anodyne. That is how it had to be. Now Ridsdale could embark on a well-earned family holiday, safe in the knowledge that he had heralded the dawn of a brand new Elland Road era which promised to be riveting, exciting and hugely successful. In the vastly experienced Venables, Ridsdale had identified and put in place a man who, it was hoped, would instantly consign to the corporation tip an *annus horribilis* in the club's history. What went before his arrival was just that to Venables – history. He started with a clean sheet which, in theory anyway, would quickly become the blueprint for United's future on the field.

Venables was introduced to the squad against a background of feverish activity. With captain Rio Ferdinand still non-committal about his future, Lee Bowyer set to join Liverpool, Olivier Dacourt appearing to be Juventus-bound and Jonathan Woodgate apparently putting pen to paper on a lucrative new deal, Venables was hardly off to a quiet start. Venables jetted into Leeds/Bradford airport, where he was greeted by club secretary Ian Silvester and met up with coaches Eddie Gray and Brian Kidd and chief scout Ian Broomfield. Along with club officials, they talked long into the night over dinner at a luxury hotel. The following morning, Ridsdale accompanied Venables to the club's training facility at Thorp Arch ahead of an afternoon media conference. Venables urgently wished to know the intentions of Ferdinand, who said:

> I'm looking forward to meeting Mr Venables and hearing his plans. People have said a deal has been done to sell me but it hasn't as far as I know. It makes me feel quite uncomfortable that some people have seen me as the man in the middle in what has happened at the club, because I haven't done anything. I've never asked to leave and the club haven't told me they are selling me. I spoke to the chairman before I went to Las Vegas on the first part of my holiday and we agreed to talk when I got back to training. I won't go into details about what was said, but I am still a Leeds player and I haven't asked for a transfer.

Within days, Venables was saying that he tried everything to keep Rio Ferdinand at the club before finally admitting that he was fighting a losing battle. His first few days in the Elland Road hot seat were dominated by the saga of Ferdinand's £30 million move to Manchester United, and he confessed that it was a difficult time for everyone connected with Leeds:

> Me and the chairman were on the phone a lot during the Ferdinand situation. It was a very difficult time for us because we didn't want him to leave and we made it very clear to him. We decided in the end that we were fighting a lost cause and tried to do the best we could under the circumstances. I think, in the end, he left us with little choice and we did well to get the money we did. We had to sell him and we did very well.

Ferdinand stepped out with Manchester United manager Sir Alex Ferguson after becoming Britain's most expensive footballer and pleaded with Leeds United fans to forgive his move to their arch-rivals. Clutching a Manchester United shirt, 23-year-old Ferdinand admitted that his transfer across the Pennines would make him a villain in the eyes of Leeds fans who idolised him. Eric Cantona, the last player to defect from Elland Road to Old Trafford, in 1992, had never been forgiven by Leeds supporters and Ferdinand knew he was likely to face a similar backlash. He said:

> I'm not sure how they will react to me. I like to think they will be nice, but you never know. I took all those things on board when I came here and you have to be big enough to take it on the chin. I would have liked the situation to have been resolved in a better way and I could go there and get the kind of reception I get when I go back to West Ham, but who knows? We'll have to wait and see.

Ferdinand made a point of thanking the Leeds fans for their support during his 20 months at the club, saying:

> I made a decision to come here as I thought it was a step on the way to improving me as a player. It was a bold step, but something I'm pleased to be doing. It wasn't an easy decision. I spoke to my family about loyalty. But, at the end of the day, it's a short career and opportunities like this don't come along all the time.

Ferdinand signed a five-year contract with Manchester United, in a deal believed at the time to be worth as much as £30 million. Ferguson said he believed Ferdinand would develop into the best centre-half in the world at Manchester United. The England defender, who had impressed in that summer's World Cup in Japan, was unveiled as Britain's most expensive player at Old Trafford following his transfer from Leeds. The deal was Ferguson's first major purchase of the summer and meant, if the public figures were to be believed, that at the age of 23, Ferdinand had changed hands for £48 million in less than two years. Ferguson said:

> When you can identify a potentially great player you try to think about how you can get him. We knew it was a hard road, but we've got to the end of it. He is going to be a fantastic player. At 23, Rio has great potential. We're confident he will mature here and develop into the best centre-half in the world.

Ferdinand said:

I'm delighted to be joining one of the biggest clubs in the world. I have come here to improve as a player. That was the first thing on my list. I have to be able to cope with what is put in front of me. It is going to be tough but hopefully I will thrive in these situations. I enjoyed my time at Leeds and I hope to enjoy it at Manchester United. I was always confident in my ability and I was confident at the World Cup. I know this is a big challenge. I hope to prove any doubters out there wrong. I want to fulfil the potential I have. I know the management here will work me hard and demand they get the best out of me. My mum and dad gave me advice. They said, 'Go where your heart says you should go – go where you can improve as a player.' My brother had his say as well but in the end it is down to me – it was an easy decision. Opportunities like this do not come that often. I don't want to sit around thinking about what I didn't do in my career. I went to Leeds for a lot of money; I don't think about it. It won't play on my mind at all.

Ferdinand, whose first taste of action for Manchester United was in a tournament in Amsterdam in early August, added:

I'm really looking forward to the new season and I can't wait to run out in a United shirt. I am leaving a great club in Leeds and I appreciate what they've done. They went out on a limb to get me and not many would have done that. David O'Leary brought me on as a player.

Ferguson added:

A transfer like this had to be difficult simply because Leeds are a big club and one of our fiercest rivals and there were three years left on his contract.

The *Yorkshire Post*'s John Woodcock, meanwhile, considered the new start for Venables this way:

So Terry Venables has come back for more. Why? Could it be that boardrooms and courtrooms, punditry and showmanship, wise-cracking and crooning, creating detective stories and running flash bars, have been only a game to Tel Boy? Distractions from what he does best? Only fools and horses would attempt to answer that one. Trying to pin down such a streetwise, elusive character is a mug's game, but in the quest for clues let's look at the form-book. He grew up on a council estate near the Ford plant in Dagenham, and given his questionable business dealings since, maybe not everyone would buy a second-hand model from him. On the other hand, give him a team of more than useful footballers and you'll find admirers of his judgement everywhere from Barcelona to Middlesbrough, including those at the Football Association who entrusted him with England. Doubtless, he has already blown any chance of a knighthood. They will not care a jot about that at Elland Road, though, if next season Venables overtakes Sir Bobby Robson's Newcastle, and particularly Sir Alex Ferguson and Manchester United, en route to the Premier League title. Any silverware would do, for that matter. The lack of it, having spent tens of millions on a fruitless quest, cost David O'Leary his job. Can Venables do better? With some of the finest players in the country – British, Irish and foreign – to work with, his record suggests he can turn underachievers into something more. His TV analyses on the World Cup may sometimes have taken a simple game to a level best understood at Sandhurst, but when translated to the pitch, his tactics have a habit of making sense. Depending on which media version you believe, Venables was third choice, if not lower, for the Leeds job, and yet he is now reportedly the highest-paid manager in the country after the chap at Old Trafford. It would be stupid to suggest that money wasn't a major factor in luring him from the sharp suits into a tracksuit, but, equally, the man has always been attracted by a serious challenge, and at 59 he has some unfinished business with himself. He was a clever player, even shrewder as coach and manager. He won championships with Crystal Palace and Queens Park Rangers, where his ambitions led to him becoming major shareholder and managing director. His record with a modest club in west London attracted interest in Catalonia and he took over at

TERRY VENABLES — A MARRIAGE MADE IN HELL

Barcelona, guiding them in 1985 to their first League title in 11 years. His signings there included Gary Lineker, but then finishing second in Spain and being beaten in the European Cup final was considered failure. Venables was sacked and returned to his London roots as manager of Tottenham. It was to be an interesting era for the club. He signed Paul Gascoigne, developing him into a world-class player, was joined again by Lineker and commandeered an FA Cup victory in 1991. Off-the-field developments were even more dramatic. Venables, ever one for the main chance, was a partner in an unsuccessful bid for the club, before becoming chief executive after computer tycoon Alan Sugar won a battle with Robert Maxwell for control of Spurs. Subsequent boardroom wrangles saw him ousted in 1993 and reinstated, before defeat in the High Court. Later that year, BBC's *Panorama* programme alleged various misdealings connected with Venables' businesses. He responded by offering money to charity if they could prove them, and threatened libel action. With that background, most careers would have been rushing downhill. Not for the first time, the chirpy East Ender confounded expectations and headed the opposite way. Such was the FA's desperation to create a successful national side, they overcame their instinctive caution and appointed Venables as England coach. The risks were obvious — within months, police dropped their inquiry into allegations that he had paid Brian Clough a 'bung' to arrange a player's transfer — but legal problems were mounting. As our hosting of Euro '96 approached, Venables announced that he would resign afterwards because of pending court cases. England's tournament appeared to be heading for disaster, especially as the team's preparations were dominated by antics starring, who else, but Gazza. In the event, Venables' team reached impressive heights and on the way Gascoigne scored a wonder goal. England seemed to have every chance of winning the trophy, until the Germans defeated them again in a semi-final penalty shoot-out. Venables' reputation as a coach was further enhanced, but again it seemed that his ambitions behind the scenes would mark him out as a chancer who was destined to lose. During an unsavoury spell in control of

Portsmouth, where his company received big money but the fans saw little success, he was taken to court by the Department of Trade and Industry and subsequently agreed to an order banning him from holding company directorships for seven years. The sometime scriptwriter, crooner and host at London celebrities' bar, Scribes, was in the spotlight for all the wrong reasons. The jokes were wearing thin, though the Aussies thought they recognised a brash but gifted operator in their own image when they gave him the job of leading their national team to the 1998 World Cup. The partnership ended in recrimination when his side failed to qualify at the final hurdle against Iran. There was an uninspiring return to Crystal Palace, and when the England job became available again after Kevin Keegan's resignation, this time there was no call. Today's man was Sven – Venables was yesterday's. Or so we thought. When Middlesbrough found themselves at the foot of the Premiership in December 2000, seemingly doomed to relegation, they appealed to him to work alongside Bryan Robson. It looked like mission impossible, and perhaps it would have been for anyone else. The opportunity revived Venables, the coach. After an 11-match unbeaten run he was named Manager of the Month, and Boro's season was rescued. He rejected efforts to keep him, citing his ITV commitments. On the face of it, a sofa in a television studio and an audience of millions was more compelling than a dugout on a dismal Saturday afternoon in January, trying to plot a result against Southampton or Blackburn Rovers. And yet . . . the football man inside him has called out, and again Venables has answered. Maybe South Korea and Japan were his inspiration. Having spent a month telling millions of us what was tactically good and bad about the World Cup, could it be that the chance to put his words into action, to work with Rio Ferdinand and co., to persuade Lee Bowyer that the new season represents a new start for both of them, was too good an opportunity to resist? Leeds' formal announcement to the Stock Exchange of his appointment reflects how far the game, and the boy from Dagenham, have travelled.

TERRY VENABLES — A MARRIAGE MADE IN HELL

Before the end of August 2002, Venables was looking forward to ending a 15-year exile from European club competition with Leeds set to take on Ukrainian side Metalurg Zaporizhya in the first round of the UEFA Cup. Venables had not experienced the thrill of coaching a side in Europe since being sacked by Spanish club Barcelona in 1987. Although he was involved with Tottenham's European Cup-Winners' Cup campaign four years after this, team affairs at the time were being handled by Peter Shreeves. Venables was now at the helm of a Leeds squad who were clear favourites to beat a side who only finished fifth in the Ukrainian League the previous season and who only managed to score 25 goals in 26 games. Not surprisingly, Venables admitted that he would need time to do some homework on his first-round opponents but he was looking forward to the challenge of once again pitting his wits against the best in Europe. 'It would be great to lift the UEFA Cup,' he said. 'It is still an important competition, and if we can keep the squad fit and healthy we have a good chance of doing well. It will certainly be a good test for the young players and will give them more experience.' Venables was grateful for Leeds simply being in the hat for the competition. 'It looked at one stage, from what I could see in the League, as if there wasn't a possibility they would be in it. Then they ended up with a few wins which got them in there, which is great,' he said.

At just about the time, some 40 years previously, that Venables began to make his name as a Chelsea player, Leeds United were in the formative stages of what was to become their golden era under Don Revie. Midfielder Venables was to see plenty of action against Leeds and he recalled this in our interview two months into his tenure at Elland Road:

> Billy Bremner played for Scotland Schoolboys at 15 and I played directly opposite him for England. I was right-half and he was inside-left. We both got into our respective teams at the age of 17, and that Leeds side started at the same time as ours. We had some great matches against them and I think, in fact, we used to have the edge on them when we first started. We got to two semi-finals and we maybe did too well too early because Tommy Docherty began breaking the team up when we failed for the second time to reach the final. Where Tommy became

impatient, Don Revie did exactly the reverse. He stuck to his guns and they became the Leeds that we all know. And love. In fact, Chelsea had a third semi-final, against Leeds, when I'd left for Spurs. They won that, met us in the final and we beat them. You never know what's going to happen in this game, but it never occurred to me that one day I might manage Leeds. I did the Middlesbrough job, enjoyed that, liked the place. It was a bit different to the situation here at Leeds because the object there was just to get results. Here they expect to see a calibre of football which I would like to put in if we can, and you've got to try to get that balance, which is always difficult.

Venables contended that his position was made more difficult by the 'Bosman ruling'. Jean-Marc Bosman was an out-of-contract player in the Second Division of the Belgian League. He wanted to move to Dunkerque in France. Dunkerque didn't offer his Belgian club enough of a transfer fee, so they said he couldn't go. In the mean time, he was on reduced wages because he was no longer a first-team player. He took his club to the European Court for restraint of trade. After many months, he won his case and won the right, for all EU players, to a free transfer at the end of their contracts, with the proviso that they were transferring from one EU federation to another. The Leeds manager contended that the FA's regulations on transfer windows (whereby players can only be transferred during two specific months of the football year) occasionally combined badly with 'Bosman frees' to adversely affect a manager's ability to buy and sell players:

> Before the Bosman ruling, I thought transfer windows would be a good idea. But now I think it gives you a problem. You could normally let a player go a few weeks into the last year of his contract if he or the club were so inclined, but now nothing can be done until January, by which time the player thinks that he has only got to wait another four or five months and he is a free agent. There's lots for and against transfer windows, but I just find myself, on the whole, against them. Having said that, they helped me while at Barcelona. I had 36 players and a lot of the other clubs didn't, so it was in our favour. You couldn't buy a player during the whole season in those days, so all those

players were with me for the entire campaign. When we could, we bought and sold only one player. Out went Maradona, we made a £4 million profit and won the League! I don't think that had ever happened at the Nou Camp – they always liked spending money! My parting was done in an entirely grown-up way with the chairman, vice-chairman and myself round a table and agreeing that it was in the better interests of us all for me to go. I'd done three years, which was the longest anybody had ever been there. Three leavers in a year was the record, with one of them never even reaching the first game of the season! Since then, Cruyff has broken the long-stay record, of course. The thing about being in Europe this season is that you just hope you're geared up for it. No one has been in this period of four months without being able to bring in a player, and you never know the right amount of players that you are going to need – especially when you get hit by injuries in the same position. When my predecessor here was putting five on the bench in European games in which seven substitutes were allowed, citing a lack of bodies, the fact was they could have gone out and bought players then. You can't now, so we'll just have to see really. I think the current financial climate in football is going to get worse. Some time a little further down the track there will be fewer £30,000-a-week players. There will be some, but managers will be presented with a budget with which they must decide what to do – whether you want to pay the big bucks at the top or spread it around. If budgets are not adhered to, as we are already finding, there are lots of clubs who will be in trouble. It used to be that the supporter and the shareholder were the same person. They can be, but that is not necessarily the case any longer in public limited companies. They want to see the results, and if they are just shareholders, and not supporters, there's a conflict. The supporters want you to buy the players, the shareholders want money in the bank and that's where something's got to give. I haven't set any targets here at Leeds because I have nothing to target against. If I'd had a year under my belt then I would have something to compare it with and know who and what I am dealing with. I've just got to gain experience with the squad. I've been pleased with the way they have gone about their work, but there's an awful lot to do. The Ferdinand thing was something we didn't want to happen because I felt that his presence would have made us very strong at the back. He had to go, though, and then we had to do the best we could. We've got some good defenders, but we needed cover and that's concerned me a bit. And, of course, you always want good players. You want to increase your staff. We've got good players, but you also want cover in every position.

Venables had certainly been putting in the hours since his appointment on 8 July 2002. 'I've been leaving the hotel at eight in the morning and not leaving the office until seven thirty at night to try to get up to speed with everything,' he said. 'Then down to the restaurant at night for a meal and straight to bed. That's how it's been. But I've moved into rented accommodation in north Leeds in the last couple of days and we've rented long enough to take the pressure off needing to immediately buy a property.'

On the day we met I reminded him that, as Kim Basinger might say, he had been in situ for nine-and-a-half weeks. 'Is it really?' he asked. 'How come I've only been paid for a month!' It was Tel at his best. He went on to talk to me about tactics and teamwork:

It's a good challenge. We have a lot of good young players. We have got to learn very quickly. As talents, they are very good but we've just got to make sure that our teamwork improves. But they are receptive and we have put a lot of work in, considering the short time we've been together. There haven't been many days off because I want to know what they can and can't do. When you haven't got a year behind you, it's very difficult. Coaches always want time and supporters can't wait, but you understand that and we've got to try to perform to our optimum as soon as possible. Tactically, if you've got 4–3–3 it doesn't take much to make it 4–5–1 and vice-versa. I want the players to be flexible and to know how to change a system, albeit very simply. It can make a difference. We have already changed systems when we have played and it doesn't affect, for instance, the back four. We haven't done anything in that area, as I would have liked, because we simply haven't had time. Once the season starts it's like you can't do too much the day after a game because you're just loosening off and you have one day in which you can't do too much because you're playing the next day. There's a lull now because everybody's away on international duties and all this is the real frustration for me at the moment. Saturday, Wednesday, Saturday is a lot of games in a short period and there's no time to do anything. That is the beauty of having had a team for a while. They know what you want. I'm still at the stage of trying to implement what I want.

In late July 2002, Lee Bowyer was assured that he still had a future at Elland Road – if he wanted to stay. The troubled midfielder's proposed move to Liverpool broke down, leaving him in limbo. Reds boss Gerard Houllier called a halt to the deal as he questioned the player's hunger to play for the Anfield outfit. It was yet another twist in a footballing year Bowyer would surely care to forget. With the long and protracted talks sunk in the River Mersey, Bowyer limped back to West Yorkshire where – unsurprisingly – he was met with open arms by club chairman Peter Ridsdale, who now hoped that contract rebel Bowyer would put his past problems firmly behind him and sign a new five-year deal which would finally see one of the Elland Road favourites commit his future to Leeds. Supporters, having seen Rio Ferdinand leave for Manchester United, would no doubt have been delighted that there was a strong chance of Bowyer and Leeds kissing and making up and looking to the future together. Ridsdale had told Bowyer that his deal was still on offer.

Whether Lee stays a Leeds player is now down to him. We want him to stay and have never suggested otherwise. The offer of a new contract has always been there for him and we hope that he will now sign it. The only reason he was placed on the transfer list in the first place was because he refused to sign a new deal with the club and we faced losing a potentially valuable player on a Bosman free at the end of the next season. I can't go into the reasons for his move to Liverpool falling down, but I do now hope that Lee will come back to us and talk about signing the new deal.

Bowyer said he was looking forward to a season of unprecedented success at Elland Road after seeing his move to Liverpool collapse. He insisted his heart lay with Leeds and predicted a rosy future for the club – despite Ferdinand's transfer. Bowyer said:

> Rio's move to Manchester United is a loss, but it also means that other players are less likely to leave the club and I think we have a strong base to build on. Although it looked as if I was going to leave, I always had my doubts – and I knew it would be hard to find a set of supporters as loyal as the ones we have at Leeds. I think they will see that the best is still to come from this Leeds team. I never asked to go on the transfer list and made it clear to Mr Ridsdale that I had reservations when they accepted Liverpool's bid. So it is probably in the best interest of all parties that the deal did not go through. The arrival of Terry Venables was also a major factor in my thinking that this was not the right time to be leaving Elland Road. With the players we have and with Venables as manager I genuinely believe we have an excellent chance of winning something this season.

Houllier decided not to continue with his bid to take the 25 year old to Anfield after days of talks. A club statement said, 'Liverpool have decided not to go ahead with the proposed transfer for a variety of reasons. Manager Gerard Houllier was not convinced the player had either the hunger or desire to play for the club, qualities which are essential for any Liverpool player.' Ridsdale said, 'There is very good reason to feel confident about the future. We have a very good coach, we have great players already within the squad and now we have money to invest in the transfer market.' He refuted claims from some quarters that Leeds were in the midst of a financial crisis but admitted that there could be further departures:

> The only people talking about a financial crisis have been the press. I said in February that I felt the squad was top-heavy by four players and that we would like to bring in funds through the transfer system during the summer. That is by no means a financial crisis. If the Rio deal goes through then we still have two or three too many in the squad but at the same time we

have overtaken our target for a funds influx. I believe we are financially prudent.

When the Ferdinand deal had been signed and sealed, Peter Ridsdale believed it was time to look forward to the new season with great optimism:

> I have mixed feelings. I am excited that we have done a good deal under the circumstances, but I would have preferred those circumstances to be very different and for Rio to have wanted to stay with us. This has been going on for some time now and it has cast a shadow over our preparations for the new season. Once this deal goes through then it will be the first time that I can safely look forward to the new season with excitement. Once this is all over then I believe there is genuine reason to feel confident about the new season. We have to look forward, and under Terry Venables there is a great prospect of success for Leeds United. I would expect new faces to come in within a matter of days.

Just three games into Venables' tenure, Sunderland had plundered their first win at Elland Road in 41 years. A month later, Arsenal looked on a different planet as they left Yorkshire with a 4–1 victory in their fancy pants. A month after that and Liverpool went to the top of the League with a single-goal Elland Road success which did not please the home crowd. Come November, Everton were the latest to raid full points from a journey over the M62. But worse was to come. Three days later, First Division Sheffield United slotted in two goals in the four minutes of added time to dump Leeds out of the Worthington Cup. And now, serious questions were being asked of the man with the Permatan who was supposed to be a tactical genius. The *Yorkshire Evening Post*'s Paul Dews wrote:

> The vultures have already started to circle, but Leeds United boss Terry Venables is determined to stay calm while all around start to fret. Speaking less than 15 hours after United were sent spinning out of the Worthington Cup at the hands of First Division Sheffield United, he remains a determined individual

who is not prepared to let the doubters or critics shake him. The Whites have picked up just two wins in ten games and, while there is growing talk about the club slipping into a crisis, the former England manager is attempting to put a brave face on things. The Cockney charm is still very much in evidence, although the twinkle in his eyes may have faded somewhat since his much-heralded arrival at Elland Road back in July. The lynch mob are already baying for his blood – there is increasing speculation surrounding his future – but there is a steeliness about the one-time Barcelona boss and a genuine belief that Leeds will get it right. 'Do you know Brian Clough and Jock Stein were both at Leeds for the same amount of time?' muses Venables. 'Forty-four days. That's amazing.' If some had their way, Venables would have completed an unwanted hat-trick of 44-day managers, but the wily campaigner insists he is not at Leeds for the short-term and is looking to the future. There have been suggestions that Venables is already considering scuttling back to the safety of the TV studio but, while he could be forgiven for considering that option himself, there is no serious indication he is about to turn his back on Leeds. Unsurprisingly, he has been taken aback by the speed in which the fans have turned their backs on him. 'They were at me after the third game,' he says. 'But fans are fans and they are entitled to their feelings.' However, Venables is not one to be deterred by the reaction of a minority and is determined to shrug off any ill-feeling in a bid to stay focused on what is becoming a tougher mission than perhaps he first expected. The United faithful, usually renowned for their patience, have jammed radio phone-ins and newspaper letters columns with their comments about the United boss. Aside from the hot potato issue involving the absence of David Batty, an issue the manager believes he has explained fully, it appears that Venables' legacy as a tactical genius has exploded around him and the fans want to know what is going on. The midfield stronghold of recent seasons appears to have evaporated this term and Venables is being accused of tinkering for tinkering's sake. He explains:

*A lot of our changes have been down to injuries. Matteo
has played while injured and Radebe has played while
injured and one of the things you have to do in situations
like that is maybe stiffen up injury areas by playing a
certain way. Some lads have played when you wouldn't
normally play them. They didn't have to do that and
we've tried to cover that up by playing midfield players in
front of the defence and therefore it has reduced our
chances of going forward. You're then relying on what the
forwards can do and rather than rely on two when we've
got three I'd rather rely on three to see if we can sit more
defensively. We also have Lee Bowyer who can get
forward and back.*

At this point, Venables reaches for a sheet of a paper, a glint in
his eye, to demonstrate the system he is trying to impose on his
front players. People have accused him of not being interested,
but as he scribbles furiously there is no doubt he knows where
he is going. 'When the ball's on the right, Kewell gets in the
middle and on the left Smith gets in,' he explains.

*That way you can fit in more strikers than in a 4–4–2.
I've tried things to see what suits us the best because in
the early days I thought I should do that. You can't play
all the strikers and some will be unhappy, but we played
4–4–2 on Wednesday and for most of the game we played
well and should have come home with the win.*

There have been accusations that Venables has blinded his
players with his science and suggestions that the midfield are
struggling to cope with his ideas – but the manager is quick to
dismiss such talk, and he insists:

*I don't think we should spend too much time talking about
tactics. They are there to have a pattern and a shape. I'm
trying to have a good defence. Apart from the Arsenal
game, we haven't let goals in. But, at the same time, we
have not scored as many as we should, which surprises*

me given the players we've got, and that has been disappointing. I don't want to start getting flummoxed and I've tried to lay it out as simply as I can. Sometimes, we'll play three up and sometimes one behind. In the long term we will have to change a lot during the game and be ready to adapt. Everyone is changing their systems. [Chelsea boss] Claudio Ranieri's been accused of changing his system four or five times during a game, or after ten minutes. When you see something causing a problem you have to do something about it, but you can't keep pulling rabbits out of the hat. Liverpool have played the diamond as well and Manchester United had lots of changes last year. Look at Arsenal – they'll play Wiltord up front or on the right side but, unlike with Smithy, they don't go on about that. They don't say, 'Why is he on right wing?' It's ridiculous.

While Venables is keen to explain how he sees United progressing tactically and the reasoning behind what some have viewed as radical changes, he is firm on his stance that he will not be drawn on individual players. Sections of the United faithful have singled out individual performers this season with contract wrangle star Bowyer provoking mixed emotions among the supporters, but Venables insists what happens behind closed doors stays behind closed doors. 'I read an article on Wednesday saying that we had a team meeting behind closed doors in private – I mean, do they expect me to invite the public in?' However, that meeting failed to provoke the response Venables was looking for when his injury-ravaged side failed to see off the threat of Sheffield United and finally succumbed to two injury-time goals. The manager was pleased with the way his team performed for large parts of the Worthington Cup tie, but, as is becoming the norm this term, Leeds left with nothing to show for their efforts. The final whistle was greeted with dismay by the fans and the chants of 'Venables out' rang out loud and clear around Bramall Lane while the manager and his players were ensconced in a dressing room post-mortem. The critics are wondering how a squad which has only lost the services of Robbie Keane and Rio Ferdinand is languishing in the lower reaches of the Premiership and has suffered an early exit in the Worthington Cup. But Venables firmly believes that changes needed to be made and he explains:

> *It's fair to say that Leeds were not playing well for a long while last season. The players and the staff own up to that and it's got to change. We've had a good look at each other and we've spoken candidly about what we have to do to improve, but other teams are also out to fight their corner and they obviously won't make things easy for us. We've got to get our confidence up now. The hard work will be there, but we've got to pass the ball better and that's something we all agreed on.*

It was an injury-hit side which turned out in South Yorkshire on Wednesday and the treatment room was bursting at the seams yesterday after more players picked up bumps and bruises. The manager still refuses to use the knocks as an excuse for United's failing in the results department and, equally, he won't be drawn into a debate over alleged misconceptions over the club's financial position when he was appointed. It's true that United were sitting on a potential £60 million windfall in player sales but all those deals, bar Rio Ferdinand's move to Manchester United, fell through and any cash bonus for Venables was reduced. The sale of Robbie Keane did raise further funds but, aside from the arrival of Nick Barmby, the Leeds boss has been unable to make any serious moves in the transfer market. Brazilian World Cup midfielder Kleberson is thought to be among the manager's targets when the transfer window re-opens in January, and Venables is clearly hoping to strengthen. He says:

> *I've spoken before about our imbalanced squad. I can't do anything about it right now. I believe I've got a group of players who could do really well and the addition of two or three would make a big difference. The club do realise*

that and they've said they will try and do their best to do
something for me. I'm optimistic come January that I will
be able to do what I want to.

In March 2003, with Leeds staring relegation in the face as just eight games remained, Venables was gone – sacked for the first time in his career. He will forever look back on his time in West Yorkshire with horror. Never can there have been a more public stand-off between chairman and manager as in the media conference following Jonathan Woodgate's departure to Newcastle. The body language was explosive. Venables' retake on his lunch with Peter Ridsdale in Spain in July 2002 in which he agreed to take on the role of Leeds manager was, 'It didn't look like this in the brochure.' Clearly, Venables hadn't wanted his young star defender to go and indeed believed that he would remain in the backbone of the side he was hoping to build. Within a rudely short period of time, Venables had lost arguably the best central defensive pairing in England in Ferdinand and Woodgate. Lee Bowyer, Robbie Keane, Robbie Fowler and Olivier Dacourt all followed them out, the latter with an offer from Venables to 'drive him all the way to Italy myself if I have to'. Venables' fall-out with Leeds hero David Batty was so severe that he would not even play him in the reserves. For Venables and Leeds, it had been a marriage made in hell.

CHAPTER SEVEN

PETER RIDSDALE – SHOT TO PIECES

Always immaculately attired, well groomed and perfectly mannered, Peter Ridsdale certainly looked the part. He played the part, too, making himself readily available for countless hotly pursued newspaper, magazine, television and radio interviews concerning the affairs of a Leeds United which had become greatly elevated in the football world during his tenure as chairman (from 1997 to 2003). So obliging and comfortable in the public eye was he, in fact, that he unkindly earned the nickname Publicity Pete. These, though, were the great days of high-profile matches, big-name, big-money signings, sold-out fixtures and journeys throughout Europe, as well as the dire days of murders in Istanbul and stomach-churning court cases involving his players. He was in constant demand. Not a day passed without some hint of excitement, a drop of controversy, a development here, wild speculation there. Our daily conversations – some days there might be half-a-dozen exchanges – were never dull. Ridsdale combined his Leeds United duties with his commitments to several Football Association committees and the role of chairman of Education Leeds. Having been swallowed by a python on the snakes and ladders board he dropped two divisions – from chairman of Leeds United to chairman of Barnsley. In an interview in a Leeds hotel in April 2004 we pored over his time at Elland Road:

> It was not until we got to the semi-final of the UEFA Cup – when, at the time, we fancied our chances of beating

Galatasaray — that I became convinced of Leeds United's abilities to once again become a power in European football. I never really thought of us progressing as far as we did. But suddenly it became reality because we found ourselves in the semis against a team we thought we stood a good chance of beating. We had avoided Arsenal in the semi-final, and we really thought then that there was a real opportunity of doing something not only in Europe but challenging at the top of the Premiership. Everything was being geared up to us becoming a fixture in European football and the key was that we finished fifth in the Premiership under George Graham and went on to finish fourth, then third under David O'Leary and reached the semi-final of the UEFA Cup — a major European competition. I think that, for the first time, we realised our bunch of players stood a real chance of challenging on a consistent basis as we'd established a pattern for it three years running. George Graham's departure could have interrupted the flow of things, and I was disappointed when he left because he had come in and stabilised a team that everybody thought had declined under Howard Wilkinson. We had that awful season in 1996–97, the year before I became chairman, in which we scored only 28 goals and remarkably survived, but then in my first full season we came fifth and got into the UEFA Cup and it was only very early into the following season, in October 1998, that George decided he wanted to move on. Obviously, I was disappointed, because George had only recently signed a new contract and all I asked of him was that if you sign a new contract you see it through, and anything after that was fair game. Clearly, he fancied going back to London and the Spurs job attracted him. We had written a clause into the contract that said we got compensation if he left and, ultimately, the Spurs chairman, Alan Sugar, handled it straight down the line. I have no argument with Alan. The minute he paid we said to George, 'You are free to talk to them,' and off he went. The difficulty in football, as I have now found to my cost, is that it is very easy to say you need to change a manager and very difficult to successfully change a manager. It's no secret that we tried to get Martin O'Neill at the time from Leicester.

Frustratingly, we weren't given permission to talk to him and of course David O'Leary, who had initially said he did not want the job, was left temporarily in charge. As the weeks wore on, it looked more and more as if he was enjoying it and the players enjoyed playing for him. I don't think any of us could have anticipated how well that initially went, and when you change a manager for somebody you have got in-house there's less disruption anyway. Therefore, it was a seamless transition which worked exceptionally well until, in my view, the end of the trial. That, and the tragedies in Istanbul, were big smacks in the teeth. Yet subsequently, and in the wider world, it's funny how people viewed the incident involving Leicester City players in La Manga and the problems they brought on the club. How on earth, people reasoned, were they going to cope with an away fixture at Europe-chasing Birmingham when they were in such deep relegation trouble and now facing the world with red faces? Human psychology is strange, because what did Leicester do − they went and won and people raised their eyebrows. I didn't raise any eyebrows because Leeds, during the two years between the incident outside the Majestyk nightclub and the conclusion of the trial, became a very close-knit unit. I think we decided that the world was against us and what we would do is all stick together. The end of the trial would be the turning point where we could relax and fully focus our efforts back on the football.

If you look at our results from the end of the trial, we went from the top of the League on 1 January 2002 to being knocked out of the FA Cup five days later by Cardiff, and then not winning again for nine games and slipping down the League and missing out on the Champions League. That was the beginning of the decline. Some people are trying to make out the beginning of the decline was when David left. David left because the decline had already started and the mistake we made was that we didn't replace him with a manager who could take us forward. It wasn't deliberate. We were just heading for a landslide. So the decline to me started in January 2002, not later on in the summer, and I do think it absolutely and categorically can be ascribed to the end of the trial and the publication of David's book. *Leeds United on Trial* was a slightly ridiculous title for a book which is penned by the manager of a football club who talks about his players and therefore there is no surprise when there is a backlash. I have been interestingly criticised for David's book. People keep saying, 'Ridsdale says he knew nothing of it but he did and he's lying.' The fact is that David told me at the start of the 2001–02 season that he had been asked to do a diary. I didn't think anything of it and that was the only conversation I had with him. I had absolutely no idea that the book was being published to coincide with the end of the trial. If the first trial had been concluded it wouldn't have coincided, but that collapsed and we then had the second trial. The first time I found out the title of this so-called 'diary' was when I was asked about it in the press conference after the trial had been completed. The first question was, 'What do you think about the title of David's book?' and I had no idea, so if anybody says I have denied any knowledge of David's book, then categorically I have not. I was aware he was doing a 'diary' but I had no idea of the timing and absolutely no idea of the title or its content. David knows I was disappointed with that but, again, I am sure there are things I have done which other people are disappointed with as well.

You can't go through life pointing a finger at people. A lot of people are still trying to point a finger at me. If you make mistakes you should hold your hand up and say 'I've made a mistake'. People criticise me for saying I have never apologised for what happened at Leeds United, but on occasions I mention that we've made mistakes and I take my fair share of the blame for that. I think to suggest that I was unique in making mistakes is inaccurate. I think there were plenty of others involved in the club at the time, from the manager to the rest of my colleagues, who ought to also acknowledge that they were part of that journey and they at times made mistakes as well. I think we went for it – we articulated the strategy, we said what we wanted it to be and every year it came off, until it suddenly didn't. And if you want to know when it didn't I think I have pinpointed the time it started to go wrong. We tried to correct it, but we didn't correct it.

On the plus side, Ridsdale is generally perceived to have had his finest hour as chairman in the aftermath of the Istanbul tragedies, but he says:

> I think it's difficult when people start saying it's the finest moment as chairman, etc. A tragedy occurred which I never want to see occur at a football match again. I did what I thought was right at the time. The memories of seeing dead supporters and the effect on their families is something I never want to happen again because I can't forget that night. I can't forget seeing dead supporters lying there in a cabinet in a hospital, so those memories will live with me forever. I did what I thought was right and I probably got more credit than was due because it was what was instinctive.
>
> I think that some of the criticism I have come in for takes you out of the realms of being a member of the human race. People think they can say things about you when you walk down the street. Anywhere in the country they say things to you as if you aren't listening: as if you're not there and you can't hear them. I've said that I made mistakes. I also think that I have done some things well. It's very disappointing when, on the one hand, people praise you and see you as a figurehead during events such as Galatasaray (though I was certainly not looking for praise there; the only people I cared about were the families and supporters) and on the other hand, people castigate you when things go wrong. I don't think I deserved criticism to that degree.
>
> The fact is we had a strategy. It worked, and then it went wrong for all sorts of reasons, some of which were not of my making. And the plan B? Of course we had a plan B. We had the squad independently valued at £200 million by someone who is one of our biggest critics – Dr Bill Gerrard of Leeds University. That was in the annual report as an independent valuation and, in June–July 2002, we had £60 million of offers in cash on the table. Had the players gone – we accepted the offers, so clearly we would have liked them to have gone – the financial position we subsequently found ourselves in would not have been created. These proposed transfers were Lee Bowyer to Liverpool

for £9 million, Robbie Keane to Sunderland or Middlesbrough – both offered £10 million – £2.5 million for Gary Kelly to Sunderland and Olivier Dacourt to Lazio for £14 million. At the time, we hadn't received a bid for Rio Ferdinand but everybody was talking about it being £20–30 million. At £30 million, the combined incoming revenue would have been even higher. So you're talking about £65 million of offers on the table and that would have transformed the club's finances. The fact is that the Keane and Kelly deals fell through, as did the one involving Dacourt. Bowyer turned his back on Liverpool, so £35 million of potential income disappeared overnight. On top of this, we missed out on the Champions League for the 2001–02 season, although we were still in the UEFA Cup. We had been enjoying around £1 million previously for the Champions League from television and now the offer we got from Channel 5 was just over £100,000.

The next problem was that we weren't performing on the field under Terry Venables. I think we got four televised games that year, each one of them worth £685,000. We had been enjoying £11–12 million the year before. In fact, the television revenue for three or four seasons before that was very good. Now we're 16th in the League rather than in the top five and if the reward for each place is worth around half a million, that's 11 places, making £5.5 million. So there was £5.5 million lost out on there, added to television revenue of about £5 million. Bang. There goes £10 million. The UEFA Cup was not worth a lot of money and we saw what could have been £15 million disappear before our very eyes. Add £35 million in lost transfer money to this, too. Now when you explain these losses to people, and say what you have done, nobody's got an answer. They just criticise you for it and they say, 'Well, you shouldn't have taken the risk,' but at the time we didn't think it was a risk. Otherwise, we wouldn't have done it. We were gearing everything towards Champions League football. Of course we were, because we were that close. Now when you are that close you don't turn round to the supporters and say, 'We'll settle for fifth because we daren't take that one step by investing £10–11 million.' You think you can make it. There are four places available and the manager believes he can make it and the supporters believe you can make it. Do you go for it or do you say, 'I am happy with things as they are'? In fact, nobody was saying, 'Don't do it'. And the backstop was in the transfer market. The fact is that when the transfer windows came, the players wouldn't go when we got offers for them. Then we brought in a new manager who we hoped was going to move us forward with £15 million revenue and the team goes backwards.

In my years as chairman, on the day we appointed Terry Venables as the new manager we had never been out of the top five and, until January 2002, when David's book was published and the trial finished, we were top of the table. If we had remained at the top of the table, or second or third, we would have added another £20–£30 million of revenues and, in fact, it could have been more than that. Looking at the people who were prepared to put up the money to fund our ambitions, so that we could go into the transfer market, we were offered £100 million by the three parties. We could not afford that and settled for £60 million over 25 years in the end. That would have been fine had we continued to be in the top three or four. Had we therefore enjoyed the revenues, that would not have been an issue, and we believed that if it did become an issue we could sell players accordingly. But the transfer market collapsed completely. If you had told me that a team which finished every year in the top five, had just been to two European semi-finals and had a couple of players, particularly in the case of Robbie Fowler, that had an outstanding goal-scoring record; if you had told me we would have gone backwards, I wouldn't have believed you. But we did. Ray Ranson came round and said, 'We have a mechanism for helping with finance in place.' We had a policy of ideally buying British or Southern Irish players and, if not, Scandinavians or other Europeans. If you bought British players, or players from British clubs, at that time, you had to pay the whole transfer fee within 12 months. If you went to Europe to buy you could buy over five years. So it was encouraging you to buy foreign players. The policy was that the manager didn't want to buy foreign players, so we were at a disadvantage in the transfer market. If you buy a player from

Europe for £10 million and you pay over five years that's £2 million per year. Buy a £10 million player in England and you had to pay £10 million in 12 months, so Ray offered a facility to treat them as if they were European players and pay over the length of the contract. All he was doing was offering a facility, essentially, so you could compete in the British market rather than having to go foreign. It was insurance-backed. The advantage to the lender was that if you couldn't pay, the insurance policy paid out, which we thought was a good way of funding because you had a financial guarantee. I would like to put to rest the notion that Leeds never owned some of their players. Leeds owned the players all right. It's no different to buying a car on a lease purchase scheme, or the house on a mortgage. It's a method of paying over a period of time, where you still have the title to the goods. And remember, a player was never bought without full board approval – that's every director – and a player was never sold without full board approval. No money was ever borrowed without the whole board agreeing to it. With a view to our club's success, the board basically put in place huge funding for a manager to go to war with and that happened every year until it fell apart. As these policies had previously been successful, we had to ask the questions of how, why and when it fell apart. Did the poor performances on the field mean that David O'Leary had lost the dressing room? My contention, although David has always denied it, is that if you talk to the players they would suggest that the board take is probably accurate. Regrettably, we decided that David O'Leary had, indeed, lost the dressing room.

Then along comes Terry Venables, who wants to manage Leeds but barely gets a performance out of them. If I knew the answer to why that was then I probably would still be chairman. Everybody cries out 'Sack the manager' and 'Sack the board' when things are not going well or are conspiring against you, but what you have got to have is an alternative. I have got an outstanding respect for Trevor Birch. If you take the 12 months since I was chairman I don't think anybody, except Trevor, has done a better job than we as a collective board did, and time will tell how Leeds' future fares because it is dead easy to stand on the sideline and point the finger. I have often wondered what would have happened if we hadn't changed the manager and said, 'It's David O'Leary's chance to get the full support of all the players again this summer,' but we took the decision to change and that change didn't work. I went to the board and said that if Terry stayed we would get relegated, that we had to take a decision and that we should go for a short-term stopgap from the best person available and then in the summer appoint a chosen manager. I gave a short list of four for the summer and Peter Reid was readily available. I said to Peter, 'There are eight games left, we will pay you on a points basis as an incentive to get as many points as possible.' I told him that, in my opinion, even if we won all eight games it would be unlikely he would be the manager in the summer because we had other people in mind. That was almost the last thing I did at Elland Road. I was there for Peter's first match and then I left. I had been getting terrible stick from the fans ever since Jonathan Woodgate was sold. But I'll tell you what's interesting. We were getting all these headlines in the papers saying, 'Let's investigate the directors' and 'What they should have done as directors'. The fact is, a company has a responsibility to do what you think is right for shareholders. We had an offer for a player that was for a lot of money, combined with our cash-flow problem and the imminent closure of the transfer window. It was a method of raising money between then and the summer. Whether or not those offers in the summer would come back again, who knows? I'd already gone through a period in the summer where, of all the potential offers, the only one to materialise was the one for Rio. And therefore we sat down as a board to discuss Woodgate and said, 'From a footballing perspective, do we want to sell him?' Answer: 'No.' 'As directors with responsibility in a plc, do we want to sell him?' Answer: 'We have no choice.' Here was a player who cost us nothing because he was home-grown in a club with a cash-flow that required us to raise some money at some point in the future without any guarantees. At that point, we weren't even guaranteed to stay in the Premiership. So the board, in my view, legally had to sell him, irrespective of whether or not people were saying we should or we shouldn't. Terry made it clear that he didn't want to sell. From a footballing point of view, I also didn't want to sell, but from the point of view of the public company I think the board of directors and I had no option but to sell. I said that to Terry at the time and I gave him that explanation. He said that he didn't really have any view on that. He didn't care about the plc; he was a football manager and therefore disagreed. I hear what he says but you can't disagree if you have the responsibility to make the right decision. That's why when people refer to the Woodgate transfer now I am more than happy that we did sell him, because at every board meeting we sat down and looked at the cash-flow and asked what our responsibility was to our shareholders. We took what we believed was the right decision as directors of a public company. The financial balance of the club was always right in the board's eyes until we missed out on the Champions League for two years running. We lost out by one place two years consecutively, which probably cost us £40 million. In the first of those seasons, 2000–01, we were top of the League at Christmas. When the trial finished, the book came out and we started losing games. At that point, we had to take some urgent action to bring some cash in, but we had a squad of such value that we were able to do so. Offers totalling £65 million would suggest that was correct. These were not offers for Mark Viduka or Alan Smith or Paul Robinson or Danny Mills, or players of that calibre – and I don't mean this disrespectfully – but for Gary Kelly who, at the time, wasn't in the team, Dacourt whom, in David's view, we could afford to lose, and Robbie Keane. We still had strikers of the calibre of Michael Bridges, Harry Kewell and Viduka and Smith at that time – and Lee Bowyer, whom everybody believed we could afford to let go, otherwise he would have left on a Bosman.

I think if you look back at the history and imagine a few things going our way we wouldn't be sitting here talking about what the problem was. Take, for instance, Lee Bowyer. I was disappointed with Lee's reaction because clearly Lee felt I had let him down. I believe both he and Jonathan were supported 100 per cent throughout the trial. Indeed, we paid their legal fees, which they then subsequently owed us and we always said from day one that we would take appropriate disciplinary action when the incident first took place. They were found not guilty of the most serious offence, of course. Jonathan was found guilty of a certain offence but Lee was found not guilty and felt he shouldn't have been fined. Our view was that he was clearly out in the streets of Leeds, taking a non-active role in something that became a chase, which caused Leeds United tremendous damage, and we believed it right and proper to fine him. But Lee disagreed, and he felt let down and took the decision he took. I was disappointed at that reaction. Jonathan was just the opposite. He thanked us for our support, recognised we stood by him and took a very hefty fine and said he accepted that was right and proper. But there is no doubt my relationship with Lee was destroyed because of the fining, which I was disappointed at because I always got on well with him and I tried very hard thereafter to get on with him and offer support. At the time, we didn't fine him without consulting the manager. In fact, it was David O'Leary who informed him of the fine and confirmed to the board that he agreed to it. To what degree do you go, regarding breaches of club discipline? As a player, you can't be out on the streets having had too much to drink. You are a role model and it had caused us two years of grief. If a manager doesn't take that view on discipline for an individual player, then where does discipline start and finish? David may or may not have felt privately that a fine could have alienated a player to the extent that he might not in future give all he has got to the club, but the fact is that David did not say that and he was right not to say it. At the time, fines were not imposed on any player without the manager not only being consulted but agreeing.

I was always a great admirer of Harry Kewell's skills and it was surprising that there were no more approaches for his services other than, through a third party, an expression of interest in January 2003, which we were told would be followed up in summer. This was in excess of £10 million, but then I was no longer at the club and do not know the ins and outs of his move to Liverpool. I do know there was a backlash as far as agent fees were concerned, but the position with player contracts and agents is as follows, dependent upon what order it comes in. What normally happened was that if we were getting an expression of interest from a club, we would then inform the player if we were going to accept it. For example, if Liverpool had been interested we would have done the deal first with the club and if it was acceptable to us we would have then approached the player. What we would say in any situation to an agent would be, 'The more you get for a player the more we are prepared to consider your fee, so if you get £10 million your fee might be half a million, and if you get £20 million it might be £1 million.' So there is an incentive to get a higher price. There are various aspects of the football business that I don't like, but I don't think agents are as despicable as people say. Agents are only as good or as bad as you let them be. At the end of the day, an agent has got a responsibility and most agents I have met have been fine. There is the odd one that hasn't been. I haven't dealt with a number of overseas transfers because, through third party hearsay, the more complicated agents are those who perhaps deal in South America and some other countries. Most of the British transfers are fine. All they are trying to do is the best for their client and get the maximum they can as a fee. That's their job. The chairman's job is to try to get the player for the cheapest price and the agent for the best agent fee. The thing I don't like is that I do think that players sign contracts and expect you to honour them, but if they want to leave they make sure they can get out. Player contracts, certainly at the highest levels, are one-way streets and I think it's the same with managers. As we saw with George, if George wanted to go somewhere else he could inform us he wanted to go somewhere else, but if we wanted to dispense with the services of a manager we had to pay him every penny that the contract says. I don't have a problem if we sign a contract and we pay that person whatever it is, but I think the other party should also honour it and very often they don't. There are aspects of football which are very different and not great, but in every business I have been in there have been aspects of business life I don't like and a lot I have enjoyed.

Football is no different, except some of its less savoury aspects are probably unique to the industry. There was a point at which I thought, 'I am beginning not to like this very much. I can see the storm clouds looming,' and that was the day we sold Jonathan Woodgate. It was the first time we made a business decision which had a fallout which I couldn't cope with emotionally. I knew what it would mean to our supporters. Despite the fact that they now have a go at me and criticise me, I hurt as much as they did when we sold Jonathan Woodgate. But I knew from a business point of view it was the right thing to do. I should have quit that day. I tried to quit that day. I was persuaded to stay and I should have gone. I knew then I had lost the backing of the supporters and that's what mattered. I'll never get Leeds United out of my system, but the day I walked out of the office and said it's time to go, I knew I had to look forward and not back. I have been disappointed because a lot of people have failed to look forward. All they have done is look back and criticise, almost to the point of distraction from whether or not they have been doing a better job. I think in life what you do is to do your job as well as you can and as honestly as you can. To a degree, you do it well and, fine, to a degree, you make mistakes. Then you have to hold your hands up in the air, which I have. I keep stressing that I have said more times than I care to mention, I made mistakes.

The biggest was buying Robbie Fowler and Seth Johnson in October 2001. That expenditure was an expenditure too far. We were top of the League, so we believed that Champions League football was almost guaranteed. We were persuaded by the manager that that was the icing on the cake and we were guaranteed Champions League football, and it didn't happen. So clearly we shouldn't have done that. I am accused of being conceited because I said I wouldn't have done things differently. The trouble is, you can only take the decisions at the time based on what you know at the time, and in a perfect world, with the benefit of hindsight, you might turn round and say yes, if I'd known what was going to happen, or if I'd known the consequences of an action, I might have done things differently. You can't do that because at the time you have to take the call. And at the time, based on the knowledge we had, we took what we thought were the right actions, and I stress the 'we' because it was a plural board. At no stage did I go out there and say 'I am doing this or that'. People think because you are chairman you can do what you want, but that's not true. We had some very lively debates at board meetings. I was hung out to dry. As chairman, to some degree you accept that you get a disproportionate amount of flak because that's what happens, but I think I have had 100 per cent of the flak. I personally think I have been treated as if everything I did was wrong for five years, but there were some great times and everybody enjoyed the great times. I didn't write a book, I didn't chase people through the streets of Leeds on a January evening. You look at some of the one-off incidents which have influenced our future, including players refusing to leave when they know the club will benefit financially, even though ultimately they knew they were going to leave, and realise they helped to change our lives financially. Had they just gone the other way, or had something else happened, we wouldn't be the subject of such scrutiny. All I will say is that you have to judge everybody else's capabilities on the job they do over a period of time, and in the 12 months since I have left, I give total credit to Trevor Birch. In fact I tried to bring Trevor in as chief executive in 2003 and I had a conversation with him about it. Trevor still had to finish his job at Chelsea and said he would prefer to have the conversation in the summer, by which time I had gone. I knew of Trevor's skills and would have welcomed him on the management team before I left, but I don't necessarily think anybody else has done an outstanding job in the period after me other than Trevor. So I think all they have found out is how hard it is and I will stress that when I left there were 24 internationals on the books, and the squad that people say we had sold off was 16th or 17th in the League with some players that most managers in the Premiership would have given a lot of money for. I wasn't the one who was paid to train them and coach them and pick the team every day and yet I seem to have been the only one to have got the criticism. I am not whinging about that, by the way.

So is life a bit more enjoyable at Barnsley? Well, what Barnsley have given me is an opportunity. When you read people's comments on me and the mistakes I made at Leeds they talk as if I am not allowed to do anything to live and feed my family. I am a human being who made honest mistakes, and what Barnsley are giving me is an opportunity to do something I enjoy, which is to be involved in football, to learn from mistakes – because that's what I was taught, to learn from mistakes – and that's what I am trying to do. I deserve to be allowed to learn from my mistakes and I have at no stage gone out slagging people off, because I don't do that. I've tried to tell it as it is and I've tried to look forwards and not backwards. I just wish other people would do the same. I still look at Leeds matches with great interest. Absolutely. I get texted all the way through the games, even when I am watching Barnsley. I will be watching any game where Leeds are playing live on the television when I am not watching Barnsley playing. My life is now that I have got to do a good job with Barnsley, which I am now doing. But you can't just take away what I did at Leeds and pretend it never happened, and I am disappointed that a lot of the Leeds supporters seem to think that by taking it out on me and wishing me ill, Leeds will be better for it. The only way Leeds will be better is by appointing the right management, and I sincerely hope that the people who now own the club do a very good job. I have sent them my best wishes because that's what I want – I want Leeds to prosper. All I want is for Leeds United to be successful. I wanted that as chairman and that's what I want now.

I think if you look at the pressure I was under from October 2002, when things clearly weren't going well, there was the question about what was going to happen during the annual general meeting. I was then challenged by the board to raise a certain amount of money in the January, which I did, and to make cost savings, which I did. John McKenzie has taken credit for a lot of the cost savings, but if you look at the public pronouncements I had already announced some 50 per cent of them. And in terms of the cash in from transfers, I think you will find that I raised most of it during the period of the last five years because very little has been raised since I left. It's difficult when you are under that sort of pressure and I didn't sleep for four months. It was knowing you had to balance raising the cash with keeping your team alive that caused the most stress. Whilst the board were making decisions about how much we had to raise, I was personally charged with raising the money. It was a very difficult period and actually, until the summer, I had no confidence to do any of it. I left at the end of March and it completely shattered my confidence, because of the way in which people, wherever I went, whether it was the newspapers, radio, supporters and so on, talked about me. You know you have got to get up in the morning, and you have got a family to look after, and everywhere you go people are saying you did this or you did that. I challenge any human being to go through that without any adverse effect. The Barnsley opportunity, which we worked on from late May until we eventually got it completed at the end of October, to some degree allowed me to focus on something without the responsibility of running it. But I was shot to pieces and, to some degree, I still am. I am very fragile, and when you see people such as Peter Lorimer come out and make derogatory comments without any knowledge of what went on, I find it disappointing because, again, if Peter wakes up in 12 months' time and he's done a better job I will be the first to applaud him. But he will find out how challenging it is.

Peter Ridsdale's Barnsley finished 12th in Division Two in 2003–04.

CHAPTER EIGHT

ALLAN LEIGHTON – LESSONS IN FOOTBALL

A week before Christmas in 2002, with the weight of the downturn in Leeds United's fortunes as inexplicable as it was infuriating, I journeyed to the British Home Stores headquarters in London to meet the football club's deputy chairman, Allan Leighton, for the first of the two fairly lengthy interviews which I have held with him to date (the second, conducted after Leighton had left the club, is also reproduced below). The chairman of Royal Mail and BHS, he was appointed deputy chairman of the club in 1998. Typically, Hereford-born Leighton, then aged 48, would spend two-thirds of his time at home in Buckinghamshire and the rest at his Leeds base. Some 200 miles from Elland Road, he gave some candid answers to the frank questions I felt needed answering on behalf of all Leeds fans at the time. Leighton never dodged an issue and was, I felt, mightily impressive in his appraisal of the prevailing situation. Further, no one reading his responses could have been left in any doubt that a different, inferior Leeds United would soon emerge. They had been warned.

Q: What is the background to your involvement with Leeds United?

A: Very straightforward. I was running Asda and one day I got a call asking if I would like to go and be a non-executive director of Leeds United on the grounds of 1) I was a Yorkshire businessman; 2) I lived locally in Boston Spa; and 3) I love football. Leeds was not the team I then supported, but was my local team, and I was always fascinated by football. This presented an interesting opportunity to look at football from a business perspective too.

Q: You hold nine company directorships. How much time does this allow you to spend on the affairs of Leeds United?

A: I'm a different animal in that I don't allocate time. People always say to me 'What do you spend your time on?' and my reply is that I spend my time on the issues. So what I do is allocate time against issues, rather than allocate time against companies. It's a different way of thinking about it. Time isn't the issue, it's managing the issues which is the issue. This means that my involvement with Leeds can vary, but clearly in the last few months I have spent more time on the club than I would have done 12 months ago.

Q: The journey to a Champions League semi-final against Valencia was like a fairytale. What are your abiding memories of that campaign?

A: I remember being in Munich when we qualified. With 90 seconds to go I turned to Peter Ridsdale and said, 'We're playing the next minute and a half for about £15 million!' That's about £150,000 a second! There were players in that side who have not played for Leeds since, but it was a real battling performance that saw us through. Then it was Barcelona, Madrid, Deportivo, Valencia . . . we were all over Spain, with Milan thrown in for good measure. It was a roller-coaster. Tremendous. And a really big growing-up exercise for the club. I will also always remember how well treated we were by all the clubs we went to. When we went to Barcelona I thought, 'They're Barcelona, we're Leeds, what will they really think about it?' In fact, they were fantastic. All the clubs we played were very gracious hosts and not just to the directors but also to the players and the fans. After the troubles of Turkey, they were all very good experiences. We were well beaten by Valencia, but we did better than we thought we would do. After all, we lost 4–0 at Barcelona in the first game and nobody was very optimistic after that.

Q: It's a big drop from a Champions League semi-final to a

1. In the beginning . . . George Graham (left) and David O'Leary.

2. Peter Ridsdale surveys the scene in Galatasaray's Ali Sami Yen stadium.

3. Armed guards with riot shields protect Leeds United players as they emerge from the tunnel for their UEFA Cup semi-final at Galatasaray.

<table>
<tr><td>4</td><td>5</td></tr>
<tr><td colspan="2">6</td></tr>
</table>

4. Big celebrations as a goalless draw at West Ham is enough to ensure Champions League football at Elland Road.

5. David O'Leary's coaching team (from left): Eddie Gray, Roy Aitken and Brian Kidd.

6. Brian Kidd leads a Leeds training session.

7 8

9

7. Mark Viduka, whose goals for Leeds came at a high price.

8. Eddie Gray (right) makes a point to Mark Viduka in training.

9. Peter Ridsdale (right) announces the big-money signing of Rio Ferdinand.

10. Robbie Fowler, who was viewed as a signing too far as Leeds plunged deeper into debt.

11. Lee Bowyer's form peaked during Leeds' Champions League campaign.

12. Pain in Spain. The Champions League dream is over for Leeds United after they crash 3–0 to Valencia in the semi-final second leg.

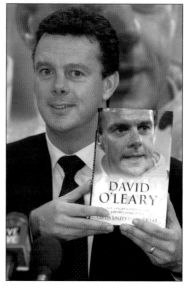

13

14   15

13. Jonathan Woodgate, sentenced at Hull Crown Court for his part in an affray.

14. Lee Bowyer, cleared of charges at Hull Crown Court.

15. David O'Leary promotes his controversial book *Leeds United on Trial*.

16. Peter Ridsdale and the rented goldfish in his Elland Road office.

17. Peter Ridsdale and the Billy Bremner statue outside Elland Road.

18. The body language between Peter Ridsdale (left) and Terry Venables following the sale of Jonathan Woodgate to Newcastle says it all.

19. High-flying Harry Kewell.

20. Harry Kewell's bargain-basement move to Liverpool sparked an outcry.

21. Peter Reid watches the action in a pre-season friendly at Burnley. But he was soon 'Away'.

22. Professor John McKenzie, who replaced Peter Ridsdale as chairman.

23. Trevor Birch, whose supreme efforts saved Leeds from the threat of going into administration.

24. Leeds' all-time record goal-scorer Peter Lorimer, who was co-opted onto the board under the Krasner regime.

pre-Christmas flirtation with the Premiership relegation places. How do you explain the decline?

A: It's very difficult to explain. There's always a combination of things. It's generally all to do with confidence and form and luck. Part of the luck is in injuries, and we've had a bad run with those – for a very long time, actually. We've obviously got players who have lost form. We're not as cohesive a unit as we were and I think that when you add up all that you lose confidence. Football's like any other sport, any other business, in that when your confidence goes you have got a problem. Clearly the players are vital in this because they are the product: they perform on the pitch, they get you the points or they don't. But it's a club thing. The club have lost a lot of their confidence. I thought it was very interesting at Bolton the other night when, after being under attack for ten minutes, you could visibly see everybody's confidence rise when Danny [Mills] scored that goal. Suddenly, this was a different team and we went on to win 3–0. Another possible reason for our current predicament is that there have been a lot of changes at the club.

Q: How difficult a decision was it to fire David O'Leary and, in retrospect, was it a correct decision?

A: It's always a difficult decision firing anybody. I'm just in the process of making 30,000 people redundant in the Post Office. That's a big decision. So you never do these things lightly. The board felt that it was the right time for a change and there's no point reflecting on whether or not it was the right decision. The decision was made, and that's that. I'm not a great one for reflecting upon the past. I'm more focused on the future. David had done some very good things for the club, but the most important thing now is what happens going forward. At the moment, we are in the bottom five and our focus is to fight relegation. That's where we have to think about what we are going to do today.

Q: The choice of O'Leary's replacement was Terry Venables who, so far, has perhaps failed to live up to expectations. Is his position under threat?

A: The only person who can determine whether he's lived up to expectations is Terry. It's his own expectations which matter.

Here is a guy who has got a good track record as a manager and coach and has managed and coached some of the best teams in the world. You don't suddenly become a bad coach overnight. In terms of personal performance, I always believe people are the best judge of their own. Are the results disappointing? Yes, they are, because we're flirting with relegation. But the issue is that there is this thing across the whole club at the moment. It is a lack of confidence. We need a few things to break for us or to change to rectify that. Basically, it's a good squad of players that we've got, but because we're not performing on the pitch we're not performing off it and therefore does everybody in the club feel under pressure? Yes, they do. And rightly so, because the measure of everything is performance. You can't get away from it. On the one hand, the shareholders need it and on the other hand the fans need it. You can see it in the profits and losses and in the points on the League table. When someone says, 'Are people under threat?' or, 'Do you have confidence in people?' that's all football terminology and that's not my game. My game is, it's very obvious that performance is everything on and off the pitch and at the moment we are not performing.

Q: The drop in share price from 28p to 4p in a comparatively short time is pretty calamitous. Why has the fall been so steep and is there any prospect of a revival?

A: I was told a long time ago not to worry about the share price, but to worry about the business. That's what drives the share price. First of all, football has lost its glitz. Football economics are under more pressure than they have ever been because you only generate money in three or four ways. One is gate revenue, and that's pretty fixed in terms of annual figures, then you have commercial revenue, and that's more difficult to grow, and the other is television. The commercial revenue and the TV tend to go with performance on the pitch, so you are restricted in where you can get your growth. That leads you to the fourth way in which you can get cash – through transfers. We all know the market in Europe has imploded. The whole economics of football are under a huge amount of pressure, and then you put into that argument the fact that we are not in the Champions League, that costs us anything up to £20 million, and you just don't magic that figure out. If you look at that very objectively, and look at the economics, then the club is under pressure financially and that is reflected in the share price.

Q: The club is said to be £77 million in the red. Is this a true reflection of the debt and what plans are afoot to rectify the situation?

A: I'm not allowed to talk about the finances of the business because we are a public company and anything I say in public gets quoted. We put our results out twice a year and that's when people see how we are performing. The debt numbers become apparent at that stage. We are going to, and have had to, adjust our finances to a business that is not in the Champions League. The transfers we have made of Rio and Robbie were to do with that. At some stage, when we get back into the transfer market, we will have to do some trading both in and out. In any business I know, if suddenly you are £20 million short of where you need to be then you can't keep running it the way that it was.

Q: Peter Ridsdale has been the public face of Leeds United for some time now but he has sunk into the background lately. Is this a deliberate policy?

A: I think that Peter, who has done a good job for the club, is in a situation where he is responsible for the performance of the club on and off the pitch, and he had a very dicey time in the run-up to the AGM, figuring as he did in thousands of column inches. When you are on the receiving end of that it's not very motivating. What Peter is doing, and I think it's the right thing to do, is focusing much more of his time on the running of the club, which is why he has given up a number of other things in which he was involved. Until there is something else to say he is in there working and grinding his way through what needs to happen. One of the issues for us is that we suffer too many column inches, and not always the right ones, and therefore at the moment the best thing is for the club to keep its head down and grind out performance both on and off the pitch. Then, when it's in a better position, we might have something to say.

Q: With Rio Ferdinand in mind, are the days of the £30 million transfer in football well and truly over?

A: I think so. The Rio deal had people saying that he's a great player and he's gone to Manchester United – something Leeds don't like. But as a business proposition it's £30 million. I always point out to people that we sold Rio for £30 million, two weeks later Rivaldo went for nothing and two weeks after that Ronaldo went for £20 million. From a purely business perspective it was a sensible thing to do. I don't think a £30 million transfer will ever take place again. Football clubs are short of cash and you can see it. There are many more loans and swaps, with people trying to find different ways of refreshing their squads and covering their injuries without imparting cash. I think the fans are aware of it, but not of its full extent. The whole economics and the fundamentals of the finances of football have undergone major changes in the last 12–15 months. The transfer market has imploded to 50 per cent of its former value and we now have transfer windows, which restrict activity, combined with huge increases in wage bills and a decline in revenue. In any business or market I know, that's an issue. We're in the limelight because of the performance on and off the pitch, but what's happening to us in one way, shape or form is happening to most other Premiership clubs. It's very difficult for the fans because I think 15–20 per cent of their disposable income is probably spent on watching Leeds United. That's a huge amount. It's not just the season ticket, it's the food, the travelling, the 'Do I take my son, my daughter, my wife?' Unlike retail, where if I don't like one clothes shop I'll go to another, there's no choice. You can only go to Leeds United. Most businesses have the fundamentals and the economics and they play a tune. Football has emotion attached to it. Instead of fundamentals, economics and perhaps a little emotion, it's high on emotion and not so much of the other elements. Fans will think, 'Hang on, I'm paying this money every week, they don't seem to have any money, they're selling our best players, they're not playing well on the pitch and I'm still coming every week because I have no choice, that is what I do, and it's costing me a lot of money. What the hell is going on here?' I understand that. We're not very good at explaining what is going on. Leeds has a very loyal, very dedicated fan base and you can see why they get frustrated and annoyed. I can't make my mind up about the transfer window. One of the good things about the season is that we have blooded some of our youngsters, and that's where we started with the likes of Smithy, Woody and Robbo. I think that's very important. The balance of squads will have to change. You're going to need 25–30 per cent of your team to come through from the youth teams, and that's why the money that's been spent on the [Youth] Academy is so important – if you get it right. We got the three I've just mentioned, and Kewell and McPhail, for nothing. You can't afford to run squads of 25 or 30 players where you've had to pay high rates for them with no players coming through the ranks. Football is going through a period of re-invention financially, and perhaps it has just come in time. Perhaps it will turn out that all these things have combined to make the game more sensible.

Q: With rumours of several big clubs going broke, how important is it for United to avoid relegation and how damaging would it be missing out on Europe?

A: We started out this season thinking that we must not miss out on Europe. Now our first task is avoiding relegation. And unless we think of it like that then we won't achieve our first objective. And our first objective is that we cannot be relegated. The Bolton match was very useful for us in terms of the points we picked up and the thing that came through, which is needed across the club, was that there was a bit of fighting spirit. We've been a club divided, in a strange way. I don't know how that's happened. We've had the fans versus the manager versus the directors versus the chairman. There have been rumours of players not getting on and that's bad. At the AGM, I said that if anybody thought that any of the directors felt any better about what's going on than they did then they were wrong. We felt exactly as they did and that is why we are determined to do something about it. But the only way you get out of these types of situations is by grinding your way out of it. There is no magic, there's no wand, it doesn't suddenly come right. You work for your breaks. You work for your luck. Bolton was a start, but the question now is whether we can string some results together. We need to. In the next four or five weeks there are some very big games for us. It is a very important period and we have got to get some results out of it. Objective one is getting ourselves out of the bottom quarter of the table. Objective two is getting into the top half and objective three is Europe. But our sights have got to be set on getting out of this predicament first, rather than go round saying, 'The objective is to get into Europe.' From where we are that might be tough. European football is very important, because that is where the television is and, consequently, the money. The UEFA Cup is quite good, but it's nowhere near the Champions League. We have a squad and a payment system which is there to provide Champions League football. We haven't got Champions League football and that is why we have got to cut our cloth accordingly. It's like any household budget. We can't spend money we haven't got.

Fast-forward 15 months to Cheltenham Gold Cup day, 18 March 2004. Best Mate had just completed his big-race hat-trick when Leighton and I shook hands at the start of my second interview with him, which was conducted in his office at Royal Mail. He had opted out of football club affairs by then and was in reflective mood:

> When I first came in to Leeds United, Peter Ridsdale was chairman of the football club, not the plc, and they were looking for a couple of non-executive directors. I was at Asda in Leeds and they approached me and Richard North. George Graham was just going. When I lived in Leeds and was at Asda over a period of five or six years, I used to go and watch the games. I have always loved them and I like football generally. When they asked me to join them I thought it would be a good idea, though all my friends said to me, 'You don't want to get involved in football. It never works.' That's true, unless you're Manchester United, Celtic or probably even Liverpool, where there is natural wealth. It is true that the involvement of businessmen in football has never worked. We have seen a lot

of casualties along the way but, speaking personally, I have gone in at quite an exciting time for the club. Leeds were involved in European football at that time: the UEFA Cup. David O'Leary took over as caretaker-manager and they went off to the Portuguese club Maritimo and won in a penalty shoot-out. When they came back, Peter phoned me and I agreed to his request for a meeting. He said, 'Look, I've been very impressed with David O'Leary. I think we ought to give him the job on a full-time basis.' We talked it through, then we talked it through with the others. Basically, I think you have to support the chair, so it seemed to me that David got appointed off the back of that. At the start of his first full season in charge, there was a 0–0 home draw against Derby and then a big 3–0 win at Southampton. I thought they played well and everything looked good. The club looked solid, as did the team out on the pitch. Hasselbaink went for a healthy £12 million or so and everything seemed set fair. The previous season, they had finished fourth and got a UEFA Cup slot again and then the Champions League was to follow. With credit to David, a lot of the young lads he'd brought into the team were really performing. Early in the 1998–99 season, just after George had gone, I can remember going to our game at Nottingham Forest with a youthful Jonathan Woodgate in the side. So we had Woodgate, Smith and Kewell coming in to play in an increasingly young team. I always remember the most amazing thing. When we qualified for the Champions League, I was looking intently at the warm up in the Olympic Stadium, where we had to get through a qualifier against TSV 1860 Munich. We had to win or draw and, in fact, we won with an Alan Smith goal. But we had Matthew Jones playing, and a lad called Evans – I don't know where he has gone now – and that was very interesting. You're looking at arguably the most successful time for the club, yet we didn't have a lot of the big names. I always feel it such a shame about Michael Bridges getting so badly injured. Smith and Bridges were playing up front and scoring goals for fun and Lucas Radebe was playing very well at the back. But what David did was to bring in all these young lads to play. He gave them a game. He bought Eirik Bakke for a snip and there was a freshness, urgency and vitality about the whole place – you could see it in the players and in David himself – and that got us into the Champions League. Was it the same in the boardroom? I think so. Peter Ridsdale was in his element, really, and managing the ups and the downs. You think of the Galatasaray thing, which he handled really well. But around the whole place, everybody thought what was going on at the club was fantastic. Going to work must have been a pleasant experience. It's one of those things I only dipped in and out of, but you know if you were there every day it must have been terrific. If you're not there on a daily basis and you don't get to all the games you just try to keep in touch. It was good. It was also very profitable. We had our best set of results ever: something like £8 million operating profit on a turnover at the time of £65–£70 million.

So it was pretty good. We were talking about doing the bond, getting in £60 million, which I think was clearly a good move at the time. This was when we got the bond to securitise against the gate money. It's a mortgage. That's the strange thing: the debt is high but if Leeds were profitable today and were profitable in ten years' time the club would still have £60 million of debt. It's like a mortgage in that you don't pay it off until the end of its duration. So you would always have this debt there. So, providing you service the debt and pay the interest it is no problem. We got the £60 million from N&G, the Pru and Teachers. Everybody bought into the strategy that we would primarily invest in players at the time – you generate revenue from success on the pitch, and the squad was independently valued at £200 million. One of the things that went wrong was the transfer market. You buy liquid assets, not fixed assets, and the transfer market imploded. Take Mark Viduka. Two years ago, we would have got £15 million for him and you'd probably get £5 million today if you're lucky. So two things happened to us. One was that we missed that Champions League spot by one point in 2000–01, and that was a £20 million hit. You could survive that, but then we had the double whammy that our League form deteriorated so badly over a period of two years. We went from a top-six team to a bottom-six team. All the money which goes with that, you lose and that's where we started to come under real pressure.

Then you start to try to sell some players to give you some breathing space, which has a double effect in that you lose the player and, because the market imploded, you are never going to get what you thought you would get for them. Harry Kewell was being talked about in terms of a £20 million deal and ended up going for a net £3 million. Should he have been sold two years previously? Yes, probably. But that's hindsight. In that 12- to 18-month period the transfer window had that effect. Suddenly, everybody ran out of cash to spend in the transfer market. Certainly, if you take Chelsea out of the equation, the market is probably 10 per cent of what it was 18 months or two years ago. If you think of it in terms of the ball-bearing market, and not the football market, suddenly you are down 80 per cent and you have a bit of a problem.

We probably bought two players too many to guarantee that Champions League place, and it was no guarantee at all. That £20 million today would have been very useful and, with it, we wouldn't have been in the position in which we found ourselves. Should Peter have been better able, again with hindsight, to say to David, 'No, we can't afford it' or, 'We don't need them'? Well, I do think Peter feels the same way. He does think that Seth Johnson and Robbie Fowler were two players too many. I think he has the ability to say no, but I think, at the time, we were top of the Premiership and this was a way of cementing that. And when you take on board all the forecasts, that's what you look at to determine what you can do. You would have been able to say that, in reality, we are the top of the Premiership, we are going to buy these couple of players, we will certainly be in the Champions League next year, certainly with these two in the squad, so actually the future looks pretty good. The problem arises when this doesn't happen. You miss by one solitary point. David O'Leary always said, 'I will be judged by my plc on whether or not we make the Champions League,' and, in the end, he was. It was a very difficult decision to remove him and, in my mind, it was 51–49. With Peter and David I think their relationship had broken down and you can't have the chairman and manager at loggerheads. Therefore, you have to back one in the end and Peter felt strongly that that was what should happen and the board went with that. I think it was a close decision. And when I reflect back, sometimes I wonder if it was the right decision. That's not a reflection on either Terry Venables or Peter Reid, because they came to the club in different circumstances.

But, you know, getting to that Champions League semi-final was wondrous. We had that 0–0 draw in the first leg, so we went to Spain for the return leg with one foot in the final. Financially, the implications of not winning through did not amount to a lot, though it probably cost a lot in terms of sponsorship. If you're the Champions League champions you've got a guaranteed year's sponsorship. There's a big spin-off on the back of that, but the most important thing is to be in it the following year rather than winning it. Failure to make it in 2001–02 required a major re-budgeting operation. The way you have to do it is to make assumptions. Rightly or wrongly, we didn't assume that we would be in the bottom six and the difference between that and the heady heights of the previous season is huge. That's when you struggle, and as we started to get towards November of 2002 we started to think about where we were going to end up in the League. Then, in January, there's a new problem because the transfer market in itself is a problem. You have only four weeks to sell somebody. You have to make a call on how much cash you need to generate because it's the only chance you have got to do it. Peter was looking to try to get £10 million in on that window and in the end a deal to sell Seth Johnson fell through. With Robbie Fowler, it was a case of was he/was he not going to Manchester City. That's why Woody went. The big mistake here was Peter sitting alongside Terry Venables and saying that we didn't need to sell Woodgate. The fact is that we did need to sell the player. We needed £10 million. That's when Peter finally lost it with the fans. What he should have done on the Woodgate thing is to say, 'Look, we needed to raise £10 million and so we had to sell Jonathan Woodgate. It was a financial decision. But we had to do it.' So then he lost it with Terry. That relationship started to fall apart and he lost it with the fans. But the fact remains, we had to sell Woodgate.

Regarding the other big-money deal, the signing of Rio Ferdinand, we believed that bringing in Rio would be funded by a second season in the Champions League. He, we thought, would be the difference between qualifying and not qualifying. But the generally accepted figures involved in his purchase and subsequent sale to Manchester United were not quite accurate. It was presented as an £18 million incoming transfer from West Ham but there were, in fact, £3.5 million in top-ups. So we actually paid £21.5 million for him. Then there is this idea that we sold him for £30 million. We didn't. We sold him for £26 million and top-ups. Rio cost £21.5 million and we got £27.5 million, so we made £6 million. The size of the agent's fee was an issue that came to a head later, on top of the Woodgate transfer, making Peter's position impossible, although the internal inquiry cleared him of any wrongdoing. He was so stressed out he was actually ill. He couldn't sleep. I felt sorry for him, I really did. He is a nice bloke underneath it all (yes, and his heart is in Leeds United). When he was 11 years old had somebody said to him, 'What do you want to do when you grow up?' he would have said, 'I want to be chairman of Leeds United.' This position was the best thing that could have happened to him. But then it's hard. He has now had to reinvent himself, really. There had to be a parting of the ways and Peter resigned, having said a number of times, 'Should I stay, should I go?' I think in the end he felt it was just becoming impossible for him personally. Terry had gone and it is to Peter's credit that he identified Peter Reid as a worthy successor on the basis that we should keep him for eight games to keep us up, with the proviso that we shouldn't necessarily keep him past that. We agreed and he did the job, including that sensational away win over Arsenal in May 2003. At the same time, there were not a great many people volunteering to be chairman of Leeds United. We brought Professor John McKenzie on board and he agreed to do it. If you're the new chairman at a company which is frankly not performing very well, then the first thing you do is to identify the problems. The great thing about the Prof is that what you see is what you get. He is very straight and he started off like a house on fire, but again, he just didn't have much luck. With the Kewell transfer to Liverpool, everybody accused him of being a Muppet, but he didn't have a choice. I don't know what else he could have done other than sit on Kewell and, like Lee Bowyer, get nothing for him. As the performances on the pitch deteriorated, the Prof and Reidy lost their relationship and Reidy went.

Football revolves around that chairman/manager relationship. The whole steerage of a club is in that axis. There's got to be a real bond there. Absolutely. They are the most important people in the place: 1) with the purse strings, and 2) with the delivery on the field. In football, you can do all you want off the field, but when the players cross that white line there are so many imponderables. That's why now, when you run other companies, there isn't a single thing you can't influence, but this being football you can't influence the most important bit – the results out there on the pitch. Peter Ridsdale was the chairman and the chief exec and people get nervous about that, particularly when things aren't going right. You also need to share the load. Basically, we were in the mire. We had always talked about getting a chief executive officer but, at the time, when the Prof came on board it was very difficult to get one because there weren't any real runners. When Trevor Birch came out of Chelsea I said to the Prof, 'He is a guy who is really good, particularly in these situations, and basically everybody in football speaks very highly of him.' So I phoned Trevor up and I said to him, 'Do you fancy coming to Leeds?' and he said, 'I don't know. Do you think it will be all right?' I said, 'We are trying to work on some re-financing and I think we can get some money in and restructure it. It's not a bed of roses but will you think about it?' He said, 'Look, I'm a bit bruised at the moment,' so I left it a couple of weeks. Then I phoned him again and we had a chat and eventually we got him in, in circumstances which he was happy with. It would have been very good to have had him in earlier, but I am glad we got him in anyway.

If the club survives, a lot of it will be down to Trevor and his particular skill in finance. He deserves credit for that. It has helped immensely that he has been a professional footballer. He came up around Liverpool when they were the best club in the land and he knows how a good club works. He has got that football mentality combined with a very good financial mind, and that is an unusual, if not unique, combination. That's what I think makes him so good. He is very good with the players because the players know that he was a player. He knew from day one that he would face an uphill battle to save the club. We were in discussions with creditors and we were trying to raise a lot of money. I was going to put some money in and Sheikh Abdulrahman bin Mubarak Al-Khalifa, a lifelong fan, was supposed to put some money in. If that had worked out it would have been a platform on which to build. The Sheikh, though well intentioned, never came up with this money. I think the other thing is that, when you bring in a CEO, you have to let him run the company. I didn't want to compromise what Trevor was doing. He is the CEO, he is a good guy; let him run the organisation. Then the first thing he did was to try to pull it together to try to get a standstill arrangement so we could look at restructuring the debt whilst at the same time trying to find a buyer. That's why I stood down, because it is very difficult to be a prospective buyer when you are sitting round a boardroom table. The other thing was that I tried to give Trevor a clear run without any baggage around his neck, and I was part of that baggage. So here we are today. It's ironic, but when I went into the club those years ago I didn't know that one day I would bid for it, and secondly that the club might not survive. Mine was a substantial bid and we'd have been able to do the transaction by the following Thursday. It was neither accepted nor rejected.

Looking back, the strategy to try to grow revenue and profits through success on the pitch was not flawed. Buying players to support this was not flawed. That's why people invested in the strategy. However, performance on the pitch did not support the wage structure in place, and the ability to generate cash from a squad once valued at £200 million was diluted by the transfer market implosion.

Player contracts are a one-way street and are not performance-related, and when the club signs players up and puts them on a contract, they know that. You can cry foul but, on the other hand, everyone knows the rules before they start the game. I also think the transfer window is a big change in the ability of football to finance itself. Five-year contracts were signed before the window came in. I hope there is some learning for all of us in the Leeds story. What has happened at Leeds has made everybody think about the finances of their clubs. Where Leeds have incurred £80–100 million debt, lots of clubs have £20–60 million of debt and it was interesting to note that our former opponents from the Champions League, Lazio, had their shares suspended recently. Football finance is a global issue, but there are lessons to be learnt for teams the world over from what happened in Yorkshire.

CHAPTER NINE

PETER REID – SPAT'S LIFE!

On a sunny day in May 2003, in my first face-to-face meeting with him, I reminded newly installed Leeds United caretaker manager Peter Reid of his recent visit to Elland Road as Sunderland manager, and he was quick to crack into a smile. For 90 minutes, the referee's decisions had gone fully Leeds' way and, in one of my more abiding memories of post-match inquests, Reid had reacted by saying, 'I'm chewing hard on my chewie, hoping it will stick my teeth together to stop me from saying what I want to say!' A diamond, heart-on-sleeve geezer is the man who was the manager of Leeds for not very long and, in his temporary office at Thorp Arch on this day, Reid was quickly into his stride:

> If I think a referee has had a bad game, I find it difficult sometimes because if you criticise him in public it can get even more difficult. But rest assured, I will have let the referee know my feelings and what I think about his performance. But certainly, I try to keep a lid on those things as much as I can. Now there are times when you have to blow your top, because I think if you keep it bottled up inside it has to come out in some way that you might not have wanted. Football . . . I love football. I love winning and I don't like getting beat, but when you look around the world there are other things happening. I'm not being schmaltzy, but you look at Glenn Roeder (the then West Ham manager who had suffered a serious illness) and

conclude that that's a fact of life. It happens all over the place. Nothing gives me more enjoyment than winning a football match but I'll tell you what – I like a day out at the races, and I've got to say that York is the finest track in the country, in my opinion. I have had many pleasurable days on a racecourse and there's nothing wrong in going out, having a good time and partaking of the odd liquid refreshment. I know that's frowned upon in some quarters, but I find it very enjoyable. Of course, athletes have got to look after their bodies, and alcohol doesn't help that, but I've never minded players, and I'm talking about players because they make football, having the odd one. As long as they do it sensibly there ain't a problem. And certainly it does everyone a wee bit of good to unwind every now and then. You've got to enjoy life. I'm not bad with a form book in my hand and I have had a couple of ownership dalliances with Niall Quinn in his Manchester City and Sunderland days, although I think I got the rump end! It hasn't been done in a business way. More for pleasure. I enjoy my cricket as well, though perhaps we shouldn't go too deeply into that, me being from the Red Rose county and all that. I find immense pleasure in watching England play and the Roses matches are very special. I know Darren Gough, and a lot of other cricketers, very well so there's always plenty to talk about. In fact I like all sports and, being from its hotbed, rugby league is dear to my heart as well. I love the big occasions. At Everton, in that wonderful team we had, I played in three cup finals on the trot – won one and lost two – and in a European final in Rotterdam. I played for England in the Aztec Stadium in Mexico and there's something about big sporting occasions that is unique in life. Certainly to play in them. Look, I'm a council house lad from Liverpool. I was brought up in Huyton, which was Harold Wilson's constituency when he was prime minister, and I'm proud of that. I'm proud of my roots. My mum and dad still live in the area and I often go back. I was there last week when my dad was out at the bowls and I had a pint with him. And that's me. I surprised him, so there was a smile. I enjoy having given him the pleasure he has derived from my involvement in football. You know, his lad's played for England. And when my mum was at Wembley, with the national anthem ringing out, her son was playing. I think she may have shed a tear up there in the stand, although I was more involved in trying to win the game with my Mr Miserable face on. At Sunderland, of course, I had that song, 'Cheer up, Peter Reid', sung about me and, of course, anyone who knows me is aware that I'm a party animal, really. It's just that when you're on the pitch as a player, or on the sidelines as a manager, you've got this face that portrays you as a model of concentration. It might just be that I've got one of those faces, with lines. I'm usually enjoying myself, though. It might not look like I'm enjoying myself, but truly I am. I've been well paid at football. Really well paid. But some of those big-occasion things you'd do for nothing. You can't put a price on them. If I hadn't made it as a footballer I would most probably be working in a factory in Liverpool, having a few pints with my mates, watching the Reds on a Saturday and playing on Sunday. I was brought up a Kopite, watching Liverpool against teams like the great Don Revie side at Leeds. I watched many great games and I was there when Gary Sprake made his famous 'careless hands' howler. I had a nightmare four-year spell with injuries as a player – cruciate ligament, broken leg, broken knee-cap – but I fought back. I was an England Under-21 international, played for Everton and won trophies, played for England and, although I have been fortunate in that football has brought me a great standard of living, I reckon that you only get out of life what you stick in. You've got to earn your rights, and I think I've done that. Howard Wilkinson was manager of the England Under-21s and I did three games with him while I was manager at Sunderland. But it's too much. Being a club manager is a 24–7 job and while Howard was having meetings with me, my phone was constantly buzzing on silent. I've known Howard for years. When I was caretaker manager at Manchester City, my first match was against Leeds, who won 3–2 with Howard in charge. And when Leeds won the title, we played them at Maine Road and beat them 4–1, leaving the City fans booing because they thought Manchester United were going to win the championship for the first time since 1967! But Leeds won it all right, and the lives of Howard and myself seem to have been intertwined for some time. His name, and that of Don Revie, are imprinted on Leeds United history, and I hope that in years to come there are reasons for my name to go alongside theirs. This has been a difficult period for the football club, but it is a fantastic football club.

When you look at a club you look at the fan base, and I've got to say the fans have been remarkably patient. The gates we have had since I joined have been fantastic, as has the away support. I've only been here a short space of time, but I think we've all had a reality check. The priority was staying in the Premiership, and now that we've achieved that I think we need to get down to basics and I'm sure it can be turned around. The one principle I would have as a manager is that you should only have people who want to play at your football club. Otherwise, the message is, 'No matter what your ability, no matter how good you are, if you do not want to be at this football club then you know where the door is.' If you're honest about these things you get more out of it. I've already started planning for the summer in the hope that I will get the job on a permanent basis. I think you've got to. Then, if you get it, it's not a surprise. I want to say to the powers-that-be, who have been very honest with me, 'There you are. That's my plan.' It's not a quick fix. You can't do that. But I've got to say that the academy, the youth set-up, is fantastic. There are some good young 'uns coming through, so if you can consolidate for a couple of years and make a team that's hard to beat, then in the future there could be a big turnaround. The fans deserve the truth, and the truth is that we are trying to get a good side and a winning side, but it's going to take a lot of hard work. While we are going through that process, we need their continued support. I think the Leeds fans will understand that and appreciate it. The next manager of Leeds United, and I hope it's me, will be doing a lot of wheeling and dealing. But so will every manager. I know we have financial problems, but rest assured, it's not a cash-flow industry out there. Not that money will change hands, but plenty of players will be coming and going. It will be a different transfer market involving loans and swaps. Industries have balance sheets and the results are six months or yearly. My results as a football manager are every Saturday and sometimes on a Wednesday. That's the industry we're in. We know the pitfalls and we get on with it. But this word 'pressure'. I won't hear of it at all in a football context. I think if you've got children and you're paying a mortgage and you get the sack, then that's pressure. In the end, I got hurt by Sunderland. I had seven and a half great years there, and that's a long time to remain in one place as a manager. Even though they've gone down now, when I joined there was an average gate of 12,000. It's 48,000 now in a £40 million new stadium. A new training ground has just opened. If you leave a club in a better position than when you started, you've done all right.

But when you look back and have time to reflect then maybe I was there just a wee bit too long. Maybe I got a bit too close, but I have no qualms about that. It's just the way I am. I had a seventh and a seventh, and when I was at Manchester City I had a fifth and a fifth – the best both of them had achieved for years. At Maine Road, I was a young boss and I think I've learned a lot since then. I was a bit headstrong, a bit fiery. You can't put out the fire, but you learn when it should be full blast and when it should be a slow burner. You learn, also, that there are many ways to skin a cat.

Reid, appointed by Peter Ridsdale in March 2003, was fired just eight months later by Trevor Birch. Then chairman Professor McKenzie had a role in this decision, of course, along with the board of directors, but as he was away on holiday at the time it came down to chief executive Trevor Birch to deliver the news. Reid will forever be remembered for saving Leeds from relegation in 2002–03 courtesy of a fabulous away win at Arsenal, which he recounted in our interview at a Manchester hotel in March 2004:

Leeds had a game on the Sunday and I got a call on the Friday from Peter Ridsdale asking me if I would take the job. He said it was only for eight games. I said 'Yes, no problem' because I did the same with Sunderland when I first got that job. Even though people might think it's a gamble, well, it is a gamble but you back yourself. I was in bed at home, and it was a nice thing to wake up to. Peter didn't refer to the financial situation. He didn't say, 'Look, Peter, there are difficulties.' He just said, 'We need to stay up,' and that was it. That was my remit: 'Keep us in this league.' I knew what had happened with the selling of Woodgate and other players because at Sunderland I tried to buy Robbie Keane and Gary Kelly. So I knew Leeds were trying to get some money in. I knew there was only a certain amount available, but obviously the club itself needed to keep in the Premier League and that was my first concern. We managed to do it, with Mark Viduka, in particular, playing magnificently.

When I looked at the fixtures for Leeds United, it was always going to be a difficult job to avoid going down. Certainly, it was one that you couldn't turn down from a professional point of view. Managing Leeds United is one of the big jobs and, to be perfectly honest, I didn't realise how big a club it was until I got there. I mean, I had always realised it was big, but although I was aware of the financial situation, I don't think I realised, to be perfectly blunt, just how bad it was. I knew it was imperative that the club stayed in the Premiership for obvious reasons – because of the amount of revenue and guarantees – but I certainly didn't know the extent of the debt and some of the salaries the staff and the players were on. It was a club that definitely needed restructuring from a manager's point of view. I wrote a report before I left and gave it to Trevor Birch. I had been doing it since I got to the club, and in it I assessed all aspects of the club other than the actual playing staff. It was going to be a long haul; it wasn't just going to be one season. It was going to be a longer job to get the club on an even keel. Looking at the financial situation, albeit not as an expert, I am still not sure how you get out of being £100 million in debt. On the football side, the main thing was keeping the club up.

That 3–2 win at Arsenal was one of my great days in football, and so totally unexpected. My first game, at Liverpool, was a bit of a disaster. We were poor and, to be fair, the players responded well and not many clubs could go to Charlton and win 6–0. People forget about that one. But 3–2 at Highbury was a fantastic job; they were up for the title and Kewell and Viduka got very important goals, and we got one off a dead ball, which was really good. That shows you what we were capable of. It probably begged the question: if we were capable of beating Arsenal 3–2 away what had happened previously? I just think that professionals should get on with the game and not worry about financial implications with a football club if they can, but subconsciously it gets to you and that's a fact of life. I think, as well, when you lose players who are all quality – and United had lost some from the dressing room – that has a bit of a demoralising effect on confidence. Basically, that's what happened, and once you get into a rut or into a sequence in which you're getting beat, it becomes very difficult. That was the case with Leeds. At first, I managed to get a bit of enthusiasm, but certainly, when I took the job permanently, Paul Robinson was going to be sold and then he turned down the money. Mark Viduka asked for a move and I told him to put it in writing. Having said that, he got me the job, but when he asked for the move after the season's end I had a meeting with Inter Milan who offered, I think, 4.5 million euros for a loan. I recommended the deal to John McKenzie but with the REFF deal, I think it is fair to say, we owed on a loan so it wasn't feasible. Now I didn't have the cash to generate extra players.

After that, it was just a matter of trying to get players off on loan, i.e. Danny Mills and Stephen McPhail, just to generate a bit of cash to get some loan players in. I just needed an injection of blood because at the time Lucas Radebe and Michael Duberry had got injured, Eirik Bakke had missed half a season, Seth Johnson had played only two games the previous season and Dominic Matteo hadn't played the previous season. So there were players there who hadn't played enough recent top-class football. Gary Kelly hadn't played a lot of games and it was Paul Robinson's second full season. Alan Smith had injuries, so I just tried to get more people in the squad to give me more options. It was a matter of beg, steal or borrow. It's not as though I didn't have people lined up. I had got Patrik Berger lined up but, at the time, I couldn't take him. I spoke to Markus Babbel's, Paolo Di Canio's and David May's agents but I was told, 'Hang on, you can't do anything at this moment in time.'

John McKenzie had to get rid of plenty of money from the football side – off the wage bill. That was during the summer, which we did. I think it fair to say that the assistant manager, Eddie Gray, and the first-team coach, Brian Kidd, were on a lot of money. I had to prune the staff down and it was difficult, you know, releasing players. First of all, I had to get rid of Brian and Eddie to calm down the financial situation, and that was a fact. They were on too much money, so they had to go. After they went, I had to get another sizeable amount off the wages. So now you're talking people like masseurs and physios. That's always very difficult, but as a manager you've got to do it. So dealing with that, and then trying to get new players in, made it a difficult time. In pre-season, I brought Kevin Blackwell in as head coach. I wanted something different. I felt that we had to get the fitness level up and, without knocking anyone in that position, I just felt that Kevin and Dean Riddle, from my Sunderland days, could do just that. I didn't know Kevin. I was just watching how Sheffield United had done and things like that, you know, and then, having got permission to speak to him, I thought he was the man for me. I still think he is a fine coach and we were on the same wavelength. I honestly think the players enjoyed the training under him. But trying to change that mentality of the A team of two years before, when they had gone downhill, was very difficult and even I couldn't do it. Had they become lazy or had they become used to a routine? No, I just think there were a lot of them there who had been on the fringe of games – you know: Kelly, Duberry, Harte and so on, who hadn't been first-team regulars – so it was a matter of trying to instil confidence and trying to change their mentality into a winning one. But pre-season, even though the training went well and we had injuries, we were very, very poor in the games. Hence the loan players coming in and, to be fair to the players, at the start of the 2003–04 season against Newcastle, Middlesbrough and Southampton, they did great.

But the 4–0 defeats in the Everton and Leicester games were really poor – poor performances which simply were not acceptable. Speculation was going on about my career and things were made public by McKenzie. I think he had a difficult job, but that was particularly wrong. We managed to beat Blackburn, but the next four fixtures were Manchester United twice, once in the Carling Cup, and then Arsenal and Liverpool – very, very difficult games. I thought we were unlucky in a couple of them. In the Liverpool game, at 1–1, Mark Viduka got a great chance and missed it. I'm still not sure about this offside ruling, but when Jeff Winter awarded a goal to Liverpool when there were three of their players offside, I thought it was crucial. Also crucial to my future was that 6–1 drubbing at Portsmouth, after we had done OK in the first half. In the second half, we just fell apart, which did not add to my popularity and, obviously, I had made decisions about Mark Viduka. There were a couple of well-documented bust-ups resulting from my unhappiness with his time-keeping – he just kept turning up late. We were trying to be as professional as we could and I just thought Mark, whether or not he was disillusioned with the football club, could have done better. There were a few times when he was late at training and he was once late for a game – against Arsenal. I just left him out. When I first got the job we had a big game against Fulham and he came late that day, so whether it's in his make-up, I don't know. But we needed to get the best out of him and I gave him the benefit of the doubt. I just said, 'Go get me a couple of goals.' We won 2–0 and he got the goals. I am not a tyrant on the training pitch, because I like the players to enjoy it, but you have got to have some discipline and I think Mark overstepped the boundary lines. It doesn't matter whether he was disappointed that he didn't go to Inter Milan on loan. His attitude wasn't the best and, it must be remembered, that's talking about a player I admire. When I first got there, I liked him and I still like him as a player now. As a manager, I recommended him to a certain other manager who asked me about him. I just think he felt his time was up at Leeds and he wanted to get away and, because he couldn't get away, he felt he had already done his bit. Mentally, at the start of the season, Mark wasn't with us. But, on the outside looking in now, it seems that after he went away to Australia to be with his sick father he returned with a clear mind. Certainly, he came back a different player. So that came to a head and, with everything else on top, it was a difficult time. The Portsmouth result was the straw that broke the camel's back. Trevor Birch, who had just come in, decided to change things. A manager lives and dies by his results and mine hadn't been particularly good. But I had kept Leeds up the season before. I think I had tried to get a new structure within the club. I had to cut costs, which the chairman wanted, but didn't get sufficient positive results. I have got to say that. I was left with egg on my face over the loan signing of Roque Junior who, I think in time, would have handled the Premiership. But Leeds United didn't have time for a cultivation exercise. Some people thought I had made a mistake and brought in Roque Senior instead, but when I look at Edu and Forlan, who came in from South America and both do well, Roque Junior is a better player. You don't get a World Cup-winner's medal and a European Championship medal if you can't play and he certainly didn't show his true capabilities at Leeds. It was all a bit hectic. I think some of the other lads I brought in on loans are decent players but need time to settle. Lamine Sakho is a good player, and I certainly think Jermaine Pennant, Zoumana Camara and Didier Domi are decent players. As for Jody Morris, he is a player who had troubled times. I gave him a chance and he didn't take it.

Yet ultimately, as a manager, it comes down to results, and certainly the Portsmouth one did for me. They got a deflected goal just before half-time. They looked dangerous from the crosses so I said to the full-backs in the dressing room, 'Stop the crosses. Just stop crosses. Keep playing your football. I thought you were the better side in the first half. I thought you were unlucky.' The second half was a disaster. I remember turning to Kevin Blackwell after their fourth goal and saying, 'That's me gone.' I was a manager and it's something that, as a football manager, I accept. I just think if I had been given time I would have got it right, but time wasn't on my side nor the club's side. When Harry Kewell went, I was of the understanding that we would have got at least some of the money to bring in new players on a permanent basis. It was a depressed market and there were some bargains to be had. Sheffield United's (now

Tottenham's) Michael Brown, for instance, would have been an automatic target. I know him well having signed him as a kid at Manchester City and it was that kind of player I was looking at. Paul Robinson could have gone because I would have kept Nigel Martyn and, hopefully, generated money to try to do something else in the market. I think Arsenal, Manchester United and Barcelona were all interested in Kewell, as well as Liverpool, the club he chose. They are not all going to be wrong about his abilities. I still think he hasn't reached his full potential, but certainly the amount that Leeds got as a club was disappointing. In that deal, I certainly thought that wasn't the going rate. However, the going price is only what Liverpool would agree. He was adamant he was going to Liverpool, so that was the only club we could do a deal with. Our hands were tied. But certainly, with a year left of his contract, we had to get some return because we had lost out on Lee Bowyer. I felt during my time at Leeds that it was a club riddled with cancer. I just think that when you look at the players, there are a lot who have been there a long time and I thought that situation needed to change. I just think that the whole ethos in terms of the work ethic is something you must have. I am not saying the players are bad pros. I just think that for two years it was hard luck and a bad story to tell and we had to change that mentality, somehow, because people were getting used to losing and it was becoming a habit. In the overall structure, you have got to get people out there and enjoying what they do. I brought in afternoon weight training and pool work – just a different structure on a football basis – but certainly I have got to say there were a lot of players overpaid and underperforming. And, I think, if the players have a look at themselves they would agree with me.

Another unfortunate episode was my private meeting with John McKenzie, which became very public. There was speculation in the newspapers – and I have a good relationship with newspapers, but I never leak any club business. I am very professional in that I try to have a good working relationship with the press and try to mark their cards about team matters. I think a lot of people knew about this meeting. I know at the training ground at Thorp Arch there must have been 20 press and camera people, so we couldn't have the meeting there. It was my suggestion to have it at a certain hotel. I think there were a couple of the posse following me but – I don't know if it's because I am from Liverpool and have a cynical nature – there were a couple of roundabouts and I managed to shake them off. I got to the hotel on the outskirts of Huddersfield and sat in the bar. After ten minutes, I'm having a glass of wine with the Professor and all of a sudden 20 pressmen are there at the hotel reception. I asked them out of courtesy to leave us alone, but I think it is fair to say that they followed the Prof's car from Elland Road, which was disappointing. But that was a meeting in which I was told that the club were waiting for a phone call about my future from a bondholder who was away in India, which I found very disappointing. I got the impression that they wanted me to go and, certainly, I think the way it was publicly handled gave me the impression, rightly or wrongly, that they wanted me to resign – which I would never do. Subsequently, I asked for support from the board and I don't think I got that publicly. That does affect you. It affected me at the next game against Blackburn, which we won, and I think that was the beginning of the end. I have been in football long enough to know these things and I went away from that meeting in Huddersfield not knowing whether I would be the Leeds manager the next day. I had a phone call at seven o'clock in the morning asking me in. I think they were difficult times for the Prof and I think he was naive and inexperienced in football matters. I don't think he realised what the media do and how football is portrayed in the media. I got a phone call after this meeting, thinking I was a goner, with an order to attend work. This was hardly a confidence booster. I went along and did my job but I have been in football a long time – since I was a little 15 year old – and that was one of the most bizarre times in my career. There were a couple of players who asked me what was going on and when the manager says to the players, 'I don't know,' it doesn't inspire anybody. That was virtually the end – the Blackburn game. Even though we won it, I knew there was no way back. I am not being smart or clever, they were the facts.

I think Leeds United is a fantastic club which just needs to go back to the basics. If I went back I would say to the board:

Get the structure right and get the players to work. You've got to earn the right to win football matches — forget about selling this, selling merchandise, doing this, doing that — that all comes in time. It's what happens on the pitch. You've got to get it right and if it means changing personnel, you change personnel.

The training ground at Thorp Arch is fantastic. To go there and work every day is a pleasure and the facilities are great. The basics are there and the training set-up is fantastic. They are lucky lads. Everything is there; it's just the mentality. Players have got to buy into that. It has to be everyone together, otherwise it doesn't work. It has to be said that the Champions League is a dim and distant memory. To get European football back at Elland Road is a long, hard road. When I was Sunderland manager, Leeds were at the top of the League and we beat them 2–0. But we didn't get to the Champions League and I thought it was the beginning of the end. When you used to play Leeds in those days it was hard and that's what they have got to get back to. Unless they get back to that, it is going to be very, very difficult, but certainly the fan base and the club is geared up to all that. It's fantastic. But it's going to be a long job and it's not going to happen overnight.

Peter Reid was appointed manager of First Division Coventry City in May 2004.

CHAPTER TEN

PROFESSOR JOHN MCKENZIE – A BLOODY REIGN

It was when Professor John McKenzie decided to scale down his international work as a financial adviser, leaving him with more time on his hands, that he embarked on a route that was to eventually see him in the unlikely role of chairman of Leeds United from April to December 2003. He lived, as he still does, in nearby Ilkley and was urged by his wife, a keen bridge player, to find a new interest in life. His short, controversial and bloody reign, in which he cut £20 million from the budget, was over when he talked to me at length in a Leeds hotel in March 2004:

> At the end of Leeds' heyday, the seats in the stand were not well placed. I thought, 'How do I get to sit in better seats?' and so I bought some shares and ended up with four million of them. I still have three and a half million now – for loyalty to the cause, not for anything else! I got to know the directors a bit and I think Peter Ridsdale was nervous about the AGM 18 months ago and the prospect of getting voted off. He invited me to join the football board. I might have met Allan Leighton a few times, but I didn't know him and I think Peter would agree that he brought me onto the board himself. Then, of course, within eight weeks we reached a situation where the half-year losses were desperately bad, the full-year losses were nearly £50 million and they were jumping up and down saying something had to

change. Leighton, I think, asked Peter to step down and me to take over to try to stem the losses. The last thing I wanted in the world was to be chairman of a football club. I wanted to sit back and enjoy the football. Leighton was very, very supportive of me when I was chairman. He may have been very busy but he presented a lot of time and backing to me. It was something of an eye-opener to me when I had taken my place as chairman. It was clear there would be some task to perform. The club was haemorrhaging money left, right and centre and I really think the urgent business was to stop the haemorrhaging and make the books balance and to find a new management team. Previously, people didn't take their feet off the accelerator and put it on the brake as quickly as they should have done. The operational side of the business was worse, and was certainly going to get worse still. Neil Robson came on board very quickly, first as an adviser to me and then as finance director, and he came into a very unfortunate situation. There were too many highly paid staff and too many indulgences and I have always felt that the indulgence permeated the way in which the team played. Players were getting high salaries which were unrelated to their performance and we would have probably been all right in terms of the remedial steps if the team had been playing well. But it wasn't, and never really has since on a consistent basis. I didn't appoint Peter Reid as temporary manager; Peter Ridsdale did that. But I made him permanent. I think Peter Reid did a very, very good job in keeping the team in the Premiership at the end of the 2002–03 season and I'd rather hoped, given that we had survived, that he could fire up certain people. The team, on paper, was better than any Sunderland team ever was, and he would be able to use that in a permanent post. In hindsight, in view of the Kewell situation and given the Reid situation, we may not have made the decisions we did. As a temporary manager, Reid did a fantastic job. He inspired the players and won back their spirit, and Viduka, in particular, was very positive at the end of that season. I think Peter should have been very good as a permanent manager but, clearly, things went wrong almost immediately following that. He was very good at acting on and tidying up the excesses off the pitch. There were too many physios and too many staff around the place. He dealt with the indulgences off the pitch, which was a start. But it really started to go wrong almost from then. Pre-season was really bad and then the team was producing a set of results and playing in a way which gave rise to a lot of discomfort. The 4–0 defeat at Everton in September 2003 was embarrassing and I thought it was about time that the manager and I had a chat. I asked Peter to meet me but he wouldn't meet me at the training ground. He chose a place which was very public and our cars were followed by the press. It made what was to have been a private chat into something of a media circus. I wasn't happy about the way it happened. It is bizarre the way the football world is. I mean, I have been involved in the structure of a lot of businesses, particularly in the education field, but never in the public eye. I am uncomfortable with it. I am not a particularly public figure and I'm certainly not out to be on the front or back pages of newspapers. With some exceptions, the press is not easy anyway. With ten pages to fill on football, you're not allowed to get in the way of a good story. When I was first chairman, I thought it would be low-key but, in reality, at Leeds that's an impossibility. With Peter Ridsdale having been so high-profile, it was impossible to work away quietly, out of the media glare, and I think on the financial side it inhibited what we could achieve. I certainly don't think it helped – because of the size of the debt and the inability to spend – and the restructuring was undoubtedly inhibited by it being a public arena exercise.

Clearly, there had to be new finance coming into the place, and getting re-financing and having a break-even situation in trading terms was absolutely critical because then the City could see that we had turned the corner and were progressing. Also, you have got to have a team that is at least middle of the table in terms of that, because then you have sufficient money coming in. We had processed it through to a position in which we assumed, and had every reason to assume, that we could make agreement with the bondholders which would involve a deferment of payments to the end of the season. There was to have been an input of new capital at two levels: bringing in

£4.4 million in December, firstly, and then going to the existing shareholders and potentially new shareholders for more capital towards the end of the season. That would have taken us through and would have helped the situation so that we would have traded our way out of difficulties. We were within 24 hours of that happening. The exact date when it should have all happened was 24 November 2003. Everything was in place. The bondholders, REFF and everybody else agreed and a circular was ready to go out to shareholders. I had to pull it because the £4.4 million was based on £2.2 million coming in from two different sources and we couldn't guarantee to the Stock Exchange that one of these inputs of £2.2 million would come in. And so it had to be pulled. If that money had come in, Leeds would be in a different situation today, although the team would have had to survive in the Premier League. If those two amounts of money had been put in place, then we would have traded through the capital. There would have been an injection and we would have been going to the shareholders in the late spring saying, 'Look, this is where we are. We need some more money.' There would be another £5–10 million coming in and the problem would have been solved. But it wasn't because of that one thing. The reality was that the board could not be convinced that the money would be in before 19 December, and you can't issue to shareholders a document to vote on if you are not convinced that the money is copper-bottomed. The Sheikh was saying he could guarantee his £2.2 million would come, but it wasn't in his holding company at that time. He is a very genuine guy and he believed it would materialise. So we believed we were very close to our solution, but it didn't happen. It was a grave disappointment, and after that things went a bit downhill. That was the time when we also got the new management team in place. My annual report, which is published, had to be announced on 30 October 2003. We were positive – cautious but positive – and then we had got the new management team in post-trading. Hopefully, the football team were going to do all right and most of this £4.4 million was likely to come in. By 24 November, when it got pulled, the situation was now quite different because the new management team had to look for cash elsewhere and move more towards sales, and it had to look for inside cuts which are actually contract-breaking cuts. I am not being negative about that, because that's what every administrator does. When Trevor Birch took up his post on 1 November, I stepped back to being non-executive chairman. I never wanted to be executive chairman – that was certainly not my intention – so to move back to being non-executive chairman, with Trevor chief executive and Neil finance director, was fine. With the vision of a good, strong football manager and a strong performance from marketing to support the trading, getting to break-even and then to get the capital growth up, we were very nearly there. And then we fell apart.

It has been suggested that I could have played hardball a bit more over the Kewell transfer to Liverpool, but I don't know the answer to that and other people who have been quick to criticise don't know the answer either. The reality is that if you compare it with the Bowyer situation, it is not dissimilar in many ways. Bowyer didn't go, for various reasons, one year before the expiry of his contract. He then went at Christmas for £300,000. We were faced with a situation in which Kewell really wanted to go – I don't think there is any question about that – and the fact that he was only ever going to go to one place was something we didn't know until right at the end, when it was said that, besides a different contract, he was also prepared to have a new contract with us. The only contract he was prepared to countenance with us was one which he could terminate at any time he wished, getting himself 50 per cent of the transfer fee. Well, that's no contract with anybody. So, we specifically asked ourselves the question whether we should have got £3 million, or £4 million or £5 million and whether £3 million was good. I don't think anybody could ever tell. It's very easy to say we should have said, 'Right, you come back and you play for the reserves.' He was never going to play for the first team again. You remember the notorious television trailer in Australia in which he said he had always wanted to play for X and it stopped short of revealing the club? We couldn't say where it was because it hadn't been signed at that time. But they said they had been talking since Christmas. There was no way he could play for the first team again in those circumstances. The fans would never have accepted it. So, if we had been richer, I guess we would have hardballed Liverpool and Kewell's negotiating team and maybe we should have done so. But we got £3 million, which we needed, and lost £2.5 million off the payroll. I don't particularly defend that situation. It's unfortunate it was the first negotiation I had to do, but I was cosseted by advisers, all of whom recommended me to do that. The board discussed it at length and had to accept that deal. Whether it was right or not I doubt we shall ever know. He wanted to go and needed to go. It was nothing like the Woodgate situation. He didn't want to go, I am sure. Whether the money for Kewell was right or not I don't know. I don't think anybody helped particularly. I don't think the agent was as constructive as he might have been. In the press, he was heavily critical. We showed remarkable forbearance in not going into several personal bits and pieces. I certainly had a different view from Liverpool on what they actually said. I don't think it was a commitment, but I certainly think it was moving towards an understanding.

I think one of the great perceptions among Leeds fans is, 'Look, there is all this revenue coming into the club from crowds of between 35,000 and 40,000 per game, there are various big money transfers that have taken place over the last three years, so why is it that the debt continues to grow?' It's not quite as simple as that. We even had Dr Bill Gerrard's criticism that we weren't going anywhere when we were, in fact, 24 hours away from pretty well sorting out the whole thing. You get into debt, and you borrow more money to service the debts and the debts get bigger, so when you get to the Woodgate scenario, I now know, and I didn't know then, that pretty well the whole damned team was for sale and they needed to sell somebody to survive. The money is simply used to help pay the interest on the debt to service the debt itself. Is there any way out of that? Not when you have borrowed money to a depreciating asset. I am not suggesting they knew that asset was going to depreciate. But if you borrow money to buy a house, unless it's in a particular crisis period, you know that five years later if you find you can't service that debt you can sell it off at a thumping profit. If Leeds United had invested the money in a new stadium then you might have been able to borrow more money against the stadium, but in reality what they did was to spend most of the money on buying players and then more money in servicing the debt for those players and it's a completely vicious circle. It's never going to improve until you can in some way trade to break even, which they hadn't got towards. For goodness sake, stop anticipating you are going to be in the Champions League – they would still be in financial difficulty there – and try to raise money to reduce your debt or get your creditors to take a big cut. Somebody should have said a long time ago to Peter Ridsdale, 'Stop this, I can see a doom scenario here and you are going to have to stop buying players and get a more realistic handle on the finances of the club.' I think you might ask Leighton and Richard North, the finance man who was a non-executive director, what their perceptions were at that time. What was the case for buying Seth Johnson and Robbie Fowler? I don't see how you can defend it when, within six months, they're having to sell Woodgate in order to survive financially. It might have been all right if players had been sustaining the levels of money. Even with Ferdinand it's not the great deal it seems because if you pay £18 million for him, you then add £2–3 million in agents' fees and the like, your interest on servicing the debt and then you sell him off and you don't sell him for £30 million, as has become apparent recently, but he knew anyhow, but £26–27 million. Then you get extras if Manchester United win a cup and things like that. You didn't get £30 million so, at the time of the sale, you've probably made £2–3 million net. Everybody thought the profit was £12 million but that is totally wrong. Viduka has loans against him of something like £8 million so, theoretically, if you sell Viduka you don't have £8 million. The only people you could sell and make money on are the ones who have come up through the home-grown ranks.

Given the scale of all that and the question of the spiralling debt, it has been speculated that being put at the helm of Leeds United must have been enough to make my hair curl. I don't really think that anybody was quite aware what was happening until I got four or five weeks into it. I never saw Ridsdale as a man who was particularly close to the figures. I get the feeling that he just decided to do something and the then finance man, Stephen Harrison, found a way of making it happen. From the outset, when I took over it was always going to be an incredibly difficult situation to deal with. I had not seen the likes of it – the scale of it – anywhere before. Football is a different sort of business anyhow. It's very much gambling-based because you are putting all this money on players and there's not necessarily a return. You pay to train the squad and pay for their performance and it's a very big gamble. By the time I came in, it was obviously a gamble that had failed. Then one was into damage limitation. My only sadness is that we came so close but didn't quite do the damage limitation I would have liked to have seen, and now, essentially, however good Trevor and Neil are and however good the new consortium is, it's all dependent on the team performing a bit more. That's the real unpredictability that is not normally around in business. Did it ever occur to me at any time that the players weren't giving their best? Well, it was apparent from the Venables period. I didn't particularly see a problem with O'Leary. The book seemed a bit odd, but I was surprised when O'Leary was fired. I did think Venables might be all right, but I would rather have had Steve McClaren or Martin O'Neill, obviously. The team always looked a bit lethargic and that's where I thought they were not playing as a team other than in short, stuttering moments. They didn't find any level of performance really in the two seasons after O'Leary left, except in all-too-brief efforts like the win against Arsenal that kept them in the Premiership in the 2002–03 season. They were not consistent and I always felt that reflected a measure of indulgence in the amount they were paid, and maybe with an attitude which had been cultivated by the overall management of the club.

From what I saw of Venables, he appeared to be out of touch with his players. He certainly had an office a long way away from them. Reid was closer, but then seemed to lose the plot. I think that the relationship between the chairman and manager is absolutely critical but I always took the view, and

Reid was very strong about this, that he would be the one to deal directly with the players. And just as I wouldn't go and talk to a member of the catering staff – I would say hello and chat to them but I wouldn't see it as my job to talk to them about their work, that's the catering manager's job – I felt it was better to leave the formal relationship with the players to the manager. Maybe that, in football terms, is not a good thing. Certainly, that's how one would run most businesses. It doesn't mean I didn't talk to players on a one-to-one basis. I did talk to them on a personal basis but I didn't ever talk to them as a team because I would have seen that as straying into the manager's role. Maybe that's a criticism that could be made of me.

My view of football as an industry, now I have been on the inside track, as opposed to the view from the stand, has accentuated the view I already had. It's a very inefficient business. It's a jungle to a large extent – a bit like the stock market was 40 years ago when you all stood in a ring with a piece of paper and shouted at each other. The transfer market is totally unsophisticated. The boardrooms are full of quaint symbolism. There are huge egos and scrambles for status, and anxiety among many managers about the way the business goes. It's a very old-fashioned business in some ways. I don't think it is going to change very easily. An awful lot of questions need to be asked about agents and agents' commissions. It's almost impossible to write an accurate budget because of the way in which you eke out money. You get money from television and so on, according to how you do. In one sense, that's right, but it means that to budget is almost impossible. You either budget to be bottom of the League – and who wants to do that? – or you budget for being in the middle of the League. Budgeting is very difficult. The relationship between success and merchandising and revenue in the ground is critical. It's a very difficult business to make any money out of and people get emotionally involved in it. It's high profile. But was I pushed to one side? No. The decision to bring in both Robson and Birch were my own decisions and I have always manifestly made that clear. I made the conscious decision to bring Trevor in on the basis that he had the time and energy and commitment relating to age which I probably couldn't provide.

Undoubtedly, you might raise the question as to whether our approach to things was the same. You might think that I don't have a great affinity with shareholders. In fact, I am a major shareholder and also there are 18,000 fans as shareholders. In the end, I have stepped right out of it. I was not convinced that the operation was enabling me as a director to continue to fulfil my duties as well as I should have done, given my other responsibilities. I felt also I could possibly do more things to help if not being constrained as a plc director. But that aside, there are many other things to do and I think it was right to give Trevor a free hand. The only interest I have got, and this is from the beginning, is in sustaining this football club. I didn't go into it to make any money.

I had to drop a great deal of consultancy work to take this on. I didn't apply for it. The issue of the advanced payment to me which has been talked about was modest, compared to my other consultancy work. There are not many consultants at Leeds United who don't have similar terms. It's really to guarantee a position in a very vulnerable situation. The figure in question is a lot less than that often quoted. I suspended nearly half a million pounds in contractual payments to me when I left. I've never publicly said that because I didn't want to get into a row about it, but theoretically they should have paid me, and continued to pay me, in the same way as former players and former managers get paid. And with them, you're talking huge sums of money. Also, I've stuck with my 3.5 million shares even though they are now virtually worthless. Anyway, I would not have wanted to be emotionally in the position of selling Leeds United shares. Getting involved in the first place? I think if you regret things, you don't do anything and you don't get experience. I think I could have done it better with the experience I now have but that's true of many things in life. I found it a very interesting learning experience and it came very close to being a successful ending. Sometimes you win and sometimes you lose in business, and it's sad that Leeds

United did not come up to everybody's preferred position. That would have been much better than having to sell to someone else. I suppose the other thing I regret is, to some extent, the loss of my sheer unadulterated fan's enjoyment of the football because you spend so much time worrying and getting emotionally involved. My wife talks very much about the morning before the Arsenal match at the end of the 2002–03 season. We were in danger of going down then and we were going to lose about £25 million as a consequence. I spent most of the time on that morning with Leighton trying to work out how we would survive in those circumstances and it was so traumatic. She went out from our flat in London for a walk to relieve the tension. That was before a ball had been kicked and then, after we had won, the emotional trauma had us almost all on the floor. You can't enjoy it in quite the same way ever again as a fan when you are involved at that level, but if you think you have done the best you can at something and if you think you had a chance to try and put something right and use your skills, you have given all you can. If other people don't think it is good enough then that's for them to say. I think there is a lot of greed within that industry, a lot of self-serving. It's a drug really. Peter Ridsdale is heavily addicted to the business and to that visibility issue, and lots of other people are like that. You make some good friends in football and with Leeds it opened doors for me. But it's a very strange world, totally artificial and all-embracing. You haven't time for anything else. I went to Premier League meetings as chairman, for the first time in my life, and my impressions of them as a body from those meetings were that there are a great many egos, a few very bright people and some people who ought to have given up quite a long while ago. With 20 different strong views, the meetings were very idiosyncratic. All the members were very self-opinionated, including myself. Better discipline was needed. Socially, they were very pleasant people, but they didn't really hang together as a large business team. But then, football doesn't have to be business. If you look at it now it's moving more and more away from public companies who are responsible to a large number of shareholders.

PROFESSOR JOHN MCKENZIE — A BLOODY REIGN

If I did it again, I would maybe do it better, but that's true of every job you have ever done, isn't it? For instance, Bill Gerrard of Leeds University is a very intelligent man. I think he has an agenda and I don't know to this day what that agenda is. I don't know what his early career was like, but we would have embraced him to some degree and would certainly have welcomed his advice. He didn't seem to like me for some reason, but then he didn't like Peter Ridsdale either. Yes, if I did it again there would be no rented goldfish in the chairman's office, nor anywhere else for that matter. The story of Peter Ridsdale's rented goldfish caused great mirth up and down the country, but in fact they were symbolic: symbolic, that is, of the excesses at Leeds United. The measure of indulgence across the board, on and off the football pitch at all levels, amazed me. I should have perceived it better than I did. All these guys on expensive salaries and things. I am not allowed to comment on confidential items like the closing deals with Ridsdale and Harrison, but it's all in the annual report. Peter is a nice man, an engaging man. I enjoyed his company. He's a bit obsessive at times. He was on the phone every five minutes to me. He had a little boy scout's enthusiasm. On the face of it, he's rushing round like mad and completely convinced of himself and yet, when reality comes, it's not like that at all. He came within an ace of winning something, which Leeds have not done for a very long while. O'Leary did too. One view is that Peter is to be admired for having the balls to have made the gamble and that, having provided £100 million of funds for the manager, the manager has then failed miserably in his duties; that if you give somebody off the street £100 million and say, 'Go buy a football team,' a lot of people could have done a lot better. I think where criticism must come is that I don't think that Peter exercised sufficient measures of financial control over expenditure. For instance, if I want flowers in my office, I pay for them myself. All of these salaries are twice as high as mine. You can add in all this so-called dispute over forward payment. My biggest criticism would be that he didn't shut the speedboat engine down as, clearly, he was going towards the rocks and that, in a business, is a terrible mistake. And then you come back to the non-executive directors (Leighton and North) and whether they can step aside from overseeing these actions. They are independent referees put in by shareholders to monitor and control the executive. And the executive is vulnerable, particularly when you have got the chairman and chief executive in the same post for long periods of time. When I was in Liverpool in the Hatton crisis, I sat in a meeting with all of the senior management of the place and was sent to the City Hall to be present at the vote in which it was decided to go for the redundancies. I suppose it was supposed to be a salutary exercise. And Hatton and the others sat there surrounded by a group of cronies, just clapping and patting them on the back and, like many politicians, this removes them from the realities of the world. Having got the money, and got himself into the semi-final of the Champions League, I think Peter removed himself from the realities of the world and didn't realise that you couldn't go on living that life when you were not performing that well. He invited me out to a lunch with some other businessmen when he was chairman. I had met him a few times but I knew that the club was not doing as well as it was and should have been. They picked me up from the railway station in this stretch Mercedes S500, which was only about a week old, and I said to myself, 'There is something not quite right about this.' I didn't know if my journey was paid for by the club or by Peter Ridsdale personally, but the fact is we didn't need a stretch Mercedes. It's this general indulgence which was a problem. I think it is important that you stay in touch with the realities of the business – especially when it's a business making losses at the rate of £50 million a year.

At the end, while we had made savings of £20 million a year and I had put in an excellent management team, there was still an enormous amount to do. Now it was up to Trevor Birch and Neil Robson; Eddie Gray and Kevin Blackwell . . . and, above all, the football team!

CHAPTER ELEVEN

ADAM PEARSON – HULL OF A JOB

West Yorkshire-born Adam Pearson was only 39 years of age when I interviewed him in February 2004, but he said he felt a lot older. He started his working life in retail with Marks & Spencer in Hull at the age of 18 as a trainee, eventually transferring to their London headquarters and spending eight years in buying, merchandising and marketing. He left to become commercial director of a sports company supplying sportswear to M&S and other high street stores before joining Leeds United as retail director, becoming commercial director when media company Caspian Group plc (subsequently renamed Leeds Sporting plc) took over the club. Leeds Sporting plc was the holding company of Leeds United Football Club, which obtained a stock market listing by way of a reverse takeover, in August 1996, of Caspian. Leeds Sporting differed from other quoted football clubs inasmuch as there was no dominant shareholder – there was, instead, a wide base of institutional and private shareholders. Leeds Sporting's principal activity was, of course, football and Leeds United had a tradition of success stemming from the 1960s and 1970s that few other British football clubs could boast. More recently, the club saw a resurgence in its fortunes. Third place in the 1999–2000 Premiership, together with a semi-final place in the UEFA Cup, were followed by progress to the semi-final stage of the Champions League.

The club's annual report for the year 2000 read as follows:

On the basis of this success, Leeds Sporting is implementing a strategy of growing the power of the Leeds United brand. A high quality playing squad is crucial in this regard. It is being achieved both through investment in the necessary infrastructure to nurture the 'home-grown' talent that Leeds United's well-respected youth academy has been consistently producing, and through the judicious purchase of players whose abilities and personalities complement the Leeds United ethos. The quality of the playing squad is underpinned by two key factors: prudence and continuity. Leeds Sporting acknowledges that investment must be made in the playing squad. However, that is tempered by the need to control wages paid to staff, recognising that, ultimately, there is a responsibility to shareholders to control the cost base of the entire business. Leeds Sporting has also secured the entire playing squad on long-term contracts. Most importantly, the manager, David O'Leary, has committed himself to Leeds United for six years. Off the field, strict systems and controls have been introduced throughout the business and Leeds Sporting's financial record illustrates the effect. Every part of the business performed strongly: commercial revenue, TV income and gate receipts were all significantly ahead of last year. Moreover, the strength of the Leeds United brand is evidenced by lucrative sponsorship agreements with Nike and Strongbow and the strategic media alliance concluded with BSkyB, who acquired a 9.9 per cent stake in Leeds Sporting. In summary, Leeds Sporting is performing strongly both on and off the pitch and is building a platform for further success and growth. The intention is for spectacular performances in the Premiership and the Champions League to become a regular feature every season. This should generate revenues to create a virtuous circle of ongoing investment, brand development and long-term success which, when combined with the strength of management and systems and controls already in place, mark Leeds Sporting as a business to be reckoned with.

Pearson, a dashing young man, was a major off-the-field player in raising the Leeds United profile before becoming chairman of Hull City back in 2002. His team went on to gain automatic promotion from the

Third Division in 2003–04. Despite these new commitments, Pearson found plenty of time to reminisce about his days at Leeds when we met in his office at Hull's spanking new stadium:

> In 1999, the finance supremo at Leeds United was Natalie Martin, a New Zealand girl who ran a very orderly accounts department. She wasn't a high-flier, in my opinion, but she was a good book-keeper. She ran a very tight accounts team and provided good financial information on a regular basis. Everything was fine. I think there was a feeling that because it was a plc they wanted to introduce someone who had financial experience of dealing on a plc institutional side as well as just running a tight ship. What they should have done was to leave Natalie in place and appoint somebody at senior level on the board capable of doing that. But the decision was taken to appoint a financial director instead of Natalie Martin so that, immediately, the experience within the club on the financial side was completely removed. There was no experience within the company with regard to key financial management issues on the ground-floor level, and if you haven't got that on the ground floor then you are really going to get yourself into trouble.
>
> It was felt that making a clean break by bringing in a financial director who would appoint his own team was the way forward. The choice was Stephen Harrison, who had been working in the spectacles industry following a spell at Asda with Allan Leighton. I think that to have to build a new accounts team within the club at a point when it was expanding so rapidly made the club vulnerable. From my own perspective, it is always so much easier to be successful commercially when the team is successful, and the team was about to embark on a very successful period. People in Leeds, and nationally and internationally, could see that. But it was a very tight commercial team and one that worked extremely hard to secure some good, sound deals for the football club both in the short-term and long-term. Packard Bell had been our sponsors at that time and we had just switched to Strongbow, which was a fantastic deal financially for the club. Obviously, it had some

171

ramifications with it being an alcoholic brand, but they were easy partners to work with in that they had a similar target market as the football club and so it fitted well. Financially, we were talking top three or top four in the Premier League, which was great. Away from that, we put a whole cross-section of business partners together in a similar way to what they subsequently did at the Football Association. We had a level of six platinum sponsors below Strongbow who all contributed very significant funds to the sponsorship pot.

So commercially, the club was doing very well, and the retail side of the operation doubled overnight. The deal with Nike took the merchandise onto a different platform in that, from dealing with secondary brands, we had teamed up with the number one. The spin-offs on the retail side, as well as the cash injection, were enormous. The whole range of merchandise became credible, so we were now not just selling the shirt but the training kit, the tracksuits, the sweats and the polos, because of the Nike brand on them. To get Nike for Leeds at that stage, when their only associations were with Arsenal and Glasgow Rangers, was a significant breakthrough for us. Peter Ridsdale and I worked hard at the deal. After it, the retail operation, which had a very good manager with a lot of experience in charge of it, did fantastically well. The Leeds and Nike brands together meant that the leisurewear flew off the shelves. The input from Nike and Strongbow was over £3 million a year, which moved us from a top-ten or top-twelve commercial club to a top-four, and every deal we tried to structure from that point onwards was geared to a top-four strata. Eventually, we got to a turnover of £80 million and £10 million net profit. Those figures finally came through in 2001, when the club was financially at its peak. Leeds had never been anywhere near that financially, and to beat, in monetary terms, big clubs like Liverpool and Newcastle put the club into new territory.

The club was on the crest of a wave: financially secure and ostensibly set for a very rosy future. It was also a club with a wage structure which was beginning to creep up but, at the same time, was still entirely manageable. When looking at reasons why this situation changed so dramatically in such a short time it has got to be understood that the financial climate in football changed overnight. The collapse of ITV Digital when it was the sole competitor for Sky was very significant in that there was no long-term certainty about the media revenues. This unsettled the transfer market and wages went ridiculously high, so that particular market was inflated. There was also the issue, and this was not unique to Leeds United, that some very long-term contracts were being offered to players. When you are bedding down a young team which has basically come through the ranks – people like Alan Smith, Harry Kewell, Ian Harte, Paul Robinson and Stephen McPhail – the security of extended contracts plays a key part in a club's future and is a sensible course of action to take. If you can get those boys off comparatively low wages and onto a five-year contract and have them fixed at that, then great. The problems started to arise when those deals were never allowed to run their course and wages were increased on a regular basis until the thresholds became too high. If they had been left on those original contracts it would have been fine, but they were being renewed annually.

The chairman of the club's remuneration committee was Allan Leighton. At that stage, Peter Ridsdale obviously wanted to keep the players happy, but there's a balance, isn't there? I think the ultimate problems started to arise when the club started to buy players whom they a) couldn't afford and b) didn't need. Competition for places is great, but when it becomes a factor in lessening motivation and creating problems you have gone too far. I think this was probably the case. Four forwards for two places is great, but six forwards for two places isn't so welcome, particularly when, at that point, the financial information is showing that perhaps we couldn't afford those transfers.

Pearson enjoyed his time at Leeds, and played a very significant part in the club being recognised as a European power. Perhaps not unnaturally, he began to harbour ambitions of owning his own football club. He reasoned, 'When you've been party to engineering £80 million turnover with £10 million profit, then where do you go from there?' Pearson looked at the spiralling wage bill, a decreasing transfer market and a policy of buying players from the status of that top-three echelon and decided that it was time to move on. He put four clubs under the microscope – Cardiff City, Plymouth Argyle, Burnley and Hull City – and recalled:

> Cardiff and Burnley were being moved on and Plymouth is extremely well run, so that just left Hull, which was a shambles. Hull therefore became the perfect target, so I borrowed the money and away we went. March 2001 may not have looked like the plateau for Leeds to everybody else, but hindsight is a wonderful thing and I obviously didn't realise that the club was going to get into the mess it did. Yet perhaps that was its peak. I don't know whether it was vision or gut feeling, but I decided to go. The company ethos had changed away from maximising revenue and minimising costs to an attitude based on, 'Let's build a beautiful football team'. Maybe that is not quite how it should be done.
>
> There was constant talk of building a new stadium. The original Caspian dream was to build at Elland Road a multi-sport venue with an arena on the back for ice hockey. My view all the way through, my considered opinion on it right from the start, was that the West Stand should be redeveloped, putting in corporate facilities which would take it onto a different level, matching the Manchester Uniteds and Newcastles, and that the stand should become a twin of the East Stand in size and capacity. That deal could have been put to bed on the back of the 1999–2000 season very easily, without hocking the club up to the eyeballs. A £15 million investment at that point would have produced a fantastic stadium. To me, there was no need to do anything else, because you would then be looking at a stadium of 45,000 people, a capacity which would only be tested by the visits of Manchester United, Arsenal and Liverpool. Another 30 private boxes, which always helps, and you would have got yourself some great hospitality facilities. You would have also retained what is still a not badly networked ground in terms of accessibility. I could not see the logic in hocking the club

to the tune of £60–70 million for a stadium that may have only 5,000 more seats than Elland Road.

In retrospect, Pearson pondered over whether the decline of Leeds United was a shock, an indictment or a puzzle and declared:

> It's a shame. A crying shame. It's sad that Leeds United is now there as a model for everybody to study and analyse the subject of how not to run a football club. It was for a number of years a club going fantastically well and everybody looks at it now and appears to enjoy pouring scorn and derision on it. There have been an enormous number of people on and off the pitch who have benefited financially from the club, and when you have that ethos you are swimming in very dangerous waters. Players were coming in for renegotiation of contracts on a six-monthly basis and to me this appeared ridiculous. Agents were therefore being paid every six months on renegotiation of contracts. It seems bizarre, but it also helps when you look at the most stable Premier League clubs that the principals, the chairmen and the directors, have significant wealth. I think that's pretty important.
>
> The most expensive signing when I was in situ was Olivier Dacourt from Lens at £7.2 million. What a good player. He didn't exit very well under the managership of Terry Venables, but in the climate of the time you would not have said that was a bad buy. To be fair to everybody there, you thought, 'He looks a good player. He's value.' You have to look at some of the later deals – for instance, Seth Johnson from Derby County at £7 million and Robbie Fowler from Liverpool at £11 million – and wonder about the value. Did the club really need them? It is going to be extremely difficult for Leeds United to recover. To me, the only way they could get out of it would be to go into administration. People have got different ideas on that, but going into administration can be a positive situation, as we have seen at Hull City. You can come out of it debt-free, streamlined, a lot thinner and more in control of where you are going rather than being saddled with heavy debts which have been incurred by previous managements. At Leeds, there

seems to have been a distinct determination not to go down that route.

Much of the blame for the situation in which Leeds have found themselves has been laid at one man's feet – Peter Ridsdale's. I think it always goes to the chairman of an ailing company and you know that before you get into it. You know that you get paid a nice amount of money and enjoy all the perks that go with the job because you are ultimately responsible. I think Peter would be the first to admit that. It certainly cannot be attributed to one person's decisions, but unfortunately as chairman you do have to take responsibility, whether or not you have been responsible for all those decisions. You do set the ethos and the tone of the company and you do have ultimate fiscal responsibility. I think if any company gets itself into financial problems then the board as a collective is responsible. The plc board at that time was very experienced and had a lot of wherewithal and ability. It got carried away by the success on the field. Football has a habit of sneaking up behind you and biting your bum. You think you're in control and making the right decisions on behalf of the football club, then all of a sudden the financial climate changes. I could get caught out tomorrow. I've got my players on one-year contracts and some good players on two-year contracts. Say that, out of the blue, the financial market changes, people have got their houses in order, they've got a few bob to spend and the transfer market reopens. The Premier League clubs start looking at Football League clubs instead of going abroad and suddenly I'm very vulnerable. What appears sensible today could be a ridiculous decision tomorrow. There's always an unknown quantity in football. One week, the team looks unbeatable and the next week they look as if they couldn't win to save their lives. You can't legislate for it because you are dealing with human beings who are fallible and have moods and peaks and troughs.

The Bowyer/Woodgate trials had a sapping effect on the club. I was in Hong Kong with Peter Ridsdale on the night of the incident in Leeds city centre at a time when the phrase being used was that Leeds United were everybody's favourite second team. Everybody liked watching this young, bright team with its emphasis on attacking football and I think what happened gave the nation a reason, or an excuse, to change their minds on the team. All of a sudden, people started concentrating on the bad aspects of the players, the team and the club and it was the first piece of negative public relations they had had for a long time. People latched onto it and from there it was a cycle with people jumping on the bandwagon and the perspective on Leeds getting worse and worse. I think over the past four years a total of nine Leeds United players have been arrested, charged or both in connection with various criminal matters and that, as a lone fact, is just totally unacceptable. Leeds had been transformed from everybody's favourite second team, to the team everybody loved to hate. It is staggering and begs the question of just who is applying the discipline at the football club. The manager and the chairman have to be completely focused on these highly paid employees who must adhere to the behavioural standards that every other employee has been set.

Some of the decisions made at the club post-Peter have left a lot to be desired. I would put somebody in charge of the football club who knows something about running one. I thought it a quite staggering decision to put an individual from academia in charge of a football club, and my opinion is that it was lit up like a neon sign internally in football that there were rich pickings to be had at Leeds. Everybody, particularly agents, could see that there was a club which was ripe for the picking, and, as a Leeds United fan, do you look back on a single one of those deals which went through under the chairmanship of Professor John McKenzie with any pride? I think Leeds United fans have been sold down the river. And they do not deserve it because they have always given support which at times has been unbelievable. I sometimes think that they have, if anything, been too loyal. I have been at recent games, most memorably the 3–0 home defeat by Middlesbrough, where they have stuck with the team when the players really needed telling that the kind of play they were producing was totally unacceptable. All the businesses were working well. The financial services side was profitable, the travel company was thriving, the publishing company was doing OK, the lottery company was doing all right. All the different companies we set up were profitable, and all had a business manager in charge with responsibility to me. They were taken apart and destroyed overnight, because nobody could be bothered to manage anything that wasn't football. Everybody wanted to be a football manager. They should have been concentrating on the retail business, the lottery business, the financial services, publishing, travel and commercial. All those strands and they all needed managing and watching. At the end of the line was a financial department which was supposed to give you the information to be able to manage them properly. That collapsed, and it closed down the rest of them. You're left with the retail, and turnover drops by millions. So it's not just escalating costs; it's somebody not driving the business as well.

To lose more than 30 per cent off your turnover in three years, from figures of around £80 million to about £55 million – and that's what appears to have happened – is a scandal. It also means that somebody is not working very hard. The issues concerning what Leeds United own, and what they do not own, are interesting. The city council sold the ground back to the club after buying it from them 15 years previously, but retained some of the land. Although the club retains half of the land, it would be fair to say that the more valuable land belongs to the council. This is an ongoing difficulty. The two bodies need to get together, because a poorly performing football club will have a demoralising effect on the city, lessen external investment and have a knock-on effect on the council, as we have seen in recent elections. It is very important to the city council to have a nationally and internationally successful football team. In Hull, the council is well aware that the goodwill factor around the city is coming from two sports teams – the football club and the rugby league club – doing well, with a great new stadium also featuring big international matches and rock and pop concerts. The whole feelgood factor is helping them to establish themselves politically. On Monday mornings, the factory workers go onto their production lines and, because Hull City are top of the League, there's a cheery, 'Good morning'. They're happy. There is some pride back in the city, and that reflects on the city council. Only recently, Leeds was buzzing. It had become the financial centre and property centre of the north and the football club was flying. Everybody was saying, 'Let's get to Leeds. It's the place to be.' Not any more.

CHAPTER TWELVE

TREVOR BIRCH – CREATOR OF CHANCES

Less than a fortnight into his new post as Leeds United chief executive, blue-eyed baker's son Birch, in collaboration with Professor John McKenzie and the rest of the board, had already fired manager Peter Reid. Birch found himself at the helm of a club in total disarray. The task ahead was mountainous and his early take on matters when we first met in his newly acquired office at Elland Road's South Stand in November 2003 was as follows:

> During those successful UEFA Cup and Champions League campaigns involving Leeds, I, along with everybody else, looked on and thought, 'They're an up-and-coming force in football.' I don't think anything in football surprises me because it is such a crazy world, but to the ordinary person it is inconceivable that you can reach such heights and plummet to such lows in such a short time. But things can happen so quickly, and once a club's on the slide it is incredibly difficult to arrest it. There are factions and frictions within clubs and when you're doing badly, the cracks get wider and become exposed very harshly. If you're doing well, it gets glossed over. Fans really couldn't care less about what's going on off the pitch, and why should they? It's an entertainment business and they come here on a Saturday to be entertained. The level of income or revenue that a club can generate governs and limits the capabilities of that club. In the long

term, then, for Leeds to get back as a top club it needs a new stadium.

Leeds will never be a leading club again unless it's got a state-of-the-art stadium in which 5,000-plus of the 45,000–50,000 seats are taken by corporate hospitality. Otherwise, it cannot generate the revenue. These are the hard facts of life these days. Leeds' gate revenue is £12 million, Chelsea's is £30 million, Newcastle's £35 million and Manchester United's is £60 million-plus. Unless you have got the stadium, you can't generate revenue sufficient to sustain payment to players. OK, in time, player salaries may come back down again, but still those clubs that generate the most revenue will, on the whole, be the most successful. As we currently stand, no one else will ever win the League other than Manchester United, Arsenal or Chelsea, or possibly Liverpool, and you can throw in Newcastle. But that's it. That's not good for football and something might need to change to sustain football long term.

The most important thing is to have a very strong Premier League, and we are seeing polarisation within it. The Champions League is having the most significant distorting effect in that equation, as is relegation. For some clubs, relative to their cost base, the financial impact of not securing Champions League status is worse than actually being relegated. You're looking at an average of £15–20 million for Champions League qualification and that's a massive input of cash. What you can't have these days, unless he's a billionaire, is a local benefactor. He isn't going to make the difference. Here at Leeds, the new stadium is when the good times are going to return. It's vital, although the number one priority at the moment is surviving in the Premiership. You can't think of anything else this season other than survival, because the ramifications of failing to achieve that are too horrible to contemplate. And yes, administration would figure very highly in those ramifications. It's disappointing. I know Peter Reid, and I did look forward to working with him, but his position became untenable and unsustainable. We had to act and I think Peter realised that. I just hope the players realise the significance of where we are and what might happen. They have a duty not only to the fans but to themselves to start to perform. Once you start spiralling down, it becomes difficult. It's a vicious circle because you lose matches, you lose confidence, you feel bad about yourself, you try that bit too hard to correct things and you make mistakes. You're playing at 120 mph when you should be settling it down, but there's such anticipation from the supporters that you feel you've got to be seen to be really trying and what comes of that is a reckless challenge. They've got to calm it down, start to rebuild and go back to basics. It's Churchillian, I know, but we are in our darkest hour. The optimist, though, will say that the darkest hour is just before the dawn. Let's hope so.

Birch takes us along the route that propelled him into what is currently the most difficult job the game he loves could possibly demand. Born in Ormskirk in 1958, he was brought up the middle son of three and explains:

Dad had a shop in Haslingden in which he baked all the bread, pies and cakes for all the local mills, so even though you never think about it as a child it was a distinctly middle-class upbringing. I went to the local grammar school, where I had a bit of a culture shock because the only sport they played was rugby. I became involved in that on Saturday mornings, but Saturday afternoons, Sunday mornings and Sunday afternoons were all about football with local teams. I was playing in the men's league when I was only 13, so it would be the Southport Sunday League one game and the next for the Chas Hill building supply company team and then Hesketh Casuals. Some guy who's now in charge of the Leeds Housing Trust and was in that same Hesketh team has just written to me enclosing a picture of my younger self, which is a bit unfortunate. From as far back as I can remember, I wanted to be a footballer. School was a bit of a blur, really, although I managed to pass my 11-plus and go on to grammar school to pick up a few O levels, which I thought I'd never really need because of my certainty that I would play football. My team was always Liverpool; my heroes Ian St John, Roger Hunt and Ian Callaghan. I was steeped in that football era, standing in the Anfield paddock on a little stool that dad had made out of a breadboard. It was safer watching from there than the teeming Kop. There was a European game against Vitoria Setubal and though Dad had two tickets he hadn't told me we were going and, anyway, I had a severe dose of tonsillitis. I really wasn't well enough to go, but nothing was going to stop me once I learned that we would actually be sitting in seats. Watching football in that kind of luxury was as good as it could get, even though I could hardly stay awake because I was so ill. Dad took one look at me half an hour from the end and he decided he had to get me home before I died! I was so keen I would say a little prayer before kick-off like, 'Please God, give them my strength,' willing them to win every game.

Dad was keen on his football. We used to have a piece of Accrington Stanley's stand in our garage from the day they played their last game before folding and everyone wanted to take home a little bit of history. When I left school at 16, I could have signed for any of what were then the First Division clubs, but I was never going to join anybody other than Liverpool, so I became an apprentice at Anfield. I was like Little Lord Fauntleroy. There I was with six or seven O levels among 15 other apprentices, most of whom had been up chimneys for the previous two years. In those circumstances, you have to adapt, fight and survive. Having signed me, Bill Shankly had a mental breakdown, but I'm comforted by the thought that those two events are unlikely to have been connected. He was the greatest man I have ever met. Still. Period. He's the most inspirational manager the game has ever seen or is ever likely to see. It's a fine line, I know, between genius and madness, but to be able to go up to a player the day before a game and say, 'Jesus Christ, son, I'd hate to be playing against you tomorrow,' showed an ability to say just the right thing at just the right time to just the right person. He'd be the same just before kick-off, making the players feel in control. He'd say, 'I've just seen Bobby Moore . . . he can't even walk.' Then afterwards, when you'd won, he'd say, 'Lads, you've just played against the greatest defender in the world.'

The ability to motivate players has to be the number one asset for any manager. Being involved at Liverpool was a shock to me. Sport had always come very easily to me. I was good at athletics, ranking third in the UK at 400 metres at the age of 16. I played rugby at a decent standard, I ran for Lancashire and was good at football. So, on the face of it, the world was my oyster. Then I went into a pool of players who were not only good but were hard as well. That period at Liverpool was my university of life. Their policy was that they would try to break you before they made you. They had a very poor track record at bringing players through, preferring to buy in one or two every year. It was very difficult to break the mindset that you could trash youngsters rather than nurture them. In my first few weeks there, Ronnie Moran stopped the game, pulled me up and said, 'Hey, son, you think you're a good player, don't you? Well, you're f****** s***.' That was a bit of a shock. I'd never been spoken to like that, but he went on, 'All your mazy dribbles . . . you'll never get away with that in the First Division. You get the ball, you give it and you move.' I was a bit of a runner who tried to do things, but they knocked that out of you. You kept getting knocked down and had to get up again, so much so that only two of us made pro – myself and a guy called Bill McClure who went on to play for New Zealand in the World Cup. Eventually, Bob Paisley called me in and told me that Hibernian wanted to buy me. I had no inkling that I wasn't going to make it because I was still determined to break through, and to be told that was like a bolt from the blue. I immediately said no but when Shrewsbury, who were top of the Third Division, came in for me I thought it might be a chance to score a lot of goals and make a few people sit up and take notice. I became their record buy at £50,000 in 1979 but it never really worked out and I moved on to Chester for £10,000. They weren't very good either and the thought suddenly dawned that I would never be as good as I thought I was or should have been. It was a very low point in my life. I'd done nothing from 16 to 18 but at 19 I decided to do some business studies, thinking that if I was to be the greatest player ever I would need to know what to do with my money.

At 25, by now with Ernst & Young, I had graduated with a

first-class degree in accountancy and was in the same Liverpool office as Mark Palios [Chief Executive of the FA] and Rick Parry [Liverpool Chief Executive]. After nine years, I was a partner and rose to head up the whole of the northern region as head of corporate restructuring. Then I had a rush of blood in 2002 and thought how nice it would be to get back into the game, hence my appointment as chief executive at Chelsea. Having been a footballer wasn't necessarily a route into governing football, because the administrators tended to be the club secretaries. When more money started coming into the game, people realised that those with financial acumen would be those to turn to. The chief exec. role was created and was pursued by secretaries who didn't really have the right business background to fulfil it. As soon as that happened, I thought that maybe there was a route back and kept my eyes open for an opportunity. I knew Chelsea's bank manager, who was based in Manchester, and got an introduction to Ken Bates, who seemed to like the cut of my jib. With debts northwards of £100 million, the situation was rather precarious and my remit was to steady the ship and negotiate a way forward, through restructuring and refinancing the business. Chelsea, like most of the other clubs in the Premier League, had got it badly out of kilter in terms of the wages they paid to players relative to their turnover. It should be a fairly straightforward economic model. You know exactly how much money is coming in, so how can you actually conspire to spend more than you have got? There's no real uncertainty about your revenue stream, so you should be able to cut your cloth accordingly. It's the speculation aspect of it that fools people. It's easy to think, 'Well, if I buy that player I can sell this player, but I've got to buy that player first.' One thing you learn is that that extra player never makes a difference. It's always, 'One more player will make the perfect team,' but that never happens. The way forward was to keep it calm and do everything behind closed doors away from the glare of publicity, which hasn't been the case at some other clubs I could mention. It was a good 18 months at Chelsea. We built a great heart within the club and people behind the scenes were fantastic in creating a happy family atmosphere, which I think is incredibly important for a club because if you're dealing in turmoil and crisis it spreads throughout the place. If people walk in and see happy faces and it's all smiley smiley there's a feelgood factor which is, I think, critical to the success of any business. Of course, I became an adopted Chelsea fan because you quickly become emotionally attached to it all. We put our heart and soul into it. I look back with pride that the ship became seaworthy and to see it going full steam ahead is good. Roman Abramovich had been kicking around but he only really took the decision to become involved in football after the Real Madrid v Manchester United games. He looked at Manchester United, Arsenal, Tottenham and Chelsea – Leeds United, for all I know – but Chelsea had all the right constituents for him. I was instrumental in bringing him into the club and it was a very exciting time. Fantasy football. When Abramovich decided to bring in Peter Kenyon as chief executive it was a pleasant parting of the ways between us and I wish him all the best. If a knight in shining armour is going to put untold fortunes into a business, he's entitled to pick his own people, so I've no regrets on that score. But it did precipitate a period of reflection in which I wondered what I was going to do with the rest of my life, and along came Leeds United. This club needs a chief executive and it is in financial trouble, so I would like to think that my name would have been thrown into the hat given what I had done at Chelsea. I spoke to Allan Leighton and John McKenzie and, though Leeds United is a challenge, it's a challenge that plays to my strengths. My views on Leeds as a football club were formed pretty early in life. Liverpool and Leeds were always on television because they were the two top clubs, and you'd always see their managers, Shankly and Revie. Leeds were just a great team – a strong team full of exciting players. I've still never seen anybody hit the ball as hard as Peter Lorimer, nor dance down the wing as gracefully as Eddie Gray, nor tackle as hard as Norman Hunter. There's a correlation with Chelsea in that both clubs followed a period of success by slipping down among the also-rans and then reinventing themselves, though I have to say that Leeds have a lot more traditional history. Yes, they were known as 'dirty Leeds' but maybe they played with the spirit that is needed right now. And if Chelsea can rise again, why can't Leeds?

That discussion with Birch was the beginning of a period which he later referred to as 'living a lifetime in five months'. Back in that same office in March 2004, he said:

> My remit on being head-hunted by the club as chief executive was to oversee the financial predicament in which they found themselves. Negotiations were ongoing with the major financial creditors and the experience I gained at Chelsea was to be put to use in that respect, alongside the running of the football club. It was perhaps going a longer course than I had anticipated and a rescue package didn't reach fruition. Therefore, we had to change tack and it became a little bit more compacted in terms of the timescale because you had to deal with the problems. When I came on board, administration was still a possibility. It had always been a possibility, really, given the size of the debts. The core debt was £85 million and the bits and pieces around £15 million, bringing it up to around the £100 million mark. It is generally perceived that in any other business outside of football they would, with such a colossal debt, have ceased to trade, but it depends whether you have got a business to salvage from it. Of course, here you have got a very strong business to salvage – a Premier League share – and there are only 20 Premier League clubs. As a middle order Premiership club, the guaranteed revenue is in the high twenties of millions, whereas if you get relegated then it's two or three million.
>
> Peter Reid was the starting point, really: my introduction to Leeds United. By the time of the first board meeting, I had not spoken to him as manager. I knew Peter quite well but I had not really had a chance to speak to him or understand how he was viewed within the club. Removing him was a difficult decision, so I attempted to try to put them on hold for a little while and, of course, the next game we lost 6–1. It was almost self-fulfilling, then, wasn't it? It became unsustainable. I had to

deliver the bad news to Peter but it hardly came out of the blue for him. He dealt with it professionally, as Peter does with these things. He is a great pro. In other circumstances, he might have been given a longer stretch. He had succeeded in saving the club from relegation the previous season, but he had taken some batterings at Everton, Leicester and Portsmouth and when you look at the team on paper you think it shouldn't have been in the position it was in with the players it's got. The well-being of any club is totally dependent on what happens on the pitch. Always has been and always will be. You would have to say at Leeds that there has been a period of underachieving. It speaks for itself, doesn't it? Perhaps events off the pitch have impacted on what has happened on the pitch. I think it is essential to a successful club for there to be a good atmosphere and a positive atmosphere, and what I came into here was the most negative atmosphere and a distinct feel-bad factor about the club. That impacts on everybody – most importantly, the players. You only have to look at the way Arsenal play at the moment and the air of fun and enjoyment that they exude. You have to try to achieve that, I believe, in a football club in order to achieve great things because you have all got to be in it together. All for one. And having said that, those players would really struggle to find a set of fans who would be more loyal to them than the Leeds fans are to us. There can be no criticism whatsoever of our fans. They are loyal. Throughout everything, even the players' wage deferrals which some fans may have taken exception to, there is still an unbelievable loyalty to the club. I have never seen it before and it has never wavered. You would think at some stage that the fans would give the players stick, but it has never happened. That's the one shining beacon throughout all of this crisis – the solidarity and support of the fans.

Keeping the club alive was a daunting task, though not mission impossible, because of a) the quality of the players we have got; b) the positive support and c) the fact that there were a lot of games left. So, if you put those three together, you realise you have got to be in with a shout if you can just create a better atmosphere, which isn't easy to achieve overnight. You hope that it will slowly come together, because it is all about confidence and you have got to rebuild slowly and you can only rebuild that by hard work, which we are trying to do. Our creditors had different agendas. It is a lot more difficult dealing with a group rather than one individual creditor, so just trying to stabilise the group and having them singing off the same hymn sheet has been a challenge. I have to say that they have been supportive. If you look back to what we did in December when we started that standstill arrangement, the bondholders allowed us to use £5 million when they had a choice as to whether they should put the company into administration and fund the administration with that money, or allow the directors to continue to trade to attempt to find a solution. So that was a vote of confidence in the board to achieve that and, in that sense, they have been very supportive. At any given time, these people had the ability to actually close the club. Absolutely. It was up to them. At this stage, it's not the shareholders who you are responsible to, it's the creditors because they are not going to get paid in full and so therefore they call the shots. At any stage, they can say, 'That's it, we want you to stop and pay us what you can.' The suspension of share dealing was just a natural consequence of us not being able to get formal extension of the standstill agreement in place and the Stock Exchange automatically suspends you. But that lack of formal written standstill didn't matter because of the constant discussions with the creditors about what was going on. They were supporting us and felt it was better to try to work towards doing a deal and spend the time trying to put this standstill agreement in place. It is better that shares were suspended because people were still trading at the time and we had issued an announcement saying there was no value to shareholders. The question of whether or not it was preferable to go into administration in our situation is not an easy one to answer, other than there has never been an administration in the Premier League. So there was great uncertainty about a) how the Premier League would react to administration. They could have turned round and said, 'Right, that's it. You're out of the League. We have suspended you completely.' Nobody could say for certain that wouldn't happen. Also b) we could have had an eight- or nine-point deduction. So all those things led to great uncertainty. Also, you have got to be able to formalise an exit from administration. When you look at clubs who have been in administration and the way they come out of administration you've got to do certain things and guarantee certain people are going to get paid. And are you going to come out by company voluntary arrangement or will there be a sale? We were never able to articulate at that time whether administration would come. I think in general there was sufficient uncertainty surrounding it to make it an option we wouldn't really want to pursue unless it was an absolute last resort. Having said that, there are benefits of going into administration. In fact, you can formalise your compromise arrangements with your creditors – the likes of the Inland Revenue, who wouldn't be able to compromise outside the formal process; along with the managers, ex-managers, ex-directors. All those could have been thrown in the pot, so there are certain benefits in doing that. But generally there are uncertainties surrounding it. A significant question here is, 'Do you want to be seen as the person who brought down Leeds United?'

During the transfer window it seemed inevitable to some people that the crown jewels – Paul Robinson, Alan Smith, Mark Viduka – might go. Remembering what we owed the creditors, there was huge, huge pressure to sell. But, thankfully, we were able to navigate our way through the window and were happily not having to do that. As far as the takeover was concerned, there were many frustrations. When I first arrived, the Sheikh was threatening to do something and it never happened. I don't think in any way he was being disingenuous. The desire to do the deal was very real, but the ability perhaps didn't match the desire. I spoke to quite a few individuals and groups of individuals who were interested in buying the club but it was a very difficult deal for people to conceptualise. Because of not knowing what division you are going to be in in the 2004–05 season, nobody wanted to take the chance of relegation apart from Gerald Krasner's consortium, which obviously had a cunning plan should that happen. But that has been a real problem because you basically can't use the same set of figures for Division One and the Premiership. They will have to review all options, as they say. I had similar beginnings at both Chelsea and Leeds, I suppose, in that both clubs have pursued the dream. But the one thing that Chelsea got right, which has sustained them and enabled them to go on to the next level, is that they built a stadium. If you ask me what is the one decision which was wrong, or an event that didn't happen which would have taken Leeds United to the next level, or even saved them, it would be the redevelopment of the ground – anywhere that would generate them sufficient revenue to keep them in the elite of Premier League football. We are talking quality corporate capacity at Leeds of less than 1,200 a year, whereas with Newcastle and Chelsea you're at 5,500–6,000 and that can make £10 million worth of revenue difference. I do believe there are people out there who would actually come and pay more money to watch Leeds United if the facilities were here. You would have a broader fan base – a wider spectrum of people coming to watch the games if the quality was better. More women watch Chelsea, for example, than any other club and that is no coincidence. The facilities – you can have a drink and go to a spotlessly clean toilet – are very nice. That's important for a Premier League club.

We're here at Leeds in the Premier League at a time when more money is coming to the game than ever before in its history, and we've come through that period and we are still sitting here in a 1930s stand. That's not good enough for Leeds. Every time I am on the train and I go past the Elland Road site I look at it with incredulity. The site is large, and there is so much space available, and no collaboration between the council and the club has happened. I am even chastising myself – and I've only been here five months – that more has not been done in that respect. That is the major difference between Chelsea and Leeds. What a chance there is to make a showpiece for Leeds. If you're coming into the city on the train and you look across and see a state-of-the-art stadium, what does it say for Leeds? It defines that this is a city that has got ambition; it is going places; it's vibrant. But what you look out on, with all the warehousing, is a dump. There may have been good reasons for not doing it, but my gut feeling is that this is a ground that needs to be redeveloped to take Leeds to the top. We are trying to take Leeds to the top by buying success on the pitch, which we nearly did. But in terms of the foundations, they were built on sand. Building a new stadium would have relaid these foundations on stone. I have had to live and breathe the Leeds job and there was one enormous area of satisfaction. We didn't sell the players and that was terribly important to me – that I gave the players the best opportunity of staying in the Premiership.

In May 2004, Trevor Birch was recruited by Everton as chief executive following the takeover of Leeds by the Krasner consortium. He left the Merseyside club six weeks later.

CHAPTER THIRTEEN

THE BATTLE FOR LEEDS UNITED

When Christmas 2003 was just a fortnight away, the present most Leeds United fans were hoping for – the saving of their club – was a long way from the wrapping paper. But there were hopeful signs among the six emerging scenarios. Sheikh Abdulrahman bin Mubarak Al-Khalifa was the only individual to have gone public over his interest. It was known that he was being backed by two wealthy Saudi businessmen and the added plus point was that he was a lifelong fan of United. The Sheikh had already said he would not support the selling of players and was known to have the best interests of the Elland Road club at heart. The Sheikh was viewed as being likely to step forward with a cash offer which would be for the purchase of shares and a reduction of the overall debt. Money, it seemed, would also be available for team strengthening. Allan Leighton, the club's former deputy chairman, was yet to declare any firm interest in brokering a deal, but was believed to be discussing possible investment with City contacts. It was anticipated that his long-time associate, Philip Green, might emerge as the public face of a bid which would see considerable funds pumped into the football club. By acting as broker, Leighton would be able to assemble a consortium which, like the Sheikh, would almost certainly ensure the club's long-term future. The syndicate would also make an initial investment in shares and reduce the debt. There were other figures waiting in the wings without the massive financial clout of the Sheikh or Leighton, hoping to seize an opportunity to take control at Elland Road. Their initial cash investment was expected to be much lower than those in options one and two and, while shareholders may have felt happy with it, it was unlikely that there would be any dramatic reduction of United's massive debt. Extra funds would be required to strengthen a business which had been forced to slash its costs and a smaller consortium was unlikely to have the cash required to maintain the club's current status. United would continue in the short-term in its present form, but without substantial future investment a sustained period of mediocrity and all that that entailed would be likely. Smaller consortiums were likely to come to the fore if United slipped into administration. An alternative to a major outright investment would have been a consortium willing to buy up some shares, but coming to a separate non-cash agreement with the creditors. For example, this could have led to a deal with the largest creditors in which Elland Road would have been handed over to the bondholders, with the club leasing it back at a fraction of the debt. Leicester City adopted a similar route and, while not as effective as the first two options, such a takeover would have enabled Leeds United to continue in its current guise. The new owners would look to generate further income through the sales of media and merchandising rights on a global basis and the club, without the major creditors, would eventually become self-financing. This form of investment was more likely to come from sources outside the UK who were keen to maximise United's branding rights. Another option – administration – would not necessarily have meant the end of the road for Leeds United and, from a fan's perspective, it would have given the club a good chance of finding a buyer who had his roots entrenched at Elland Road. An agreement would be reached with the creditors and the aim of the administrators would be to sell United as a going concern at what would be a knock-down price. However, player sales would be almost certain at the end of January – the administrators would be obliged to listen to any offers – and costs would be further slashed in a bid to appease the club's major creditors. The other concern was how the Premier League would react to one of its clubs going into administration and, with a number of other chairmen already expressing concern at the prospect, it was a risk United were desperate to avoid. The last of the scenarios was that a potential asset-stripper would creep in if no other significant offer appeared. They would buy up the shares at the lowest price. Players would be sold in order to slash the hefty wage bill – and fund the repayment of the debts – while the Elland Road stadium, a piece of prime land owned by the football club, could be sold on. Such decisions would have pleased the bankers and the creditors, but the business would be run at a fraction of current costs and would inevitably slip. However, with cash in the bank a timely decision to sell could see the asset stripper walk away with a tidy sum and leave behind an uncertain future for an underperforming club. In short, while the initial offer may be good, the future for United would be bleak.

On 31 January 2004, the *Yorkshire Evening Post* looked back on nine weeks of turmoil at the troubled club:

2 DECEMBER 2003

Leeds United is officially for sale. Chief executive Trevor Birch has an initial eight-week period to find outside investment to protect the club from falling into the hands of the administrators. The club's bondholders pledge to release £4.1 million from a 'lock box' which enables the club to continue trading. Allan Leighton also announces his intention to stand down from the plc board, fuelling speculation that he is ready to launch his own takeover bid. A Bahrain-based Sheikh also expresses an interest in purchasing the debt-ridden club.

6 DECEMBER 2003

Trevor Birch makes moves to reassure the club's staff about United's precarious position. Allan Leighton and Sheikh Al-Khalifa are tipped as favourites to launch a takeover bid and Birch says he is confident a deal can be struck. He said:

> *You have to remain confident. We won't know until they come forward, but hopefully everybody now knows we are for sale and we only have a short time in which to conclude a deal. You would have very few opportunities to buy a Premier League club and so hopefully this will be a good opportunity and somebody wants it.*

8 DECEMBER 2003

United chairman John McKenzie dismissed claims that the club had rebuffed an offer from the Middle East. Reports from the Gulf claimed that Leeds rejected a £17 million bid from a consortium assembled by Sheikh Abdulrahman bin Mubarak Al-Khalifa, but McKenzie insists no offer is on the table. He said, 'At this time I can confirm that no bid has been received from the Middle East or anywhere else.'

10 DECEMBER 2003

United officials confirmed they are in talks with four consortia – with another waiting in the wings – although chief executive Trevor Birch is keen to stress that negotiations are at an early stage. A club statement to the Stock Market said:

> The board confirms that it is currently in discussions with a number of interested parties which are at a very early stage and may or may not lead to an offer being made for the company. The board, which is being advised by KBC Peel Hunt, will issue further statements when it is appropriate to do so.

The consortia include one headed by Allan Leighton and another by the Sheikh.

15 DECEMBER 2003

United chairman John McKenzie confirmed he will step down from his post at the AGM. Fears over asset-stripping prompted McKenzie's move and the departing chairman vowed to channel his energies into securing alternative investment from the Far East in the hope of supporting a successful bid. McKenzie said:

> It is essential that we ensure not only that new funds are available, but that the club is subsequently only in the hands of owners and managers who care deeply about Leeds United. To generate these funds it will be necessary to bring potential new investors into the club and

negotiate on their behalf with the club's advisers and creditors. To date, there have been no substantive discussions with me but, clearly, any possible future involvement in negotiations on behalf of potential new investors could cause a conflict of interest if I were to remain chairman of the plc.

16 DECEMBER 2003

Chinese petro-chemicals tycoon Xu Ming emerges as another contender in the takeover battle at Leeds. Sources in China say that 31-year-old Xu, chairman of Chinese side Dalian Shide, is keen to partner his club with United. Leeds chairman John McKenzie announced that he will stand down from his post at next week's annual meeting in order to discuss potential investment in the debt-ridden club with a group of Asian business contacts. Trevor Birch pays tribute to McKenzie by hailing him as a saviour of the club.

23 DECEMBER 2003

Angry shareholders demanded an independent inquiry into the running of Leeds United at a stormy annual meeting. The meeting at Elland Road descended into a war of words as the cash-strapped club's board defended itself against allegations of financial mismanagement and over-spending. Chairman John McKenzie, whose salary-package and 'up front' consultancy fees have been criticised in recent weeks, was the target for some of the abuse. But by far the strongest criticism was levelled at former deputy chairman Allan Leighton.

2 JANUARY 2004

Leeds United chairman Trevor Birch issued a hands-off warning to clubs interested in signing Alan Smith. Manchester United and Newcastle are poised with £8 million bids for the home-grown ace amid rumours of a fall-out between Smith and the Elland Road board. But Birch dismissed the speculation as media mischief and insisted he would not sell to raise funds. He blasted, 'I know what Alan Smith means to the people here. As far as I'm concerned he epitomises everything that Leeds

United is all about. We're not interested in selling Alan and we're not inviting offers for any player. Nothing has changed on that front.'

5 JANUARY 2004
Just two weeks remain to the creditors' 19 January deadline and fears start to mount over the future of the football club. Premier League officials admit they are concerned about the prospect of Leeds slipping into administration.

12 JANUARY 2004
It emerges that £20 million could secure a deal to pay off the club's creditors and secure its long-term future. United confirm talks are ongoing with interested parties. Allan Leighton still represents the greatest hope, although the Sheikh is still hovering. A Stock Market statement said, 'The board . . . is in continuing, constructive discussions with a number of parties regarding proposals to purchase the company's business and assets or to inject funds. However, none of these interested parties' proposals contemplates an offer for the company's shares.'

14 JANUARY 2004
It's revealed that £5 million will be enough to keep the club out of administration in the short term. United are just five days away from the deadline given by the creditors and do not have a firm offer on the table to buy the club. United's poor League form is reflected by a lack of interest in the club. Relegation would leave a £25 million black hole and, at this stage, no one is prepared to gamble. The United players could be asked to take the biggest wage deferral in the history of the game in order to help the club survive.

16 JANUARY 2004
Leeds United chiefs told prospective buyers of the club, 'Show us the colour of your money.' Lifelong fan Sheikh Abdulrahman bin Mubarak Al-Khalifa is being touted as a £35 million saviour – but United officials insist no bid has been received. The

Sheikh has long been linked with a move, but the club say they have seen no proof of funds.

17 JANUARY 2004

Leeds United are set to be thrown a one-week lifeline. The club are poised to announce an extension to the current standstill agreement with creditors. With no firm offers on the table, the extension gives Trevor Birch more time to look at internal investment. The idea of wage deferrals is mooted again. There are also suggestions that Allan Leighton has had an eleventh-hour bid turned down by the major creditors because it falls short of requirements.

19 JANUARY 2004

Leeds United are granted a stay of execution by their major creditors, giving Trevor Birch one more week to investigate further ways of raising the £5 million required to temporarily stave off the threat of administration.

20 JANUARY 2004

United's high-earners are asked to take a 35 per cent wage deferral until the end of the season. PFA chief Gordon Taylor said, 'At the moment, it is a backs-to-the-wall situation at Leeds and the players are prepared to play their part as well as the fans, who are remaining very loyal. If deferrals are necessary to keep the club alive then they will look at that very seriously as other members have done in other situations.' Taylor's pre-meeting prediction falls short of what was hoped and the United players stall over offering to help.

21 JANUARY 2004

The Elland Road fans are in uproar after reports claim that the players refused to co-operate with the wage deferral plan. A statement from the squad says they will help 'if required', but a witch hunt starts against senior members of the squad, with David Batty being targeted for his part as PFA rep. The strife does little for morale with the club just four days away from meltdown and still no offers on the table. Birch is told to sell players, but flatly refuses to bow to pressure.

22 JANUARY 2004

Trevor Birch goes on the offensive. The acting chairman insists Alan Smith is not for sale and immediately embarks on a cash-slashing mission that sees all monies stopped to former players such as Robbie Fowler and Robbie Keane. Attempts to release loan men Didier Domi and Zoumana Camara are thwarted when the pairing refuse to sign their release papers.

23 JANUARY 2004

Trevor Birch continues his cost-cutting mission by informing Peter Reid and David O'Leary of his intentions to put a temporary block on compensation payments. He also writes to former chairman John McKenzie requesting he refund his consultancy fees to help the club in the short term.

24 JANUARY 2004

With the second standstill agreement due to end, an un-named Yorkshire consortium who are keen to strike a deal to save the club is revealed. They are the only party with a firm interest and that is enough for Birch to secure an additional five days to the agreement to enable talks to take place.

26 JANUARY 2004

Trevor Birch confirms an additional five-day extension to the standstill. A Yorkshire-based consortium are working around the clock in the hope of putting together a package.

27 JANUARY 2004

The Yorkshire consortium speaks for the first time publicly and insists that their main intention is to keep the club out of administration. Leeds-based accountant Gerald Krasner is named as a leading figure in the group. A £20 million offer is tabled with the club's solicitors in the hope of pushing the deal through. They are the first group, other than Allan Leighton some weeks previously, to show proof of funds.

28 JANUARY 2004

Talks between the club and the consortium are moving slowly. Birch suggests that he will return to the players and ask for further wage deferrals.

29 JANUARY 2004

The players are asked for their support once again and this time put on a show of unity. They accept the biggest wage deferral in the history of the game. United also receive a £1.5 million add-on payment from Manchester United for Rio Ferdinand and Birch is within touching distance of the £5 million required to stave off the threat of administration.

30 JANUARY 2004

United announce a standstill agreement with bondholders that allows them to continue to their next deadline of Friday, 6 February.

On Friday, 19 March 2004, Leeds United were saved from the threat of administration with the Yorkshire-based business consortium led by Gerald Krasner completing a takeover to save the club from financial meltdown. Completion of the deal saw Leeds United plc being wound up and removed the threat of administration hanging over the club. The consortium took over the assets and liabilities of Leeds United AFC. Over 100 lawyers descended on the city to put the finishing touches to the deal. The takeover saw the £80 million owed to three finance houses and a German insurance company wiped out at a stroke after the major creditors agreed to accept a percentage of the amount owed to them. Former managers Peter Reid and David O'Leary also agreed to a similar proposal, which saw them receive a percentage of the monies they were owed. The smaller creditors, including the Inland Revenue, agreed to re-structure their payments and would receive their monies in full. Krasner took over as chairman of the club with immediate effect. The Leeds-based accountant was to lead a new-look board of six which would also feature Elland Road legend Peter Lorimer. Former banker Melvin Helme was appointed corporate finance director while David Richmond, son of former Bradford chairman Geoffrey, took over as commercial director. Leeds-based entrepreneurs Melvyn Levi and Simon Morris completed the board. Geoffrey Richmond, who had acted as adviser to the consortium, was to maintain that role as a consultant on football matters. Chairman Trevor Birch was left to consider his future and his departure from the club appeared a foregone conclusion. The figures of the deal had yet to be disclosed, but it was understood that much would go to the creditors with an additional amount put forward as working capital and in personal guarantees. A portion of the finance was supplied by a company owned by former Watford chairman Jack Petchey, a stakeholder at Aston Villa, who would not be involved in the running of Leeds United. The new owners guaranteed the future of Elland Road and there were no plans for the club to move away from their long-standing home. The club's Thorp Arch training ground would also remain in its current guise, although a portion of the land put up for sale by the old regime, worth around £3 million, would be sold in the near future.

It was a long way from the heady days of Champions League semi-finals and dreams of European domination, but that mid-March Friday was viewed as the beginning of a bright new era at Elland Road. That, at least, was the opinion of the optimists, as the Yorkshire-based business consortium long-linked with a takeover of the club finally nailed its deal. While the club still teetered on the brink of relegation from England's Premiership elite, it had at last found a degree of financial stability without the dreaded plunge into administration. With the uncertainty having subsided, United fans were looking for a firm statement of intent from the new Elland Road powerbrokers and some reassurance that the mistakes of the last five years would never again be repeated. Many, however, were still wondering how the club could have fallen from grace so spectacularly.

With the new board in place, the *Yorkshire Evening Post* 's Paul Dews wrote:

> They jumped more fences than the previous day's Cheltenham Gold Cup winner Best Mate – but the Yorkshire-based business consortium sailed past the winning post in the race to take control of Leeds United. It took almost two months of negotiations to complete what is freely described by the parties involved as the most complex business deal they have ever

witnessed. Far from being a straightforward takeover, talks had involved over 100 lawyers representing creditors and bondholders from both sides of the Atlantic and the red tape had taken far longer to eliminate than was first anticipated. In addition, the successful consortium have voiced their concerns over an apparent smear campaign in certain sections of the media and dealt with a considerable amount of mud-slinging on their way to completing the deal. The emergence of Geoffrey Richmond as an adviser to the group simply gave the critics more bullets to fire, following his ignominious exit from Bradford City, but the consortium never once wavered. All the while, agreements with creditors were ticked off on a daily basis as the nuts and bolts of the deal were put in place during a painstaking process. Indeed, the Yorkshire-based consortium were the only group to actually get out of the starting blocks after others made the right noises but soon withdrew their interest in taking on a club in debt to the tune of £104 million. First up was Sheikh Abdul Al-Khalifa, who talked about an investment from the Middle East. Twice, the consortium claimed they were set to put an offer on the table. Twice, United asked to see the colour of their money. There was a Chinese consortium, headed by the aptly named Xu Ming, that never got beyond making the right noises while a Ugandan property tycoon, Michael Ezra, claimed he was heading a group interested in investing. As the Yorkshire consortium closed in on a deal, a rival group, fronted by ex-Huddersfield Town chairman Terry Fisher, expressed a serious interest in rescuing the club. With former United favourite Trevor Cherry supporting the cause, they had the right backing to curry favour with the fans. But almost three weeks of hints and suggestions came to an end when no formal offer was made, believed to be due to a lack of serious funds, and the consortium withdrew their interest. The only serious bid since the club was effectively put up for sale on 4 December came from former deputy chairman Allan Leighton, but his offer, understood to be around £20 million, was firmly rebuffed by the creditors. Leighton has maintained a keen interest in the situation and it was not beyond the realms of possibility that he could emerge with financial assistance in the not-too-distant future if required. But, for the time being at least, the successful runners and riders were today enjoying their moment of glory in the winner's enclosure after negotiating the tricky course. They have already overcome one test of endurance, now they are fully aware that another one awaits them.

Dews also wrote:

So Trevor Birch was able to enjoy a good drink safe in the knowledge that his mission had been accomplished. When Gerald Krasner's consortium officially took over the reins at United, Birch could allow himself a wry smile and relax for the first time in almost six months. The departing Leeds chairman had fought tooth and nail to keep the club in existence since December 2003, and the completion of those takeover forms brought to an end one of the sorriest sagas ever to hit football. Birch and finance director Neil Robson had saved Leeds from extinction, achieving what many deemed a mission impossible. Not only had they staved off £80 million worth of creditors, they had also fought against the chancers and vultures who had done their best to intervene in the near-death of a great football club. Birch woke up day after day to read speculation about potential investors claiming they were set to save the club, yet went to bed each evening knowing the club was a step nearer the grave. He commuted many times between his family in the south and his Leeds base, knowing that each day he headed north another can of worms would be awaiting his arrival at Elland Road. He must have spent many lonely hours soul-searching, wondering whether or not it was all worth it. Surely it would have been easier to walk away. But he didn't. He was lauded by few, but criticised by fewer. Not one to be over-confident, Birch never once championed the cause of any potential deal. Neither did he dismiss the chancers or treat them with the contempt they deserved. Privately livid at the claims of some potential investors, he simply rode the storm on a refreshing wave of honesty. There was always an endgame for the chairman but quite what it would be, even he never knew.

When the Yorkshire-based consortium first appeared on the scene, Birch had every reason to be sceptical. After all, he had seen so many wannabes come and go without showing their money. Why should this group be any different? The veil of secrecy surrounding the identities only served to add to the curiosity about their intentions. But Birch has always had the interests of the club at heart and has done his best to ensure United can now move forward. How many times he considered ending it all and putting the club into administration is unlikely to be made public knowledge, but it's fair to say he thought long and hard about pulling the plug when the creditors finally refused to extend the standstill agreement. On reflection, those creditors were probably as frustrated as anyone else and it's testament to Birch's ability, and the faith they had in him, that the club lasted so long without calling in the administrators. Birch is a man of few words and, even in his capacity as chairman, he has only spoken as and when necessary. Unlike others, though, when he opened his mouth you knew he meant it. His response to the Sheikh and other potential investors was simple and frank: 'Show us your money.'

He stood by his statement that no players would be sold during the transfer window, even if that meant turning down at least two offers for players which would have eased the pressure. Birch was in a difficult position. Should he bow to the pressure of the creditors – the people who trusted him – or stay solid with the fans, who had put their faith in him? He sided with the fans, despite knowing he could never go public and admit he had resisted attempts to prize away some of the assets. There was the Paul Robinson transfer saga, which could have been conducted better, but that was one small blip in the reign of arguably the most successful chairman the club have ever had. Chairmen are usually judged on trophies or on-field success and, sometimes, how much is in the bank. But Birch was never going to be judged on that. His sole aim was to keep Leeds United alive and he's done it. Birch would play down talk calling him a saviour and would probably give thanks to Robson and John McKenzie for their assistance along the way, but, when push came to shove, it was the former Chelsea chief who masterminded an escape route. Congratulations, Trevor, you've saved our football club. Your name should sit alongside the other greats in the club's history. You deserve it.

CHAPTER FOURTEEN

GEOFFREY RICHMOND – THE ADVISER

Geoffrey Richmond once listed his greatest achievement as selling petrol to the Arabs. The 63-year-old was born in Leeds, where he still lives. He left school to begin a career selling Arthur Mee's children's encyclopaedias door-to-door before moving into selling car light bulbs. He made his money selling car stickers in a business which became the second biggest in that sphere in the world. He sold up for £1.5 million in 1980, determined to retire to a life of leisure, aged only 39. Bored, he immediately regretted the move and bought the Leeds-based cigarette lighter firm Ronson from receivers, selling it on for £10 million in 1994. But the deal returned to haunt him because the complicated arrangements under the sale left him owing £2.3 million to the taxman. The one thing he kept from the sale was the company's share in Scarborough Town Football Club. Scarborough had debts of £600,000 and faced bankruptcy when he became chairman in 1988. But, five years later, despite having the smallest gates in the Football League, it was debt free. Two weeks after the sale of Ronson, he switched jobs as chairman of Scarborough, selling his stake for £1 with his counterpart at Bradford City where the same problems confronted him. The club was £2.3 million in the red, facing court action and was losing £500,000 annually. He set about the club like a business, shedding jobs, cutting wages and paying off the debt from his own pocket and embarking on a vigorous marketing campaign to persuade more supporters to come through the turnstiles. He was also something of an autocrat in the style of many football chairmen before him, appointing seven managers. Gradually, the Valley Parade stadium was improved, fans came in huge numbers and the club, which had underachieved for years in the shadow of Leeds United became successful, winning promotion to the Premiership in 1999. It survived by the skin of its teeth in the first season and, in the second, Richmond invested heavily in talent to prevent another dogfight. But the players failed to produce and the club was plunged into relegation in 2001. The orgy-of-spending period which Richmond himself later described as 'six weeks of madness' left the club in a precarious financial position with debts which eventually hit £36 million, sending it into administration. Richmond quit the club in July 2002, when his shares were bought for just £1 in exchange for buying a £1.87 million debt.

Rather like Peter Ridsdale, it had been the long-term ambition of Geoffrey Richmond to become a leading member of the Leeds United board, though the knowledge of this was confined to close friends and family. For various reasons, this was unattainable and for nine weeks at the beginning of 2004 Geoffrey and I shared a closely guarded secret. The deal was this. I had become acutely aware of his involvement in the Yorkshire consortium which was to eventually seize control of the club, and on the basis that I, as sports editor of the *Yorkshire Evening Post,* would be kept wholly informed of the step-by-step takeover of the club as events unfolded, I agreed to respect the confidentiality of what, in the end, became a monumental event in the club's history. On this basis, we were able to keep our readers informed of the real truth of what was going on with their rescue attempt – there was much fanciful speculation elsewhere – while at the same time avoiding the danger of spilling the beans on issues that might undermine it. Hour by hour, day by day, month by month, Geoffrey acted as adviser to the consortium led by Leeds-based accountant Gerald Krasner, bringing into play his vast experience as previous chairman of two of Leeds' Yorkshire neighbours in Scarborough and Bradford City. When the deal was finally done, the relief was palpable and so, with the new owners in place, Geoffrey and I met at the club's Thorp Arch training headquarters, where he was able, at last, to reveal the drama behind a £30 million deal which, to all intents and purposes, saved Leeds United from the threat of extinction.

He loved telling the story:

The last game of the season in May 2000 at Valley Parade saw Bradford City playing Liverpool. This, for Bradford, was a game that we had to win to survive in the Premier League. Wimbledon were playing down at Southampton and the scenario was that even if we beat Liverpool, if Wimbledon won they would stay up and we'd go down. Meanwhile, at Upton Park, the fixture was West Ham v Leeds United and the final Champions League place would be going to either Leeds or Liverpool. Leeds got a draw, but the fact was that if Liverpool won their match Leeds' draw would not have been enough. Whatever happened that day, two results would have huge consequences for four clubs. It turned out that Leeds and Bradford got the results they wanted. Leeds qualified for the Champions League, and Bradford City stayed in the Premier League. What we didn't know at Bradford, though, was that 18 months later we'd be in administration as a direct result of surviving. The six weeks of madness which affected the club did not take place until the summer of that year. If we had gone down that season we were financially strong. But we stayed up. For Wimbledon, it meant relegation from the Premier League and their long-held dream going into deep decline. For Leeds, getting into the Champions League meant that they could say, 'We are a big club. We can challenge Manchester United and Arsenal. We can be the elite of English and European football. We are going to spend serious money.'

Bradford purchased David Wetherall from Leeds at the start of that season, and after his winning goal against Liverpool, Peter Ridsdale was quoted in the *Yorkshire Evening Post* on the following Monday as saying, 'That's the reason we sold Wetherall to Bradford – there was a cunning plan to get us into the Champions League!' Though David's goal was a fabulous thing from both perspectives, on the surface it was to have dire consequences which could not possibly have been foreseen at that time. On the issue of what changed, I can speak more authoritatively on Bradford.

The first thing that changed for Bradford was that within a couple of days of surviving I took our manager, Paul Jewell, out for a celebration lunch to a local restaurant in Bradford.

Looking back, I probably didn't handle it as well as I could have done or should have done, but I was aware that this was not the same Paul I had appointed as a rookie manager two years earlier. When I appointed Paul as manager, everybody said, 'Richmond strikes again – he has chosen the cheap option.' He was virtually unknown outside Bradford for his footballing abilities, but I gave him the manager's job and then the board supported him with £5 million in the summer to mount the promotion campaign. Paul had been assistant in name only to Chris Kamara and there's a famous story locally that Paul says of Chris, 'The only thing he told me to do was to stand on the far side and when the ball goes out of play make sure it gets in quickly.' Paul wasn't actually assistant manager, he was reserve team coach. Anyway, Paul always had a saying that such and such 'thinks he's Billy Bigtime'.

He would say that about players who might have had a few games. 'Now he thinks he's Billy Bigtime.' I said to Paul at that lunch, 'Paul, you ain't the same bloke I appointed as manager. You think you're Billy Bigtime and I will be honest with you, Paul,' says I, 'if your contract was up right now, I wouldn't be offering you an extension. We have done wonderfully well. We have survived. I want you to keep your feet on the ground, though, and enjoy the summer with no pressure.' And he took umbrage at that, as I found out later. He went on his holidays the following day. He was allegedly tapped up by another club and offered the manager's job and he came back from his holiday in Canada and resigned. I then appointed another manager, the assistant manager Chris Hutchings, because I had been using this policy of promoting from within – Chris Kamara, Paul Jewell and now Chris Hutchings. Then came the six weeks of madness and we subsequently put the club into administration. While all this was happening, of course, Leeds were preparing for the 2000–01 Champions League, in which we had played no small part. We had handed them a golden chalice which became a poisoned chalice, while at Bradford the biggest bout of madness was increasing the wage bill from £5 million to £15 million at a stroke. It was spending £7–8 million on transfer fees. It was engaging certain players, like Benito

Carbone, on a four-year contract at £40,000 per week. Looking back, it was doomed to failure if we were going to get relegated. But the madness was the euphoria of surviving against all the odds and starting to believe I could walk on water. Well, Premiership football is a world identity. I was, from 1994–2000, the most successful chairman in football if you look at the number of places we moved up the League pyramid and what happened with the club in support terms, in profile terms, in ground improvement terms and going to Wembley for the first time ever. I think most people would recognise that. I was also a director of the Football League, and virtually its spokesman. Whenever anybody wanted a quote about Football League politics it was my phone that rang; it was me on the TV screen. I didn't hear any criticism, not a single word of criticism from any Bradford City supporter during the time we signed Carbone, Petrescu, Hopkin, Ward and Collymore, who made himself a legend at Bradford by the one goal he did score, which was a spectacular overhead kick which had the world of football talking. Collymore peaked in his tenth minute with us. Difficult players and difficult individuals are a huge part and parcel of this game and there are two sides to football: there is the running of the business and what happens with the players when they cross the white line. Whilst the two things are intertwined, you have no real control over the second of those criteria.

So I got it wrong, and Bradford went down at the end of the 2000–01 season. But when I say Bradford were doomed if we got relegated that's not quite true, because I was buoyed up by the valuation on our players. We had a professional valuation by someone who was recognised as a leading expert in the country on player valuations – a professional employed by REFF, the player-leasing scheme people. When we got a written valuation from Dr Bill Gerrard at Leeds University valuing our squad at £33 million, I realised that, and derived comfort from the fact that, even if we got relegated, we would be very able to shed comfortably a number of our players.

Most relegated clubs do this – cut the wage bill and bring some cash in. When reality dawned and we got relegated we could hardly move a single player on. We managed to bring in about £1 million from the sale of players and the rest of them we couldn't move anyway because the transfer market had deteriorated badly and there were fears over ITV Digital. This was an issue not only to the Football League clubs, but also the Premier League clubs who were affected by it at the time. Some of the European rights in Germany and in Italy were in disarray, with television companies going bankrupt at that time, and there was a general feeling that the value of the next Sky TV deal would be considerably south of what it was. It turned out that these fears were unfounded, but all the time it was becoming an increasingly difficult battle to stay afloat and, by the time May came around, ITV Digital had actually gone into liquidation. When it then became clear that Benito Carbone could not agree personal terms with Middlesbrough, that meant we were hit with two blows in the space of three days. Not only were we stuck with a high wage bill, but the loss of £2.7 million of TV revenue was going to affect that season and subsequent seasons. Combined, these were costing us almost £10 million. We turned to professional advisers, whose view it was that we really had little choice but to put the club into administration. So we did. That being in May, I stayed during the summer right up to August and it was all sorted out the night before the new season started – the eleventh hour. We were actually then allowed to play the first match of the season, which was in doubt at ten o'clock on the Friday night, but I was forced out at the last moment. A member of the Rhodes family had said via Julian, who was the chief executive, 'We don't want Geoffrey involved in us going forward.' I was being blamed for what had happened, and I had accepted the blame in fairness. But I was very dignified. I have never grumbled or complained about that, but I will say that every decision taken was taken by the board. The phrase, and it comes back time and time again to haunt me, is 'hung out to dry'. You're the public face of the football club and you could liken that to Peter Ridsdale's situation at Leeds. I accepted and I voluntarily put my hands up. I didn't try to point the finger. I stood up at a supporters' forum in front of television cameras – this was packed with

1,800 fans – and I said very emotionally, 'Don't blame anybody but me. It was my fault. I accept responsibility.' And then I went back and said, 'It's all down to six weeks of madness.' Yes, there were things which happened which I couldn't have had knowledge of at that time. I didn't have knowledge of the ITV Digital situation. I didn't have knowledge that the player valuation was going to be reduced from £33 million to £1 million. I don't blame myself for having no prior knowledge of these things, and I always ask people to take these things into account as mitigating factors. In front of 1,800 fans, I received a standing ovation. I was a popular chairman. This meeting was held at the club in the banqueting suite which I built and which is the largest banqueting suite in Yorkshire. Everything we did we did the right way. The same banqueting suite today is bringing in huge revenues to the club and is a major asset and will continue to be a major asset for that club going forward.

My time at Bradford followed five lovely years at Scarborough. I joined them in June 1988 and at the end of the first season Scarborough were the first team to get automatically promoted into the Football League as Conference champions. They were, however, in financial disarray. I don't know why I got the job – they had approached everybody in the world. So I was approached by the then chief executive of Scarborough Building Society (who were then the major sponsors of Scarborough FC), Peter Garbutt. He was also chairman of the club at that time. He said, 'I have got to tell you, this is the position. Today is Wednesday, tomorrow the bank will be bouncing the wages cheques and the report is on its way. We are in a mess.' I said, 'Peter, how much is it going to cost?' He said it would require about half a million to sort it out. He asked if I was interested, pointing out that there was a board meeting that night. I said, 'OK, I will do it.' It was as simple as that. They were in Division Four, as it was then, and I have got to say that over the next five years we never got promotion and we got into the promotion play-offs once. But we never finished below mid-table and had some fantastic runs in the League Cup. We beat Southampton, we beat Chelsea, we beat Portsmouth and we beat Coventry. We made a nice little profit every year and my masterstroke here was that, within two days of taking over the club, I was the very first one in football to do a stadium sponsorship. Many, of course, have been done since. I asked who was the biggest firm in town and was told it was McCain, the chip people. Nobody knew how I could get close to them so I rang them up and asked to speak to the managing director. He was very receptive and the deal was done over lunch. Steak and chips, of course! The stadium has since become affectionately known as the 'Theatre of Chips'. I left that club 100 per cent solvent, with cash in the bank, and I actually gave a £100,000 donation which wrote off a significant director's loan debt on the day I left. I loved that club and still do. I didn't do what so many have done in similar circumstances – take the ground and put it into another company and then rent it back. I left it with a future and they are still doing very nicely. Indeed, they are building a new stadium on the outskirts of the town and just because it's a small town it doesn't mean they don't deserve to have a good professional football club.

What's happened in all that time is that I've been round the block a few times, learned a few tricks and made a few mistakes. I will never make these mistakes again. I have learned my lessons. If the headmaster had been marking the end-of-term reports he or she would say that one year out of fifteen years I was the dunce. The rest of the time, I was top of the class. I wasn't the only one with a club relegated from the Premier League, you know. I am big enough to put my hands up when I make mistakes and I was criticised for taking dividends out of Bradford City and I was criticised for taking a salary out. The fact is that I didn't take one penny out of Bradford City from 1994 until the summer of 1999. I worked there full-time, and I mean full-time, and didn't take one single penny out. We were in the Premiership. Huge financial risks had been taken to get there. My fellow shareholders and I decided that we'd be paid a dividend to reward ourselves, and 200 shareholders as well, for all the hard work. When we survived, we did the same again. I drew a salary for the seasons we were in the Premier League of £250,000. Compare that with the players and the contribution they made compared to the work I put in. I make no apology for that. That wasn't the reason why the club failed. It was further down the line. It would have failed with or without that.

Now we come to January 2004. I am there with a broken heart. I'd come out of Bradford and I didn't want to come out of Bradford. I love football and didn't get a single invitation to go back to Bradford after I left. I wasn't in a position to answer the criticism coming from time to time from various sources, nor the planted stories. I knew where the poison was coming from. I very seriously thought that one day I would die an unhappy man. I had lost the things I love. I love my family most, but I had lost the football, which I loved most next to that – fifteen years of it; loving every minute of it, believing I was good at it and coming out of it. Being good at it wasn't luck. You need some luck, but this wasn't luck. I stood on the pitch at the first home game when I went to Bradford against Hartlepool United, in front of 5,000 fans, of whom 600–700 were from Hartlepool, and announced that within five years this club would be in the Premier League. There were howls of derision from the Hartlepool fans and laughter from the Bradford faithful. But we were. Despite the laughter, and there are plenty of witnesses who will confirm this actually happened, I was right. However, roll on January 2004. I was sat at home, bored out of my mind on a Monday evening and the phone rang. It was Melvyn Levi. He said, 'I haven't seen you for years.' I said, 'I haven't seen you. Anyway, Melvyn, what can I do for you?' He said, 'Are you interested in joining us? We are going to buy Leeds United.' I said, 'Melvyn, come on.' Melvyn is a lovely boy with a slight reputation of being a little bit eccentric at times. I said, 'Melvyn, don't be so silly. It's over £100 million. Forget it.' 'Well,' he said, 'there are three of us who want to buy it. Would you like to invest?' I said, 'Look, I am going to talk to you very seriously. Even if I wanted to invest, being honest with you, I have got one or two financial problems at the present time but frankly, even if I had £100 million in the bank I still wouldn't do it. I've never heard anything as daft in my life. Leave it to the Sheikh.' So he persisted and persisted and said, 'Will you come tomorrow and meet Gerald Krasner and Simon Morris and just talk about it, because even if you don't invest I am sure you will help us with your football knowledge.' I said, 'Help, no problem at all. I would be absolutely delighted to do that.' The meeting was at Gerald's Bartfields chartered accountants and corporate recovery specialists office in Clarendon Road, Leeds, in the boardroom at 10.30 a.m. They outlined their plan following a meeting with Trevor Birch, and Trevor had given them some figures which turned out to be reasonably accurate. They thought they could dispose of the bondholders' debt, which was £60 million of a total debt of £104 million, and the REFF debt, amounting to another £22 million. This would leave £22 million of debt which, with a club the size of Leeds and the assets the club have got, made it, on the face of it, a not unattractive picture. I started to believe that there was a possible deal there. I asked for and was given further information, particularly in relation to players' contracts as well as a whole host of other football-related matters which were critical in the appraisal of the situation. From that moment on, I was involved heavily day after day, hour after hour, in making the assessment of how the deal could be done. Nine weeks later, we completed that deal and I have got to say that this was an extremely brave consortium. I continued to say that I could not invest in the club but, by then, if I could have done I would have done. But the consortium members – Gerald, Melvyn Levi, Simon Morris and my son David – by that time had been in for a whole number of weeks. They were lion-hearted. Not one of them is short of money, but none is a multi-millionaire. They are all just comfortable. I know that two houses were at risk, and one business was at risk if the calculations were wrong and they had the confidence in the business strategy I put forward and the enormous input from Gerald who, not surprisingly considering his field of endeavour, is an expert at putting it all together. I was providing a lot of the information and the analysis of the information and that's one thing. But Gerald was putting all this down in a format that was easy to digest. Those nine weeks were a real roller-coaster ride because it went from a deal done to a deal not done to a deal a million miles from being done and all the way back again. The emotions of that were pretty fraught. I have been involved in my life in countless business deals – some very big deals as well. Not hundreds of millions, but big deals nonetheless. The buying and selling of Ronson was a big deal, and it was a complicated one. But that was a teddy bear's picnic compared to this. For a start, there were over 100 lawyers from 9 different firms and in excess of 60 accountants from 5 different firms involved on the other side, along with other professional advisers outside those 5 firms apart from our Walker Morris team. The complexity and the issues that had to be dealt with were mind-blowing and, looking back, had we known of all the issues we probably wouldn't have gone that far down the line. But it was the issues which cropped up as the deal progressed which were frustrating. Player values were never an issue. We had to take our own view on player values. These were more taxation issues, and issues where the other side, particularly the bondholders, weren't speaking with one voice because it was through groups of bondholders. There were insolvency issues, Stock Exchange issues, lots of funding issues on our side from our principal funder. There were also very complex accountancy issues which had to be fulfilled because of the way the deal was done, and it became a total logistical nightmare with a lot of nerves that were very frayed and with any one of a large number of parties having the ability at any time to pull the plug. We had our own issues within the consortium, because the remarkable thing is that the same consortium which started actually finished the deal. There was just one addition, very late on – a Southport banker named Melvin Helme, who joined us right at the death because we were a wee bit short and he provided that final little bit which was the last piece of the jigsaw.

The first part of the Leeds United dream has already been fulfilled because, if you look at it from the fans' point of view, the day before the deal was done the big issue for the fans was, 'Are we still going to have a club to support?' If we'd stumbled, or failed to achieve our goal, this club was going into administration. Whether it went into administration, then all the way into liquidation, was an open question. The chairman's view, as an expert insolvency practitioner, is that, almost certainly, had the highest offer come from a property developer, as against somebody who wanted to take over a football club, the administrator would have had a duty to accept the offer for the stadium, maybe to knock down the West Stand and the South Stand and the Kop and perhaps build a supermarket. And the issues we encountered doing the deal outside of administration would have been intensified within administration, and there was a serious danger the club would never have emerged from administration. So, back to the Leeds United fan. His first desire was that the club did not go into administration, which was very important, and then his or her biggest worry is no longer, 'Are we going to have a club?' but, 'Is Alan Smith going to be with us next season?' The question of whether we are going to be relegated is a real issue, but it isn't, 'Is the club going to be here next season?' any more. We are now back to normal football worries and we can give no reassurance on either. Relegation, and whether Alan Smith will be here next season? 'Who knows?' is the only sensible answer to both. But there is a football team to support, and one with some of the finest training facilities in the world of football. Thorp Arch is the future of Leeds United. The production of kids going forward is what the future of this club is all about. What are the aims? Well, I have got to be boring and say the aims are to consolidate our existing position. We still have over £20 million of debt and though, in context, that's not a lot of money it still has to be got rid of. I am confident we will get rid of it, but it does have to go. We have a number of player contracts which are a major issue. It's a big problem for us, because, on the one hand, you have got a group of player contracts concerning people who we can get rid of, but probably those are the players we would most like to keep. And then you've got another set of players who we would love to move on but whom nobody will take under the contracts they are on. The conundrum is that we could get rid of players we don't want to get rid of, but we can't get rid of the players we do want to get rid of. The fact is that the wage bill is unsustainable. We don't have the choice. The future stability of the club is dependent upon the board having to take the brave decision of going forward. Though I am only an adviser at this stage – and I will advise the board accordingly – I will be very surprised if the board doesn't take the hard decisions that I believe it has to take for the future good health of this club. I am sure they will. I've had some time, though not that much, to have a look at Leeds United's affairs over the last three years. There have been glaring errors and I think their living the dream equates every bit with my 'six weeks of madness at Bradford' statements. There is no doubt the dream was lived, and the difference between it coming off and failing was finishing fourth in the Premier League instead of third. One bad referee's decision, you know, is all it takes. It's very close, but everybody looks at the final result and the strategy was seriously flawed – as proven by hindsight again. As was the case in Bradford, I didn't hear of people during the time when Leeds were on the up and up marching the streets and saying, 'We shouldn't be buying Fowler' or whoever. Supporters don't care where the money comes from. What matters to the football fan is the 90 minutes on the pitch and nothing more. But there were definitely too many players on the Leeds United books. When I did my assessment back in January/February/March, there were 60 professional footballers at this club for 16 positions including the subs. You need a squad in excess of 16 anyway, but 60 I felt was ludicrous. Fifteen of them were on contracts worth over £1 million a year. There was a wage bill last year of £53 million, which is unsustainable, and some very long contracts, which seem to have been given out with gay abandon. I think there were some very bad errors in giving them out – certainly to very average players who finished up as multi-millionaires without even having an average Premier League ability, in some cases. There have been some very bad decisions. The reputation of this club throughout its recent history is that Father Christmas was in charge, dishing out presents to anybody who wanted one. The end result of this was £104 million of debt, and a once very proud club heading for the rocks with a support base of almost 40,000.

The loyalty from this club's fans is, from a consortium point of view, the biggest asset that we were buying, because there is no doubt at all that the future health of this club depends upon all the board being guardians of the fans' house. At this moment in time, that's what the board is: it's a guardian. We are trying to create a period of time in which the future of Leeds United will be in safe hands. Some of the criticisms have been that this consortium are asset-strippers. It's hardly worth answering, but I will. We are the directors, and all of us are Leeds people and have lived in Leeds for decades. Some have children at school in Leeds and, as I have already said, there are houses and a business on the line. We do see a fantastic business opportunity in the long term if it is run correctly. But asset-strippers are in for a quick buck. This is not a consortium from Outer Mongolia; it's not that we aren't on the spot. You'd have to be a lunatic to come with that sort of motivation. That is why the criticism has been so unfair, and so unjustified, because that never was the motive. Some of us who are involved with this are probably not perfect. But fools we are not, and you would have to be a fool to believe the motivation for this was anything other than the correct business motive. I've admitted I am not a Leeds United fan. I am not going to stand up and pretend that I am, though I might be able to be converted to being one. My two loves are my first sweetheart, Scarborough, and second sweetheart, Bradford, and I am not yet ready to fall in love again. As far as the future is concerned, I think everybody realises that the Premiership is a League within a League within a League, and the top three teams in English football – Arsenal, Manchester United and Chelsea – are out of sight now. Chelsea are bolstered with unlimited funds, and Manchester United are great because of the many years of Ferguson. They have built the most fantastic first-team squad and youth team set-up which has produced the most wonderful players and continues to do so. I believe in their youth system and they are very good at it. Arsenal are where they are because of Arsene Wenger, who, for my money, is the best manager in the game. You only have to look at his transfer activity; it is spectacular. They will be the champions for the next five years.

As always with Leeds United in this lamentable period in their history, just as it appeared that another impediment had been removed and that a period of stability may just be beginning, it did not take long for calamity to strike. Within six weeks of their takeover, the new men in charge became embroiled in a bitter boardroom power struggle. In a surprising U-turn, the club's directors rejected a takeover bid from a consortium headed up by lifelong fan Steve Parkin just 24 hours after agreeing in principle to the deal. Chairman Gerald Krasner and managing director David Richmond (son of Geoffrey) were willing to sell their stake in the club, but the remainder of the board were against the proposal. Richmond was said to be considering his future and on the verge of resigning. Parkin's written offer was worth in excess of £20 million and included provision for working capital, but the board felt the offer fell short of the club's market value and said there were concerns over proof of funds. The board were also unhappy that the consortium refused to sign a confidentiality agreement.

Parkin's consortium, however, comprised a number of well-respected local businessmen and adequate funds were believed to be in place should the board reconsider. Richmond was bitterly disappointed by the board's decision not to accept the offer and suggestions of internal power struggles were rife. So the boardroom musical chairs at Elland Road threatened to continue apace at a time, three weeks before the end of the season, when nobody knew whether Leeds United would start the 2004–05 season in the Premiership or what was then known as Nationwide Division One.

Parkin had assembled a group of like-minded individuals to put together an offer that would see them take a controlling interest in Leeds and it looked very much as though it would succeed at the first time of asking. While it may have seemed strange that Krasner's group took over the club only to listen to offers so soon afterwards, the board members then in place had stated from the start that they saw themselves as 'custodians' of the club and would actively seek investment from the very start. Krasner said on his arrival that if other serious investors showed an interest in the club, the board would consider its options and do what it felt was best for Leeds United. Of course, there would be a financial reward for any sale, giving the cynics a field day, but the conundrum was how their profit equated with the nine weeks of stress, pressure and turmoil that accompanied the original takeover. Those two months leading up to the completion of the deal were turbulent, to say the least, and various members of the consortium were put under differing pressures that could have seen it collapse at any time. They were the victims of an ongoing smear campaign and faced all manner of accusations from snipers all too keen to wreck the club's last real hope of survival. Personal lives were torn apart during those tough weeks and the pressures within showed no signs of easing.

A central figure in all the chaos was Geoffrey Richmond. It was announced that for 'personal and health reasons' the man credited with pulling together the whole rescue operation in his advisory capacity would be standing down within weeks of Krasner announcing that, 'The club is off the life-support machine and is now in recuperation.' It was to get worse for Richmond. A week after relinquishing his post as an adviser to the new Leeds United board, he was declared bankrupt.

A bankruptcy order was made by a judge in Leeds who refused a request for a 12-week adjournment to give Mr Richmond, 63, time to sort out payment of a £3.3 million debt. 'There is no indication in any of the documents before me that, even with the benefit of 12 weeks, Mr Richmond will be in a position to pay £3.3 million to the petitioner,' said Judge John Behrens, who also refused a request for the hearing to be in private. 'The highest the matter can be put is, given the 12 weeks, he might be able to formulate another offer which would amount to part payment to the liquidator,' he said. He had been told that Mr Richmond was looking into a possible termination payment from Leeds United which could alter any offer he could make. The judge said that the liquidator, acting for a company of which Mr Richmond was previously a director, made it plain he was not interested in a part offer. Richmond was not in court. The creditor petitioning for bankruptcy was Loquitur Ltd, a company now in liquidation. Loquitur became liable for a tax bill of more than £2 million after the sale of Richmond's Ronson lighter business in 1994. Judge Behrens also heard the Inland Revenue had already brought proceedings against Richmond and another director, Martin Jones, which led to a judgment last year in the Inland Revenue's favour to the sum of £3,348,009.11. That High Court judge found the duo had tried to evade corporation tax liability. Mr Jones is now also bankrupt.

Stuart Frith, for Loquitur Ltd, told Judge Behrens that the company's liquidator had now joined those proceedings for the purpose of enforcement. He said the High Court judge heard allegations that the two directors 'were guilty of misfeasance and breach of trust in relation to payment of an unlawful dividend'. Some negotiations had taken place with Mr Richmond but they had not led to a satisfactory conclusion and the petitioning creditor was now, 'entitled to payment of the debt in full'. Hugh Jory, for Richmond, said his employment with Leeds United had only recently been terminated, 'and there are now discussions about the package that will ensue from that.' He said there was also always interest from third parties wanting to avail themselves of Mr Richmond's football connections. He asked for time to investigate those issues and help Mr Richmond avoid bankruptcy. Mr Frith opposed the adjournment, saying the amount of time Mr Richmond was employed at Leeds United before his dismissal was unlikely to significantly pay off the debt. Refusing an adjournment, Judge Behrens said he had studied financial information prepared by another defence barrister, Louis Doyle, which showed the 'substantial decline in Mr Richmond's finances in recent years'. After Richmond had transferred his shares in Bradford City Football Club for £1, he had given guarantees for that club of £12–13 million. 'Therefore, his liabilities are in the region of £15–16 million.' Richmond had apparently made an offer in 2003 to pay £600,000 over five years, which was not accepted and, in April 2004, he offered £150,000 and 90 per cent of his earnings over five years, which was also rejected. Bankruptcy means his finances are now carefully examined. He cannot act as a company director without court permission or obtain credit of £250 or more without disclosing his status.

David Richmond resigned from the Leeds Board in July 2004, citing 'personal reasons'.

CHAPTER FIFTEEN

DOMINIC MATTEO – THE SLIPPERY SLOPE

While the wisdom of some of the signings made by David O'Leary on behalf of Leeds United has been called into question by various quarters, there is no such query relating to his £4 million capture of Dominic Matteo from Liverpool. Three days prior to the kick-off of the 2000–01 season, Matteo followed Olivier Dacourt and Mark Viduka into Elland Road for what was to be the club's most exciting campaign for years. The Scottish-born, versatile defender went on to replace Lucas Radebe and Rio Ferdinand as club captain, having established himself as a talismanic figure with a succession of hard-working, committed performances which proved his dedication to the Leeds cause. Matteo had joined Leeds with good credentials, and when we met after a training session in April 2004, we first of all looked back on his early days in the game.

Matteo broke into Liverpool's first team during the 1996–97 season. After an impressive run, he was called into the England squad but had to pull out due to injury. When he first started playing for Liverpool he was hailed as the next Alan Hansen due to his defensive ability and his enthusiasm for going forward. He had made his debut for the Merseyside club on the left side of midfield on 23 October 1993, in a 1–1 Premiership draw with Manchester City at Maine Road, going on to make 155 first-team appearances. Born of English parents and Italian grandparents, he was first spotted by Liverpool scouts when playing for Birkdale United. He caught the eye of Kenny Dalglish, who was watching his son, Paul, in action. Matteo joined Liverpool's School of

Excellence with another eleven year old in Robbie Fowler. He was to play in a variety of roles including left-back, centre-back and midfield. He didn't have a set position in the side as the Liverpool staff went about working out which position would suit him best. He started the 1995–96 season as a sweeper and excelled to the extent that he was handed his first international call-up for England. Unfortunately, his subsequent England call-ups coincided with injury problems and in the following seasons he was unable to make the impact on the international stage that many felt his talent deserved, even though he switched his allegiances to Scotland. Gerard Houllier saw him as a left-back in his Liverpool restructuring plans, issuing a firm 'hands off' warning to any club thinking of launching a bid for his talented defender. The 1999–2000 season promised to be vital for Matteo in terms of establishing himself as a regular in the side, and a good end to the 1998–99 season, along with an encouraging start to the following campaign suggested that, after a number of years on the fringes of the Liverpool team, he had finally made the big breakthrough and was in the side to stay. However, with Houllier opting for the experience of Staunton at left-back, he was once more faced with a fight to re-establish himself. Matteo's medical on his move to Leeds highlighted a problem with a knee injury, and it took a restructured deal with his former club to allow the transfer to go through. Although the injury delayed his career in a white shirt, he finally made his debut a month after joining the club in the 1–0 Champions League triumph over AC Milan at Elland Road. He then went on to grab his first goal for his new club in the 6–0 drubbing of Besiktas a week later, and celebrated a tremendous seven days with his call up to the Scotland squad for two World Cup qualifiers. He proved his versatility by playing in a number of roles as United were dogged by injuries, but finished the season as a regular partner to Rio Ferdinand in the centre of defence. Ferdinand's defection to Manchester United signalled an exodus from Elland Road, but Matteo remained to become something of an icon. Following a Leeds training session in April 2004, he offered an honest assessment of what life has been like in the dressing room during the club's freefall.

> The move from Liverpool was a very strange time for me because I had just signed a five-year deal at Anfield and I was

thinking I was staying there for a few more years at least. Then I get a phone call from my agent saying that Liverpool are signing Christian Ziege and he's probably going to be a first-choice player on the team-sheet. That was a bit harrowing but then he said, 'There are a few clubs that want to talk to you and one of them is Leeds.' The next day, I got up, met my agent and came to Leeds. I had a quick chat with David O'Leary and Peter Ridsdale and it was all positive stuff. I knew the club had been doing well from the previous season when they secured a Champions League slot. They pipped us for third place, so it all looked positive. I walked round the training ground and, already knowing Gary Kelly, met a few of the boys. I said hello to a few of the lads and asked them what it was like and it was all very encouraging feedback. Although I had played in the UEFA Cup before, I had never played in the Champions League. This was a big thing for me. The agent went and sorted the contract out with Peter Ridsdale and I just sat and chatted with David O'Leary about the football side of it, and that was it, really. The chairman and the manager said they would sign me on a five-year contract, which was quite reassuring for me in the respect that it showed they were keen on signing me.

I had done the pre-season at Liverpool, played quite a few of the pre-season games, and really I just wasn't expecting a move to Leeds. I'm afraid I missed those Champions League qualifiers against TSV 1860 Munich because of the problem with my knee, which only showed up on my Leeds medical. I was injured for four or five weeks, which at least gave me a chance to get to know the players. Everyone at Leeds has been brilliant, especially when I first came. I was really looked after. The club was on the crest of a wave, and the atmosphere was absolutely buzzing, even though it was the usual stuff – come in, get a bit of banter going, go out and train – the training was very sharp – finish training and go about your normal life. It was brilliant really. You couldn't want to be at a better football club. I mean that. It was absolutely terrific. The home fixture against AC Milan in the Champions League was my debut. That was the one in the pouring rain when Lee Bowyer raced through to score in the last five minutes. Their goalie fumbled it and dropped it in the bottom of the net. It was madness. It was a great day. David pulled me in the office that day and it was probably going on six weeks since I had joined. I had trained once — that morning — and he pulled me in and he goes, 'I'm thinking about playing you tonight.' I thought, 'Brilliant,' reasoning that even though I hadn't trained much the adrenalin would get me through. He said, 'Do you want to play and where do you want to play?' because he was struggling with injuries in a couple of positions. He asked if I wanted to play at the back or midfield left side and I replied that I had not had a lot of practice at playing centre-half because I had played all pre-season at Liverpool at left-back. So we decided on left-side midfield. I had played there before and had always done all right. It was fantastic. I will never forget that my debut for Leeds was beating AC Milan 1–0, so it was a perfect start really. Then I scored in the match against Besiktas, when we gave them a 6–0 drubbing, so I had played a couple of games and it was the stuff of dreams. During that Champions League campaign, the dressing room was absolutely buzzing before games. We went out and expected to beat teams every single time, and it was a great feeling. When we went back to Milan, I scored with a near-post header and that was two goals in a matter of weeks — in the Champions League! I had not scored for years for Liverpool and I came to Leeds and scored two in the Champions League. It was a dream come true for me. My first few games for Leeds were at left midfield. I knew I wouldn't be in that position for long, because I always believed my best position was at the back, but just to feel my way in it was good because David said that on set pieces I should take a chance at the post. Sometimes, when you make a run, one out of a hundred hits you on the head and goes in, and this was one of those times. It was a special moment; one which I will never forget, and probably the highlight of my career. My Italian background made this even better. Going to the San Siro was just the best thing for my dad and my family out there. My dad's family are from southern Italy, just outside Naples. It's amazing. They live in the mountains and they try to follow my career as much as they can. Some of my cousins whom I have hardly ever seen in my life look out for me. For me to score over there was a special moment for them because they could go out and say to somebody, 'Did you see the game last night?' There was a good chance that they had done and there would be a story to tell. It was awesome. Against all odds, we had qualified for the second phase and then Real Madrid came on the scene along with Anderlecht and Lazio to give us another tough group to negotiate. Again, with the odds stacked against us, we went through. We had beaten Anderlecht at home, so in the papers over there in Belgium they had said they were going to give it to us. Ollie Dacourt translated the story for us and said it was slagging a few of the players off. That piece of the paper was up on the dressing room wall before the game so we thought, 'Right, we'll show you.' I think that was probably one of the best performances I have ever played in. Anderlecht had not been beaten at home for so many games that I think they thought they were invincible. Our team performance throughout the whole campaign in the Champions League was good, but I think that one in Belgium might have been the best. The good thing about that whole Champions League effort was that we had every player playing at the top of his form. Like I say, it was a belief that no matter where we were playing we were going to go out there and enjoy it. We used to turn up at these places, Real Madrid or Lazio and the like and it was, 'Flipping heck, this is what it's all about.' So you would get out for a training session on a Tuesday or Wednesday night at the stadium and you just couldn't wait to get started. I just kept saying to myself – and I think it's what everyone was feeling – 'This gives me the chance to do something special at the top level of the game.' Everyone knew they had to be at their best and they wanted to be. We were playing with smiles on our faces and everyone was really enjoying it.

A lot of people couldn't get over Lee Bowyer's performances because he had all that trouble off the field and he was like a man possessed. Bowyer was on fire. He wasn't far off being the competition's top goal-scorer. He was probably the best box-to-box player in the country at the time in my view, scoring goals which were second to none. You know, those off-field problems might have cost him a regular England place. He hasn't shown the same form at Newcastle, but I often feel that in football sometimes, certain clubs suit you. I was at Liverpool and didn't really get a chance to show them what I could do. Yet I come to Leeds and play regularly. I think I have improved more as a player and know more about the game now. Yet I learned the basics at Liverpool. I just think Lee Bowyer for Leeds United was outstanding. It must be the same at Arsenal or Manchester United or whatever. When you leave a big club where do you go next? The semi-final ties against Valencia were basically the biggest nights in recent Leeds United history. The 0–0 draw in the first leg at home still gives you a real chance and the atmosphere was unbelievable. It was frightening at Elland Road. I think late on I headed one towards the back post and Canizares saved it. I remember thinking, 'I wish that had gone in.' Then, when we got over there and trained, you could feel the tension. Maybe for the first time you felt in that dressing room that it wasn't as bubbly as it usually was. I think it was just that final push to get to the final. I just think we didn't perform to the standards we had been achieving, but I do believe that if we had done so we might have got there. I just want to make one point about that game in Valencia. I'm still convinced Juan Sanchez put the ball in with his hands for their first goal. If it had gone in 0–0 at half-time, I think it might have been a different game. Even though Valencia were on top it upset the camp a bit. We got in and everyone was a bit down and we never recovered from that.

Though there has been a lot of speculation about the publication of David O'Leary's book and the effect it might have had on the dressing room, the honest truth is that I don't actually know what most of the other boys thought. He wrote something about me in the book concerning a little incident at Lazio, but the fact is that it did happen. To my mind, the incident was finished, and if he wanted to write about it that didn't bother me. I didn't really hear anyone say anything negative about it. We just came in as usual. Nobody was slagging him off. It was just normal. Obviously, I don't think it was good timing. I think everyone knows that. But it might have been good timing for him to sell a few copies. Good luck to the guy, but in some ways it was bad timing. I will let people make their own decision on that. It's not for me to say. He brought me to Leeds from Liverpool and I think I have improved, so in a way I should be thanking him a little bit. I wouldn't slag David O'Leary off to anyone because he's been pretty decent to me. People have different opinions about other people and that is mine. When our failure to qualify for the following season's Champions League set some alarm bells ringing financially at the club, we'd all be lying if we said we didn't worry about the team or whether we have to sell players to survive. But I don't think it affected any of us enough to detract from our performance on the field or in training. It shouldn't do, anyway. But we might, at the back of our minds, hold the questions, 'Are they going to get rid of some of the best players? Are any players going to have to go? Are we going to have to take a wage cut?' There is always something to worry about, but it is not going to affect us during the 90 minutes on a Saturday. In my opinion, any suggestion that that might be the case is a load of rubbish. Maybe one night during the week, one of us might talk about it in our house with our bird or missus, or we may discuss it with our family, because at the end of the day that's who you discuss those kinds of things with. That's the way I usually deal with things. I come to work, play football and then go home to enjoy a domestic life. We wouldn't talk about it on the training ground. We may have a laugh and a joke about it, because that's the way footballers are. That's the way I think it's happened here. I think everyone thinks we come in and discuss it and worry about not getting paid. It's never been like that. I think we've all pretty much been behind helping the club, really. I actually think the lads were pretty positive about the way in which they wanted to help the club.

In my time at the club, I have seen more than one or two player departures and, if you take five or six good players out of any squad in this country, it's going to affect the team in a big way. If you imagine taking Steve Gerrard and Michael Owen out of Liverpool, ripping the real heart out of that team, and say, 'Right, we're going out to play this week,' what do you expect might happen? Can you envisage Manchester United and Arsenal losing five or six good players? Jonathan Woodgate going to Newcastle was, for me, the straw that broke the camel's back. Here you have a quality, young centre-half, up and coming and one day going to be a fixture for England. He's one of the best centre-halfs in the country and you sell him down the road to Newcastle. That is making a statement to the rest of football. To me, if you lose your best players out of any team – believe me, you'll be struggling. I don't care who you are. The players we lost were strong characters in the dressing room as well. Lee Bowyer, Jonathan Woodgate, Rio Ferdinand, Robbie Keane . . . people like that. They were all excellent footballers, but good to have around the place, too. Olivier Dacourt is another. He's now playing for France, and at Roma he is apparently playing the football of his life. There you go. There were a lot of good quality players – and that's no disrespect to the guys who stayed. We've still got a good squad, but it is difficult when you lose so many quality players. Losing Jonathan was pretty hard to take for us and the fans. Same with Harry Kewell. He's another one. Harry could sometimes be the difference to us. He could come up with that bit of magic such as at Arsenal in the 2002–03 season. He gets by players and scores a wonder goal. You miss people like that, and Harry had been here a long time. He was another presence around the place. Even though he was quiet in his own way, he was a presence. Leeds' loss is definitely Liverpool's gain there. He's only a young boy and he's probably not playing the best football of his career yet. He may take another season to settle, or even another six months, but he's going to come good.

What I've found in my time at Leeds is that if ever a set of fans deserved a successful football club then it is them. They are absolutely remarkable. I cannot believe the Leeds United supporters. I've played at Liverpool, and Liverpool fans are great, but the Leeds fans are just frightening. Obviously, I have only played for two clubs, so I can only speak for them, but the Leeds fans are unbelievable. They just don't stop getting behind you. We could be 4–0 down and they would still be singing their hearts out. Come on! When you see them in the streets they are always positive. All they want to know is what is going on and why things are happening. I think they respect you in that way. Of all the Leeds fans I have met, obviously you get a few wondering what's going on, but the majority of them have been really good and positive towards me personally. The city is a great place to live. You're reminded again of their loyalty when you think about those two European campaigns, with fans taking off their tops and whizzing them around their heads. I remember the sing-songs after AC Milan and Lazio. I came out of the tunnel after the AC Milan game – I had been getting a bit of treatment – and there were thousands of Leeds fans behind the goal. It was just the best. I'll tell you a funny story. I was out in town and a guy was on crutches. He said, 'I want a word with you.' I thought, 'Oh my God, who have I upset here?' He said, 'You are out of order,' and when I asked why, he said, 'When you scored that bleeding goal in the San Siro I fell down five flights and broke my bleeding leg!' I actually laughed and he was trying to be quite serious and get a reaction out of me. But in the end he started laughing. It just shows you I am not a Leeds lad but I can relate to the people of Leeds. They do reckon it cost a lot of people their marriages, because the guys kept spending on their credit cards, doing all the trips, and perhaps thinking we'd get through the first phase and then the semis. People who couldn't get there by plane were getting boats and cars. It was just absolute madness. The fans, in my opinion, are the best. They do deserve to win something. They are so patient.

It's been difficult for us as a bunch of players because managerially there has been David O'Leary, Terry Venables, Peter Reid and Eddie Gray, and that's a fair turnover in a very short space of time. It's good to have a manager there every week for a good number of years. In ideal circumstances, this means he'll be there for you and you know he's going to be there for a while. Maybe it's one of the secrets of Manchester United's success that Alex Ferguson has been there for such a long time. I've been three and a half years at Leeds and I feel as if I know everyone here now. You can't just come here and expect to know who everyone is in a matter of weeks. Now I can name everyone in the office and everyone downstairs and everyone who does the cleaning. I think it takes a good few years to get to know everyone and I think it does help having a manager for a certain number of years. It has to. Alex Ferguson, for instance, has overseen the transition of youth players right up to the first team. It is quite distracting for a player when you change managers. They've all got different ideas and that's sometimes a problem. With Terry Venables, he came in and the first thing really was that he lost Woody and Rio. That hits the nail on the head. That's the kind of quality we lost. So it was difficult under Terry because that was the time when we were losing all the players. He's got a good reputation and, yes, his training was good. As a player, that's what you want. You want to try to improve on things and work on things and it's hard to say why things don't work out. Reidy's a good guy. He just suffered a series of bad results, but people do tend to forget 6–0 Charlton away. To be honest, at the end of that season I remember I sat with Reidy at Arsenal before the game and he looked at their team and said, 'They're shite these. We can beat them.' That's the way he is, but I felt he might be right and that we might go out there and beat them. He's a straight-talking guy. Peter had his ideas. He would make training enjoyable and insist that we work hard, which is always important. He also liked us to try to play with a smile. He had a good work ethic. I've always said he is a really good guy and a good football man. I've watched Peter play from the terraces at Everton and he was world class. They had a great team at the time.

There have been various interpretations of what's happened over these past three years. Some say it's a shame; others an accident waiting to happen. For me, personally, it's been like skiing further and further down from the top of a steep slope. We seem to have been going rapidly downhill ever since that semi-final night, if you look back. Even the year after that, when we just missed out on the Champions League, I don't think we were playing the best football that season. We were getting good results, but if you think back I don't remember it being like that the year before. There just weren't the same vibes about it. I think the Champions League lifted us up to its own standards. No doubt about it. You play so many games that you're not training as much, just coming in and doing a quick session and you're off again – games, games, games. With football, that's the best way, I think. Since then, we've been sliding down and it's hard to pinpoint a single reason why that is. But I do believe that the loss of so many quality players is the main factor and that's my honest opinion. I think a lot of people have missed an important point by not recognising that. I don't think enough people say that. A lot of people say it's the financial stuff. If you lose good players, you struggle. Look at that Champions League team. How many players from those games are still here? We even lost Danny Mills to Middlesbrough – another good player who was doing well – and he was a regular in the England squad. That was unfortunate, and further evidence that you can't lose quality like that and maintain the performance. You do find in football that when a slide starts it's a difficult thing to halt. It's true to say, from a player's perspective, that a big gap separates Arsenal, Manchester United and Chelsea from all the other teams. Those three are a long way ahead of everyone else. Chelsea have got some good young players and also they have got money to spend. Manchester United are massive and a lot of their team have come through the system. But Arsenal is the team that everyone is aspiring to. I haven't really enjoyed playing against them. They have been fantastic over the past few years and I think this season they have been a pleasure to watch. You've got the class of Vieira and Henry and Sol Campbell, who to me is a massive unsung hero at Highbury. I think over the season he has been their best player, but he doesn't seem to get the credit. Henry's been the most difficult opponent for me to play against. He's difficult to mark as he plays centre-forward and drifts out wide. Always the question with Henry is whether you go right on him, man-marking, or try something else. He is a clever player.

The future for Leeds is uncertain, and there are conflicting views on the best way forward. Some say we might be as well going into the Coca-Cola League and reinventing ourselves as a football club, but I personally don't believe that. I wanted to stay in the Premiership and I think Leeds deserves to stay there because of the fan base and the size of the club. Going down is scary. I would be lying to you if I didn't say I have had a couple of sleepless nights when I thought, 'Shit, I want to play in the Premiership with this team.' To those people who believe that going down and starting again might be better, I would say that it's a really difficult job to get out of that First Division. And going down means you are going to lose some of your good players. If you lose that quality, and you're playing in a tough division, it will be difficult. One satisfying point from the Leeds perspective is that there are a few good young players coming through. I train with most of these guys and there is some promising talent. Scotty Carson, the goalie, is coming on in leaps and bounds, and James Milner has a great work ethic. He's been difficult to leave out of the first team and he has been there on merit. Frazer Richardson at right-back has been knocking on the door for a few seasons, Matthew Kilgallon has done very well and little Aaron Lennon is a promising forward. There are some good youngsters here and if you can get them through with a bit of experience it may be the key. But at every club in the Premiership there are probably youngsters coming through – all the ones who just want to push themselves a little bit further. They always need experienced guys who know what they are doing to help them through. I have always said that when I was younger I was not the best player in the bunch of lads who got picked to do YTS, but I knew I had one of the best attitudes and the right work ethic to help me get on in the game. Some of the other lads had skills, but I knew deep down that I was going to get ahead of those boys because, on a weekly basis, I worked harder and tried harder and that's what it takes to click as a youngster. Football's the best job in the world. My mates say, 'Have you been at work today?' and I say, 'Work?' Fair enough, it is work, to a certain degree, but it is the best job in the world for a young lad and I think too many young lads nowadays don't take the opportunity they are given with both hands. I see people like James Milner grabbing that and it's good to see, because you don't see too many kids wanting that any more. I was at Liverpool and a good group of us wanted to get there and run that extra yard. You've got to concentrate on your own career. More kids need to grab that opportunity and go for it. The future for me is that I would love to stay at Leeds United. I would love to finish off my career here, hopefully in the Premiership. That's what I want. The knee is getting better. I've had an operation and one of the results of that is that I have had to cut my international football out. It's helped me because it means I get a couple of days off and I can rest and just do the normal thing for a few days and recharge my batteries. For me, that's it, and after football, who knows? Could be media work. I've done radio a few times and that's something I enjoy. I don't mind talking about football because I have done it all my life – since I was a kid. Ask me about anything else and I wouldn't know the answer, but ask me about football and the chances are that I might get it right. I enjoy talking about it. People say when you are out and about, 'I bet you hate talking about football.' But I say, 'Actually, I don't mind.' It's weird. I was brought up with football – my dad was a big football fan. My mum and dad, Marie and Alberto, were massive Celtic fans. They were there in '67 in Lisbon when Celtic beat Inter Milan to win the European Cup and became known as the Lisbon Lions.

Dad had a chip shop and restaurant in Dumfries. Then they had a cake shop and a sweet shop/ice cream shop. It was great for me. I used to come home from school and straight to the chippie every night. If my mum and dad hadn't moved to England, I might not have got to Liverpool or Leeds, and might be on a different path to the one I am on now, so I have got a lot to thank them for. My dad went on to be a bus driver for 20 years after the shop. They moved to Southport and he worked on the buses and my mum was a home help. She wasn't too well and now they live in Ibiza. When we are playing, Dad takes the dog out for a walk because he can't listen any more. It must be worse for them than it is for us, sometimes. I find when I'm injured and watching games it's horrible. That's because, I suppose, it's not been working out well for us. When you're out there at least you can try to do something. When you're watching it's like, 'Come on!' It looks dead easy, but when you get out there it's a bit different. Yet it's still the greatest game in the world, and I'm privileged to be a part of it.

Dominic Matteo signed for Blackburn Rovers in July 2004.

CHAPTER SIXTEEN

PETER LORIMER – NEW GOALS

The Commercial is one of those old-fashioned public houses which has not succumbed to the modern-day trend of becoming an eaterie/wine bar. Rather, it is a focal point for good ale, conversation, gossip, story-telling and folklore. Standing as it does within walking distance of Elland Road, it is never busier than on match days. Its landlord is the Leeds United legend and recently appointed club director Peter Lorimer, who offered his version of events in a chat over the bar in April 2004:

> The story of Leeds United's decline from the heady days of a Champions League semi-final in 2001 to the brink of oblivion within three years is both remarkable and disturbing. All the boardroom shake-ups have seen me installed as a director of the club some 20 years after retiring as their all-time record goal-scorer and I am only too pleased to be playing my part in ensuring that the crass mistakes of recent years are not repeated. During that Champions League campaign, I was working mainly on radio and doing a lot of work with the media and had the privilege to be in the commentary chair during that whole period. The build-up to it all started in Maritimo when David O'Leary and Eddie Gray had just been given the jobs of manager and assistant manager. It looked like Martin O'Neill would be coming from Leicester, but the directors decided it wasn't to be after that game because

O'Leary and Gray put the kids in and basically they performed terrifically well for them. I had seen the build-up to that Champions League semi-final in Valencia and it was really a fantastic period. The one thing that amazed me about the whole thing, with the team playing so well and with so much spirit, was the timing of the elevation of Brian Kidd. It was announced when we were over in Spain, just before this major match, that Brian Kidd was going to be the first-team coach. And, to be fair, everybody was totally amazed. I honestly thought at the time that the reason O'Leary was making changes was because there was a possibility, according to the rumours, that he might be going to Old Trafford. So I thought he was linking up with Brian Kidd to move on to Old Trafford. That was my thinking on why O'Leary appointed him. It was an amazing decision to make, because not only was the timing of it bizarre but also all of those players who had come into the side had been brought through by Eddie. They all had the highest regard and respect for him and I simply couldn't see the logic behind it.

United's brand of football was a joy to watch. To a degree, Eddie got them playing that way again in the battle to stave off relegation. They go forward, and that is the way he likes to play. That is his trademark, being entertaining and going forward. We were a lovely, attacking, flowing side. When we lost a ball, everybody was harrying straight away like ferrets to get it back. We seemed to change our whole style to a European system in which, when the opposition got the ball, we dropped off. So, whether David felt that that was the best way forward long-term in Europe I don't know, but I think what we had against all the other sides at that particular time was that they had never played anything like this before. They were used to the Italian and Spanish teams where the team would drop off and let the big defenders get the ball and look good and they couldn't cope with this pressure they were being put under. I thought that was our trump card, but the minute Kidd came that was over. Brian took over the coaching and we just became like any other non-European side in the way we played. We attacked, and if we lost it we all just got behind the ball and it wasn't nearly as exciting. It was a totally different game.

O'Leary and Kidd will argue, of course, that under that set-up they went on to win an awful lot of League games. Well, they would do. They had some terrific players: Woodgate was outstanding, Lee Bowyer was playing out of his skin at that particular time and there was Harry Kewell – players like this. We had top quality players in the side. They were all 22 and 23 so they were just coming into their pomp – full of life and ambition. It was a great bunch of players to work with. Unfortunately, things started to go backwards then. There was that horrific morning when we picked the papers up to read that players had been arrested – including Woodgate and Bowyer – in the previous night's fracas in town.

Everything seemed to fall apart. Woodgate didn't play for the rest of the season because of the pressure. Bowyer soldiered on amazingly well through that particular time and we weren't doing that badly. In fact, we were top of the League at Christmas time. Then we went down to Cardiff and had an awful result there in the FA Cup. This coincided with the massive mistake, in my opinion, of O'Leary writing *Leeds United on Trial*. Nothing against David O'Leary, but I don't think any manager should comment on his own players at any time.

The murderous events in Galatasaray were a very sad thing, and I do feel that, in its own way, it helped people to empathise with us. We'd lost, and I think people were behind us, but right on the tail of that were the book and the court case, which dragged on and on. The worst thing was that, when it was nearly all over, the trial was suspended. So it rumbled on for even more months. In that period, it was all negative and we became a laughing stock when we went to away games. All the opposition fans were jumping on this thing and criticising the side. Bowyer was eventually found not guilty and Woody was fined and given community service; and that was the time the book came out. That, along with other events, brought about a downhill slide from here to the end of the season. There was another fall-out from the trial, and that was Bowyer being disciplined by the club. For Leeds to fine Bowyer after he had been found not guilty was obviously a major thing, because the atmosphere changed from solidarity one minute – us against the rest – to fines and punishment the next. In my opinion, the chairman and O'Leary should have had a chat and called the guys in and said something like, 'It would be a good idea for you to give £100,000 between you to a local charity.' I am sure their agents would have looked at it and thought that wouldn't be a bad idea. But to slap a fine on them with Bowyer thinking, 'Well, I have done nothing wrong. Why should I pay it?' was obviously going to cause a bit of conflict. We became headlines again and, indirectly, Lee Bowyer's career dramatically went downhill. Whether he felt he had been let down and was disillusioned by it all, I don't know. But it was definitely the turning point of his career. In my view, he was the best box-to-box player in the country at the time. His energy and his effort were amazing. He's not a big lad but he was a real driving force. I think his fine, though, and the headlines he got, like the *Mirror*'s front page, 'You're scum and if you want to sue us go ahead', left him totally shell-shocked and, to me, he has never recovered at all. I think he has suffered a total loss of confidence and self-belief.

When we were top of the League and we lost that FA Cup game at Cardiff in January 2002, David O'Leary, when questioned on the field by the BBC, said yes, it was a disappointing result for the club. His target, and that of the plc board, was the Champions League and he said he wanted to be judged on that. In the final analysis, he failed to produce what the board had required of him. Although it must have been a very difficult decision for the board, this failure, coupled with the fact that they could not have been pleased with him writing a book at that time, made his departure unsurprising. The biggest mistake David made was actually writing that book and criticising the players, because it didn't look like the same eager bunch of young players after that. It caused a split in the camp, I feel, although this was never admitted at Elland Road.

Everybody makes mistakes. As David said himself, he was a young manager. Years before him, Brian Clough criticised our lads when he came in and he lost the dressing room. Cloughie admitted in his book a few years later that the one thing he had done wrong was his handling of the Leeds United situation. I am sure in years to come, when David looks back on what happened at Leeds, he will think, 'I should never have done that book, nor criticised players in a newspaper.' It lost him his job in the end, there is no question in my mind. For me, that would have been a major factor in the decision to let him go. I honestly think we would have got back into Europe if he hadn't written the book. It was January 2002, and we were top of the League at the time. But they were never the same side to watch. Woodgate didn't come back until the next year because he was shell-shocked, but a lot of the guys seemed to sympathise with Bowyer and felt he had been let down by the club.

Some people question David O'Leary's abilities in the transfer market and, although he did make some good buys – Dominic Matteo, for instance, was a terrific buy – Robbie Fowler was a bad buy for £11 million. I could never understand him buying Robbie Keane for £11 million and never playing the lad but having him sat on the bench. I couldn't understand his thinking there at all. Keane is a good player. He was a young player who needed time on the field. In those two players alone, there was a £22 million outlay and we got nothing out of either of them, really. Fowler wasn't an £11 million player, in my opinion. As for Robbie Keane, you couldn't say it was his fault that he didn't produce. He just never got selected to play – even though he was so eager. But when you put £11 million down on a player he should be the finished article and a regular in the starting line-up.

Terry Venables came in, and I think he knew there were problems within but felt he could go in and marry it all together. But I think the damage had gone too far. I think one or two of the players had already made their minds up, especially Kewell, that they wanted out. There was a problem in the dressing room – and it's still there. If you've had words with somebody, or they have had words with you, there is never going to be perfect harmony. According to what we hear, the dressing room was in two parts. There was a pro-lobby and an anti-lobby regarding the situation. Once that's happened, it is very difficult to resolve. You either get rid of all of one side or all of the other. That's the way it has to be, because it can spark off at any time on the field or in a training bust-up. Anything can happen when a lot of the players feel that the best way forward is to get out. Terry came into a crazy situation. He was told on day one by Peter Ridsdale that there was no way Rio Ferdinand would be going. He was staying at the club and they were building the club round him. He got a phone call to say he had been sold, so from day one he was being fed a line. I honestly think Terry would have been disappointed at that. A lot of people questioned him coming to Leeds, but I think he wanted to prove himself in the Premiership. And if you've got Ferdinand and Woodgate, you've got two England centre-backs.

You could build a team round that, no question. Then they were gone in a blinding flash. Terry has always been a technical man and I think everybody knows that. He is a different kind of coach — pretty deep. I don't think anybody expected anything less than that. He must have been bitterly disappointed to come when, on the face of it, he had a chance of proving himself and it didn't work out. He had won titles at Barcelona, but in this country he'd never proved himself. I think he felt he could do it for Leeds, and to find out in such a short space of time that those you were going to build your team around were going must have been a great disappointment to him. And for me, after that, he seemed to lose that bit of faith. When you saw him on television or in press conferences he didn't have that bubble about him. And, of course, he had that spectacular fall-out with Peter Ridsdale. He felt he had come to do a job, and you would expect that if you had been told those players would be available, and when they weren't, your prospects of succeeding in that job would start to diminish. I think the fans at that time were let down badly. It was only the day before Woodgate was sold that the chairman said it would be over his dead body that the crown jewels would be sold. Then you hear from Freddy Shepherd, the Newcastle chairman, that Ridsdale sat in the car park the next morning and pleaded with him to buy Woodgate. So why say these things? If he had to be sold because money had to be urgently raised then say that to the fans, because they deserve honesty, and they didn't get that at that time. They could see it was all underhanded, so you could well understand Terry Venables getting very fed up. Then they had the confrontation and the fall-out and, as is usual in a case like that, there's only one guy who goes and that's the manager. That was the case.

It was quite amazing for Leeds to replace Venables with Peter Reid. Everybody knows Peter's a bubbly character and a fighter, but what a disaster he had been at Sunderland. He'd had 12 months in which he couldn't win a match, and to bring a guy from that situation into a club that was fast moving into that situation seemed a staggering appointment.

But, in fairness to Peter, he got United going a little bit and they stayed in the Premiership. He did the required thing at the time, but as soon as the 2003–04 season started you could see that if this team stayed up it would be a major achievement. He was left with a very small squad and no money, because the desperate financial state of the club had just surfaced. Beforehand, very few people knew this was the case. There were rumours of the club being under severe pressure, but not to the tune of £104 million. That was a gob-smacking amount, an amazing amount of money to run up in debt. On top of this, Ferdinand, Woodgate, Kewell and Keane – four top players – were sold and still we were getting deeper in debt. That was the thing that amazed the fans. It begged lots of questions, chief of which were, 'How the hell can we, having just sold those four players, still be in that amount of debt? What was the original debt?' A certain amount was wiped off by the sale of those players. We maybe pulled in £40–£50 million for all of them put together. In spite of this, though, we were £100 million-plus in debt. Having spoken since to people who knew the situation, they say that even if we had got into the Champions League we were too deep in the mire anyway. The club wage bill and the debts they had incurred meant they would never have recovered, even with Champions League football. The debt was so severe that there was no way out, but for some reason they just kept spending and blowing more and more money.

In a very short period of time, we had O'Leary, Venables and Reid as managers and basically, right under their noses all this time, has been the long-serving Eddie Gray. The club is Eddie's life and always has been. His demotions under O'Leary and Reid came on top of his removal as manager back in the mid-1980s, and so by no means were these the first times that he had been wronged by the club. He and David O'Leary were a good partnership, and I cannot understand why O'Leary would want to break that up. I have spoken to Eddie and to this day he doesn't know himself.

He was never given any, 'The reason I'm doing this . . .' They just brought in a new coach and that was it. Eddie must have been deeply hurt by that. Yet he stayed at the club, and rightly so. He was thrown in again at the deep end as caretaker manager when Peter Reid left and did a fantastic job in a short time. The team didn't look like the same set of players under his guidance. They were hungry, they wanted to win and they were charging around. Unfortunately though, it was already too late for Eddie to really get results. It was quite obvious that Peter Reid had lost the plot prior to this, because we started getting thumped at places like Everton and Leicester, and they had to let him go after the Portsmouth game. I think Peter would have been relieved when they called him and said, 'You've got to go,' because you could see in his make-up he was totally changed.

He was shell-shocked. I think it was one of those situations when you think, 'I've lost the plot. Get me out of here.' And out he went. He did a good job in a short period. He saved us. A lot of it was to do with the debts and the associated problems and players having to go. That has got to have a major effect on the dressing room. It was then a troubled club with players wondering, 'Am I going?' People say the Leeds players are all rich, so why should they let that worry them?

But lots of these players have got families and young kids and a short career, and they have got to make it all fit. Yes, you could say financially they wouldn't have a problem, but there is more to life than finance. Your family relationship is very important, especially when you've got kids of five, six and seven who have just gone to school and met new friends. Just when you think everything is settled it might actually all be starting to fall apart. I have nothing against Peter Ridsdale or David O'Leary – but I do think they made mistakes. If either of them had ever acknowledged this, or personally accepted their portion of the blame, I would forever hold my peace. However, they have both tried to blame it on the other. If David said, 'I made a mistake at a certain time,' the slate would have been wiped clean. He was a young, naive manager working with a naive chairman. Peter had come from being a representative of a company to being on the board of a football club and then being its chairman. If we believe what we read, David O'Leary said he didn't even know what Seth Johnson was earning. And where did Peter Ridsdale have the experience to be doing deals like that? Who was guiding him? He didn't have that kind of experience. You need someone who knows the game and what the guy is worth and what he has been on before. Then you say, 'Well, we'll give him an increase. He will be happy with that.' You don't almost treble his wages.

The past couple of years have been an unfortunate period in Leeds' history. It's terrible, because I really thought, sitting and watching that young side going through to that semi-final in 2001, that it was not far away from what Don Revie did with us lot. We were all young kids who had come through and this batch all looked as though they were making their mark and would be around for a long time. Everybody in football was saying, 'Leeds are going to be the side to beat in the next few years.' They were young players and they were all English or British players. We didn't have the foreign influx that every other club was getting at the time. Everybody was admiring what Leeds had done. And within six months, from being a club that everybody was admiring we had become the laughing stock of football, both on and off the field.

CHAPTER SEVENTEEN

THAT'S RICH

Back in October 2002, *Yorkshire Post* business editor David Parkin reported that Peter Ridsdale and his fellow Leeds United directors saw their pay packets slashed over the previous year after the club plunged £34 million into the red. None of the board was paid bonuses, so Ridsdale earned £383,000 in pay and benefits in the year to the end of June, compared to £600,000 in salary and bonuses he earned the previous year. Stephen Harrison, who was promoted from finance director to chief operating officer during the year, was paid £224,000, compared to £326,000 the year before. Operations director David Spencer was one of the board who bucked the trend, earning a salary and benefits of £201,000, compared to £165,000 the previous year. Also, deputy chairman Allan Leighton, the former Asda chief executive, and non-executive director Richard North, the finance director of leisure group Six Continents (formerly Bass), were paid £35,000 each for their part-time roles, an increase of £5,000 on the previous year. The five directors were paid a total of £878,000 during the year, compared to £1.5 million the year before. Ridsdale said that, with the bonuses based on the performance of the company, it was only right he and his fellow directors had not been paid them. 'The bonuses are based on the level of profit of the club prior to transfers, so, given that we are not profitable, we didn't receive bonuses and that is quite right. We have also agreed to a pay freeze from 1 July.' He also said of the year that Leeds got to the Champions League semi-finals, 'Operating profit that year was over £10 million. We receive no bonus for the first £6 million of operating profit.' Ridsdale said that the club had to constantly maintain a 'balance between strengthening the squad and making money'. He added, 'That is a problem if we don't perform on the field.' The previous month, Leeds United published full-year figures showing taxable losses of almost £34 million against losses last time of £7.6 million. Operating losses were £7.9 million, excluding the figures for buying and selling players. The club had net debt of £78 million at the year end. The problem was caused by the club's failure to qualify for the lucrative Champions League, estimated to be worth between £10–15 million. High player costs forced on the club by the Woodgate-Bowyer-Duberry trial and long-term injuries to players like Lucas Radebe and Michael Bridges, which forced it to keep a big squad, also contributed to the losses. Leeds' wage bill in the year was up 24 per cent to £53.6 million, representing 66 per cent of the £81.5 million turnover compared with 50 per cent in 2001. Leeds wanted to get that down to 55 per cent, a level it judged well ahead of the industry average, which it claims could reach 70 per cent.

In November 2003, it was reported that, according to Deloitte and Touche, the most recent figures available showed that the 20 clubs in the Premiership owed a staggering £598.5 million between them. Leeds were lambasted for running up the biggest loss in one season in football history, on top of which it also owed £78 million of long-term debt. Leeds, though, were eclipsed in this latter respect by Fulham, owned by Mohamed al Fayed, which owed a staggering £107.9 million. Despite all the warning signs that football's financial bubble had burst, that collective Premiership debt figure went up by almost 50 per cent from the previous year's total of £416.2 million. Only Manchester United made a significant profit – £39.3 million.

Phil Clisby, of *Soccer Investor* magazine, observed:

> Most Premiership clubs make a loss and the amount they are losing is going up. The bad financial practices of the last decade, paying transfer fees and high salaries with money they didn't have, are catching up on them just when the global transfer market has collapsed and the Premier League is going to get less money from Sky from next summer for their television rights.

Manchester City admitted that it lost £15.4 million last year and saw its overall debt rise from £30 million to £50 million after buying players such as Nicolas Anelka and Robbie Fowler in a bid to retain its place in the Premiership. One observer noted, 'City are doing exactly what Leeds did a few years ago, taking out long-term debt to buy short-term assets, despite that disastrous policy having left Leeds in a terrible state. They spent over 75 per cent of their turnover on players' salaries, which is dangerously high.'

The top ten of the most indebted clubs in the Premiership as at 2002, published in 2003, read as follows: 1. Fulham £107.94 million; 2. Leeds United £78 million; 3. Middlesbrough £53.6 million; 4. Manchester City £50 million; 5. Arsenal £45.8 million; 6. Newcastle United £43 million; 7. Bolton Wanderers £33.9 million; 8. Everton £27.6 million; 9. Liverpool £20.5 million; 10. Southampton £20.2 million.

In March 2004, The Deloitte Rich List concerning the world's top football clubs was published. It said:

> Manchester United is again placed first in the Rich List of the world's top football clubs, based on income from the 2002–03 season. Generating income of over €250 million, United were well ahead of their nearest rivals and occupied the top position for the seventh successive year of the Deloitte Football Rich List.

Dan Jones, Director of the Sports Business Group at Deloitte, commented:

> The top clubs in the world's number one sport are generating more income than ever before. Broadcast income is the largest single source for most of the clubs and despite the widespread speculation of a collapse in media values, we think this is unlikely. At the same time, many of football's leading clubs have a great, and as yet underused, opportunity to significantly develop other income streams, particularly from their stadia. For instance, Manchester United's match day income of €101 million is over three times greater than their closest Italian rivals. The global top 20 is entirely populated by European

clubs, with English and Italian clubs occupying 12 of these positions. The remaining positions are filled by three clubs from each of the German Bundesliga and Spanish Primera Liga and one each from the top divisions in France and Scotland. The Italian duo of Juventus and AC Milan are in second and third position respectively, their positions supported by the largest broadcasting incomes in world football and their appearance in the 2003 Champions League final. Whilst the Spanish giants, Real Madrid, may have a reputation as the world's number one glamour club, they hold fourth position in the Deloitte Football Rich List. Schalke 04 is the only debutant in the top 20, positioned at 14th thanks to an enterprising stadium development and strong domestic performance.

Commenting on the importance of clubs generating significant income from their stadia on match days and non-match days, Gerry Boon, partner in the Sports Business Group at Deloitte, said:

> Whilst clubs are much more commercially focused than they were a decade ago, there's still a lot more that clubs in Continental Europe could do strategically to improve the venue and facilities they operate, their stadium utilisation and also the income yield they generate from their fanbase. Whilst income is the best publicly available measure of financial muscle, the amount that a club chooses to spend helps determine their overall financial position. Achieving a better balance between income and costs remains the key financial challenge for most clubs.

Dan Jones observed, 'It's a paradox that the top 20 includes a couple of clubs that are having some financial difficulty – but their income is amongst the highest in the world, so the source of any financial difficulty doesn't lie with the revenues they earn.'

Paul Rawnsley from the Sports Business Group at Deloitte commented:

> It has been generally recognised that the game needs to enhance its financial credibility and, to help deal with this, regulation is

a growing theme in European football. From the 2004–05 season, we'll see the first stages of the UEFA club licensing system in place, including a requirement for clubs to meet certain financial criteria. This may appear harsh on those who have sound financial practices, but the responsibility for the imposition of increased regulation lies squarely with those whose house is not in order.

As part of the publication, Football Business International provide a high level analysis of the income generation of US Sport teams. According to published data, Major League Baseball's New York Yankees generated more income than any other US Sports Team in the 2002–03 season, but at €243 million, this was still less than Manchester United's total. The NFL's Tampa Bay Buccaneers, headed by the Glazer family, who also hold a growing stake in Manchester United, generated income of €146 million – making them around 60 per cent of Manchester United's size.

SUMMARY OF THE DELOITTE FOOTBALL RICH LIST, PUBLISHED IN CONJUNCTION WITH FOOTBALL BUSINESS INTERNATIONAL:

Position	(Prior year position)	Club	Income (€m)
1	(1)	Manchester United	251.4
2	(2)	Juventus	218.3
3	(4)	AC Milan	200.2
4	(6)	Real Madrid	192.6
5	(3)	Bayern Munich	162.7
6	(12)	Internazionale Milan	162.4
7	(8)	Arsenal	149.6
8	(5)	Liverpool	149.4
9	(13)	Newcastle United	138.9
10	(7)	Chelsea	133.8
11	(10)	AS Roma	132.4
12	(15)	Borussia Dortmund	124.0
13	(9)	Barcelona	123.4
14	(n/a)	Schalke 04	118.6
15	(16)	Tottenham Hotspur	95.6

LEEDS UNITED: TRIALS AND TRIBULATIONS

Position	(Prior year position)	Club	Income (€m)
16	(11)	Leeds United	92.0
17	(14)	SS Lazio	88.9
18	(17)	Celtic	87.0
19	(20)	Lyon	84.3
20	(n/a)	Valencia	80.5

CHAPTER EIGHTEEN

OVERVIEW AND FINAL THOUGHTS

Leeds had taken some fearful batterings in 2003–04, most notably the 6–1 defeat at Portsmouth, the 13–2 aggregate in three League and cup meetings with champions Arsenal, the 4–0 drubbings at Leicester and Everton, and the 3–0 defeat at home to Middlesbrough. And so, with four matches remaining of a dreadful 2003–04 season, it was somewhat surprising that Leeds United still retained even a chance of staying in the Premiership. Only the frailties of Manchester City offered this glimmer of hope, and the televised Sunday morning return fixture with Portsmouth had become a must-win for a side which, despite the enforced absence through suspension of star striker Mark Viduka, would surely be fully charged and determined to grasp a glorious opportunity to escape the relegation places for the first time in an eternity. There was, however, an air of resignation about the place. The 3,000 travelling Pompey fans out-sang, out-cheered and out-shouted the angst-ridden 36,000 home contingent as the sun shone brightly, and what was to unfold over the next 90 minutes amounted to the shabbiest, weakest, dishevelled, uncoordinated, lily-livered and incompetent performance I have ever witnessed by any team in the history of the Premiership. Misplaced passes, half-hearted tackles, a lack of shots on goal, poor defence and a non-existent midfield had been regular features of Leeds United efforts throughout the campaign, but now they were so bad that Portsmouth veteran Steve Stone was allowed to look like Zinedine Zidane as he exploited large chunks of unoccupied territory. Within eight minutes, Stone had engineered the opening goal and soon the visitors' end was alive to, 'Can we play you every week?'; 'We're gonna win 6–1,' and, as James Milner missed a sitter, 'That's why you're in the Nationwide.' By the time Ian Harte tucked away a late penalty, Portsmouth had put the match beyond their reach with a second goal. There were stories that as the Leeds players disappeared down the tunnel at half-time there had been pushing and shoving and shouting and swearing among themselves and how appropriate that was for a ragbag assortment who couldn't win an argument, never mind a football match. How far removed this was from those victories over AC Milan, Lazio and Deportivo so recently achieved. The embarrassment, the hurt and the feeling of being cheated was visible on every one of the faces of the home fans who trudged out of Elland Road that day.

Leeds' fate was well and truly sealed in their next outing, an early-May bank holiday weekend clash at the Reebok stadium with Bolton, who were flying high by their own standards. The end of Leeds' Premiership tenure was confirmed by a crushing 4–1 defeat and, although anticipated, it was still a heartbreaking moment. Tears flowed from the vast army of travelling fans as the club's 14-year stay in the top-flight came to a bitter close. It wouldn't have been so bad had United put up a fight, but they turned in a second-half surrender that summed up just about everything that had been wrong with the club. The cause wasn't helped by the stupidity of Viduka, who got himself sent off for two moments of madness in the space of less than three first-half minutes. It was suicide from Viduka and probably cost Leeds their last chance of survival. It wasn't that Leeds were mind-numbingly bad – it had become difficult to expect much from a team which had spent the entire campaign lying on the canvas – it was more that there was an air of inevitability about the whole proceedings. Right from the moment Manchester City scored their winner against Newcastle, 24 hours previously, it seemed inevitable that Leeds' time was finally up. It was painful to look back on where it had all gone wrong this 2003–04 season. Those hidings at Everton, Leicester and Portsmouth had been added to by a 3–1 defeat at Wolves, where Leeds reverted to a 4–4–2 line-up from 4–5–1 and the defence was woefully exposed at the hands of a side which was also going down. Reality really hit home after the 2–0 loss at Fulham in March, while Easter Monday, when Portsmouth and Blackburn both re-discovered their fighting spirit, was a real killer. But the simple truth was that Leeds had not been good enough to compete at the highest level and, week after week, their performances were unacceptable. Still, you cannot get out what isn't in there in the first place, and, for all the times when their endeavour couldn't be questioned, the lack of quality could not be hidden. The commitment shown by the likes of Alan Smith, Dominic Matteo and Paul Robinson could not be faulted and their attitude was summed up to perfection at the final whistle when they lingered long in front of the devastated travelling supporters. Smith had been a talisman all season – he was the same again at Bolton – while no one gave more than Matteo. Their tears at the final whistle were contagious. Sadly, there had been a handful of players who could have done more to aid the cause. The lack of a creative midfielder was glaring and more should have been done before the season, and again in January, to ensure that void was filled. An often inadequate defence was also exposed, brutally at times, while Robinson spent much of the campaign seeking protection that just wasn't there. But what was more galling was that Bolton appeared to want it more than a team which simply had to win to stand any chance of remaining among the elite. That was despite the backing of almost 4,000 fans, who never stopped singing throughout. 'Going down, but we'll be back,' was the defiant salute from a group of fans who deserved far more than their team had given them. They had been shafted from all angles by all and sundry, yet, come Crewe and Plymouth in 2004–05, they will be there in numbers again. The anthemic 'Champions of Europe' chant, so common at away games, was sung with vigour at the Reebok, and that evoked the eerie memory of when it was belted out at West Brom in 1982, when Leeds had last been relegated. It took them eight years to return back then, and the spectacular fall from grace of Yorkshire rivals Sheffield Wednesday remains a concern today. Eddie Gray was a part of the last Leeds side to suffer the drop and, for all he has had his critics, it was hard not to feel for a man who loves Leeds United deeply. He could only watch in agony as reality overtook hope and Premiership survival slipped away. The hope came when Bolton's Emerson Thome hauled down Smith after 25 minutes and Viduka converted the penalty. It was a lifeline. Quite why Thome wasn't red-carded only the referee knows, but if he had been sent-off he wouldn't have been involved in the scuffle that led to Viduka's first booking. As in the pre-season friendlies against York and Burnley, the red mist descended for Viduka and, after narrowly escaping a second card for an unnecessary challenge on Ivan Campo, it was no surprise when he was sent off for elbowing Bruno N'Gotty. It was an act of silliness that effectively gave Leeds no chance. Down to ten men, Leeds looked lost and the hosts were suddenly rejuvenated. Youri Djorkaeff levelled on 47 minutes and followed up Nicky Hunt's shot to make it 2–1 soon afterwards. The third goal came 90 seconds later when Ian Harte bundled an Anthony Barness cross into his own goal and the rest of the game became a blur. It was all over for Leeds and the players and the fans knew it. The last rites were played out to the backdrop of defiant chanting from the United fans – even when Bolton still managed to add a fourth. It was Kevin Nolan who rubbed salt in the wound when he raced past a static defence to make it 4–1 with 12 minutes left. Nolan's goal was the last proper act in a devastating campaign. But oh, those wonderful fans. As the fourth official displayed '1' to signal the amount of injury time to be played they immediately struck up: 'We're going down in a minute.' The home crowd, to a man, applauded them.

The tears may have flowed, but many had prepared for the inevitable after a three-year fall from grace as painful as it had been dramatic. None of those fans who celebrated United's return to the elite 14 years previously with an impromptu beach party at Bournemouth could have envisaged what the future would have in store. The possibility of a relegation scrap was talked about, but for everyone the sheer joy at the prospect of locking horns with Arsenal, Liverpool and, of course, Manchester United, overshadowed any doubts. The chant of 'Champions of Europe' echoed around the seaside town that May evening in 1990 – but no one realised how prophetic the song was. Equally, no one could have imagined the consequences after going so close to endorsing the words of the song with a touch of reality. Those first few years back in the big time were the start of one hell of a ride. Leeds finished fourth in their first year in the top flight before achieving the unthinkable just 12 months later. Against all the odds, Howard Wilkinson guided his gutsy team of battlers to the League title, the club's first since 1974, and the city partied like there was no tomorrow. Over 250,000 hit the streets of Leeds to celebrate, and Eric Cantona wooed the fans with the simple words, 'I don't know why, but I love you all.' The departure of the mercurial Cantona was a blow, and Leeds' defence of the title flopped. There was a high when Carl Shutt scored in the Nou Camp on Leeds' return to Europe, but those dreams turned sour after Wilkinson's side lost the battle of Britain clash with Rangers in the second round. Leeds found the expectations tough, though, and finished 17th that season. Two top-five finishes followed and, in Tony Yeboah, Leeds fans found another new continental hero to admire. Yeboah scored stunning goals against Liverpool and Wimbledon in 1994 as Leeds marched towards a second successive top-five finish and hopes were high for the following season. Europe again beckoned, but PSV Eindhoven ended the expectation of a UEFA Cup challenge with a stunning 5–3 win at Elland Road. There was a chance of glory in the Coca Cola Cup, but Leeds lost the final in disappointing fashion to Aston Villa and, after some indifferent League form, the natives started to become restless. Wilkinson's response was to strengthen. Lee Bowyer became Britain's most expensive teenager when he joined Leeds in 1996 while Nigel Martyn also arrived at Elland Road. The end was nigh, though, and a 4–0 humiliation at the hands of Manchester United in September saw the curtain brought down on Wilkinson's reign. It proved to be the start of a new era in Leeds' history and the roller-coaster was about to be ridden again. George Graham came in, tightened up the defence, and the occasional verve was replaced by a regimented machine which conceded few goals and proved hard to beat. Leeds finished 11th in 1997 and conceded just 38 goals. That summer, Jimmy-Floyd Hasselbaink was drafted in and Leeds began the new campaign well. A David Wetherall goal sunk Manchester United on what was a proud day for Leeds fans, and all augured well. Leeds went on to finish fifth and, under Graham, the future was looking bright. But things are never straightforward, and when Graham walked out on the club the following October, David O'Leary was put in temporary charge. Martin O'Neill was approached to replace Graham, but Leicester wouldn't play ball with their manager and O'Leary was finally asked to take on the job. The Irishman, working with Gray, took Leeds to fourth in the table and a guaranteed UEFA Cup spot. The ride was well and truly in progress and Leeds continued on the up and up. The UEFA Cup run took in the capital cities of Europe – Moscow, Prague, Sofia, Rome and Istanbul – and O'Leary's exciting young side swept all before them as they maintained a strong challenge for the League. It was dreamland for the fans but, unbeknown to most, the downfall had already started. The arrests of Jonathan Woodgate and Lee Bowyer, the subsequent court cases and the fall-out from them was to hit the club hard. Just weeks after the incident, Leeds fans had to deal with grief of their own when two of their number were murdered in Istanbul and there was suddenly a surreal air about the club. Initially, O'Leary, his players and the fans closed ranks. Galatasaray ended Leeds' UEFA Cup dream, but there would be bigger fish to fry in the Champions League. Leeds set about going for glory in the elite competition, and, in a truly memorable campaign, United took on the likes of Real Madrid, Barcelona, Milan, Deportivo and Valencia. This wasn't talked about at Bournemouth. While the fans were living the dream, the board were pursuing even bigger and better triumphs, and this needed funding. Mortgages were taken out to strengthen the squad, and players were bought through high-interest finance deals. It didn't matter. Leeds were one of the emerging clubs in Europe and everyone was enjoying the ride. In came Rio Ferdinand and Robbie Fowler, and chairman Peter Ridsdale announced to the world that 'Leeds United have arrived'. But the prolonged court case finally came to a conclusion in December 2001 and, with Leeds topping the Premier League, it started to go horribly wrong. O'Leary published his ill-timed book about the effects the case had on the club and many on the inside took it personally. There were suggestions he had lost the dressing room. After a horrendous FA Cup defeat at Cardiff, O'Leary countered the critics by insisting he would be judged on Champions League qualification. They didn't and he went. It was a hammer blow and, suddenly, money had to be found. Players' salaries and high interest payments outweighed potential income and Terry Venables arrived at a club desperate to sell off its players. Ferdinand went to Manchester United for a £26 million down payment, and, after Leeds struggled to find any League form, the sales continued in January. Woodgate went, Fowler went, Bowyer went and Dacourt was forced through the door. The heart and soul was ripped from the team and Leeds became embroiled in a relegation battle. Venables finally paid the price after some of the worst performances during the club's stay in the top flight and he was followed by big-spending chairman Peter

Ridsdale. Ridsdale admitted he was the man who couldn't say no and Leeds were on the financial precipice. Peter Reid hastily re-shuffled the pack to ensure Premiership status, but after another summer of cost cutting, he was unable to strengthen sufficiently and another season of struggle followed. On the field, results were poor, while off the field, debts rose to £104 million and the club teetered on the brink of administration. That horrible 6–1 defeat at Portsmouth did for Reid, and Eddie Gray was drafted in for one last throw of the dice. Gray gave his all but, with off-field problems hogging the headlines and a protracted takeover occupying minds, it was no easy challenge. In the end, Gray couldn't do it and the only crumbs of comfort came from the support and loyalty of the fans. Many of those were the same people who danced with joy 14 years ago – now they were tearing their hair out. Arguments will long rage about the precise moment it all went wrong, but a distraught Gray was quick to promise them:

> We will come back. It's a sad day for everyone connected with this club, but we'll come back. This club will bounce back. The supporters don't deserve it. They've been terrific, but I think they feared the worst. A lot has happened at this club, given the players who have been lost and the financial circumstances. If you look at the quality of some of those players and took their equivalent out of other clubs they, too, would struggle. It makes it difficult, especially when there is no money to replace them. I'm sure with one or two breaks we'll bounce back, but it might take longer than we anticipate. Whatever, this is still a great football club with a great fan base. It's the only club in the city – a big city – and I hope we're back quite soon. We've played 36 games and we weren't good enough. It's quite simple. Every season someone fights against relegation – this year we were in that group and we just weren't good enough. When you look at the League it tells its own story. If you win it you deserve to win it; if you get relegated you deserve to get relegated. I've played in a side that was relegated and the financial side wasn't good then, but it magnifies itself more now given the money that's involved. It's quite obvious we spent too much money in the past. But

you've always got to have ambition in football. If you don't have that, it's a waste of time playing the game. But it all depends on how you approach things, and that was the problem: how it was approached. Obviously, it's not now going to be easy for the club, but we've got to try and make sure the academy stays strong and we produce a few young players. We will have to wait and see what way the board are going to go, but it looks as if we are going to lose players, and when that happens it's disappointing. We lost many good players from our Premiership team and we just couldn't cope with the difference it made. I'm sure the club will bounce back and get into the Premiership again. But when I say bounce back, it might not happen overnight because over the years the First Division has always been a difficult one to get out of. I don't think anybody at our club will be under any illusion about that, but the club have the capabilities to do it.

Half an hour after Leeds' fate was sealed, O'Leary's Aston Villa beat Tottenham, and the former Elland Road boss observed:

I'm very sad about what's happened. What I can't understand, when you look at the players that are still there, is why they are not a team who can finish in the top ten at least. There is far too much quality in that side for Leeds to be going down. It is a sad day for the supporters, because I think it has been proved they have been fantastic all season. Let's hope Leeds can get back up as soon as possible.

He added that he would not be joining a bidding war for Leeds' departing players because he saw them as far too expensive for Villa. 'There are players at Leeds I admire and I would love to have – but I won't be bidding,' he said. 'I haven't got that kind of money.'

Gray was relieved of his duties before the final game of the season at Chelsea, and Kevin Blackwell, the coach recruited from Sheffield United by Peter Reid, was put in temporary charge. Blackwell was to be given the job on a permanent basis ahead of the 2004–05 season.

One of those players referred to by Gray as almost certainly on his way out of the club was dejected striker Alan Smith, whose tears following the Bolton defeat said it all.

Smith said:

> I feel very, very downbeat. I've never been in this position and I hope I never am again because it's not nice. I've got pride and that hurts when you're relegated. It means you are not good enough. We've not been good enough this season. We've conceded far too many goals and that hurts when you're not good enough. But when you play like we have you don't deserve to stay up. We've had plenty of chances to get out of it, but we haven't done that and everyone is gutted. It is a major disappointment, but it's been coming for a while. Although it is certainly difficult to take when it comes. After Manchester City won on Saturday it was going to take a miracle to keep us up, and it came to a head. But it wasn't just about Bolton. Too many games have passed us by and that hurts. If we'd been as good as our fans then we'd have won the League. In the face of adversity they have given their all and we couldn't ask for more. I've played 223 games for this club and I like to think I've given everything I've got. I've always tried my best. The fans have let me off with a few misdemeanours along the way, but I've got great memories that will live with me forever. Wherever I go, if I have to go at the end of this season, hopefully I will still be able to come back to this club and it won't be the last time I am seen in a Leeds shirt. If I have to walk away then no one can say I've not been trying. I've done my best for this club and I'm proud of myself.

So would those loyal fans renew their season tickets? Well, the club had come up with a '20 years for the price of 10' season ticket offer, involving outlays of £3,000–4,000, which it hoped would raise substantial funds but which ran into difficulties because the banks, fearing what would happen if the club went into administration or even liquidation, refused to accept payments by credit card. The response was pitiful.

There were other issues for the fans, arguably the most loyal in the country, to consider. Would they be watching Premiership or Coca-

Cola football in 2004–05? What would be the quality of the team? There was much ado concerning the second of those questions. Incredulity spread among the players and fans when, with three games remaining and Premiership safety still attainable, though unlikely in view of the apparent apathy out there on the pitch, the club drafted in agent Phillip Morrison to advise on transfer matters and stood accused of openly touting their players around to raise funds and slash their hefty wage bill. Morrison did a similar job at Sunderland the previous season when the Black Cats were relegated and Leeds wasted no time in defending his involvement. The quartet of players most in demand was always going to be Alan Smith, Mark Viduka, Paul Robinson and James Milner. Hometown hero Smith, in particular, was indignant about this. The idolised striker blasted Leeds' use of an agent to handle their transfer dealings, saying:

> Everyone knows I love this club and yet it seems they have appointed an agent to sell me somewhere I might not want to go. This doesn't just affect me, there are other players in the same position who are just as disappointed about what is happening. If I have to leave – and that's not certain – it will be to a club of my choice, not theirs.

Smith had mellowed by the time he was to make his last Elland Road appearance for the club he adores against Charlton Athletic. The player had already held talks with managing director David Richmond and, with a parting of the ways imminent, he said:

> I've always said I wanted to stay here until it was no longer possible and I think that's the situation we're approaching now. Everyone appreciates that from the financial side, the club side and from my point of view it is time to move on. It was always going to take something out of the ordinary for me to have to leave and this is probably it. A few people have said that I don't have to leave, but they don't understand football. I'm at a stage in my career now where I am ambitious and I want to achieve what I know I have the potential to achieve. Any Leeds fan who knows and cares realises that we have to sell players for this club to survive. It's as simple as that. It would be no good for

us not to sell, not to come back up and maybe even go into liquidation. That would be no good for anybody. If people are going to be realistic, they've got to appreciate that players have to move on.

Smith's last home game, a 3–3 draw against Charlton in which he was captain for the day, received two player of the year awards and scored a penalty, saw the most extraordinary scenes when, at the final whistle, thousands of adoring fans broke through police and security lines to swamp their idol. All the pent-up emotions of the fans poured out as they sought one last look at the hero who had been at the club since the age of 10, and it took Smith half an hour to get back to the dressing room. If he could have said goodbye to each and every one of them personally, he would have.

Three years previously, Smith had shed tears for a different reason in the dressing room of the Mestalla Stadium. He had just seen red in the dying moments of the Champions League semi-final defeat in Valencia. His frustration at the club's exit came to the fore and he was sent off, but no one could imagine that those tears of sadness on that memorable night would coincide with the start of a spectacular downfall. Smith recalled:

> Two or three years ago, no one could have expected Leeds to be in the First Division. You just would not have imagined it. In hindsight, maybe we could have taken a step back then, but when it's all happening, as it was then, you want to push forward and build because you are striving to win something. A lot of fingers have been pointed and a lot has been said, but I'm not going to blame anyone for it because when we were in the semis of the Champions League no one was moaning about us buying players and paying big wages. The only disappointment is that we have not been good enough this season and not stayed in the top division which, for a club of this size and a city of this size, is not good enough.

Smith announced his arrival on the Leeds United scene as a floppy-haired teenager in 1998 with a Roy of the Rovers-style goal when coming on as a late sub in a stunning 3–1 win at Anfield. Few people imagined what was to follow and Smith has become a hero to the many United fans who see him as the fan on the pitch. He said, 'It's been unbelievable. It's flown by with ups and downs, and highs and lows. The fans mean a lot to me. I've been sent off a few times and got away with it because I'm from Leeds. The fans have always stuck by me and I can't thank them enough.'

Smith's commitment was never in question and his no-nonsense approach made him a firm favourite. The marksman admitted that, if it was time to move on, then he would take many memories of his hometown club to his next destination. He recalled:

> It was surreal scoring at Liverpool, but that wasn't the highest point. I think that would have to be my goal in the Champions League at Lazio. That helped put Leeds back on the map. They were nights that I will never forget. If you ask any Leeds fan if they would swap it, if they're honest I don't think they'd sacrifice some of those nights we had in Europe. The best performance I've been involved in was Anderlecht away. Everything clicked that night and it was a tremendous team performance. It was just great to be involved. The biggest disappointment I've ever had was at Bolton. I know we lost the Champions League semi, but in my life and career there's been no bigger disappointment than at the Reebok. When I say goodbye it will not be for ever, but just for a bit. I'd love to come back here. I think everyone knows how much I care about Leeds. I'd love to come back in three, four, even ten years' time because it's a club that has given me my chance and stuck by me through difficult times. I've given everything I've got and whatever happens Leeds will always be my favourite team. If I do go, one day I hope to return and thank the fans for what they've done for me.

Within days, Smith was committing an act of treachery in the minds of Leeds United supporters by taking a journey over the M62 to join despised foes Manchester United in a £7 million deal. Robinson, meanwhile, was off to Tottenham, while Viduka joined Middlesbrough and Milner signed for Newcastle.

Another crowd favourite at Leeds was goalkeeper Nigel Martyn, always greeted by the fans with the song 'England's Number One', and there had been mixed feelings about his departure for just a nominal fee to Everton. Martyn is another who holds the club dear and it was with more than a small degree of embarrassment that he turned in a sensational performance on his return to Elland Road with the blue half of Merseyside. The veteran expressed tremendous sympathy for everyone at Elland Road, even though Everton's survival in the top flight came partly at Leeds' expense. Everton's safety was assured when Leeds self-destructed at Bolton, a result which ensured both Everton and Manchester City could breathe easily again. Martyn said:

> It was sad to see Leeds go down; I was there for seven years. Hopefully they do the rebuilding part right and bounce back because the Premiership needs big clubs like Leeds in it. I didn't watch the Leeds game at Bolton, I was with friends and didn't really want to. But I did keep an ear on what was going on and it was a strange situation, because if they'd won it would have meant that we would still be under pressure. That would not have been good. In an ideal world, I would have wanted us both to have stayed up, but it was not to be. I have spoken to a few of the lads and obviously they are very disappointed. They are at a loss to know what is going to happen. It is hard. Some will be sold and some kept on. Everything is up in the air.

Martyn, who had been told by boss David Moyes that he was 'his best ever signing' and was instrumental in saving the club from the drop, went on:

> Really, what they need is for people there to act quickly so they know exactly where they are come the start of next season. You do not know who is going to be running the club or even who will be manager. The players do not know that, or whether they are going to be there. The coaching staff, too, are in the same boat. It is a horrible time for them all. They need it sorted out quickly and they will know where they are and can focus on getting back up. People have said that I got out at the right time and I have been fortunate, but that wasn't the case. If I had been playing in the first team I would gladly have stayed. It was

265

at the stage of my career when I had to be playing, and when you are offered that chance you take it.

Martyn quit Leeds in the summer of 2003 and his form has been outstanding ever since. Moyes is in no doubt over Martyn's importance to Everton, saying:

> What a terrific signing Nigel has been. He has saved us on so many occasions this season. And when you look at how close to relegation we have come, it is hard to put into words his value and contribution and what it has meant to have him here. He is certainly one of my best signings.

Martyn became a firm favourite for Goodison player of the year and he observed:

> I have just been lucky to get a chance of another go at the top level. I jumped at the chance to come to Everton, and I was determined to hang onto it. I only had a season left on my contract at Leeds, and if I'd had to sit on the bench for another season I would have been pretty demoralised by the end of it. Then the offers would not have been around to go to many clubs. If I was to start playing it was important that I did it quickly and not wait around.

Martyn could have joined Chelsea before Everton moved in, and he admitted to being delighted with the way things turned out. He said:

> Chelsea was wrong for me. I was at the wrong age to want to move my family. I could have been in the same position I was in at Leeds and just sitting on the bench behind a number one. I would have been moving for just financial reasons. I would have much preferred to be playing rather than to uproot the family. Joining Everton I have not had to do that and the family have stayed where we have always been.

That, of course, is in north Leeds.

Leeds United could, and should, have been a top-six Premiership club with a real prospect of involvement in European football for years to come, and in assessing why that will not be the case, several factors must be taken into account. Bulls in china shops have never rampaged so chaotically as Leeds went about spending their newly acquired funds. Theirs was meant to be a 25-year strategy and, as such, instead of at one time having six strikers on their books, why did they not adopt a policy of cherry-picking one significant signing, two at the most, per close-season to bolster and freshen up an already successful team? They were carried away on a tide of extreme optimism, an inner-sense of invincibility almost, by a richly rewarding Champions League campaign in 2000–01 and their failure, by a single point, to effect a return to its illustrious environs the following season had tumultuous repercussions. Peter Ridsdale had provided, by various means, all the funds necessary for a manager to assemble a top-three team and now it was over to David O'Leary and the players to ensure it was achieved. It was not; and the manager paid the price. While not absolving Ridsdale of blame, it has to be said in his defence that he provided the wherewithal for a dream journey to a Champions League semi-final in a campaign which will never be forgotten by all who witnessed it. Maybe he should have been more alert to the old adage that there are never any guarantees in football, nor in life. Perhaps he should have been more assertive when O'Leary made requests for the signing of certain players. 'No' is a big word. But what of O'Leary? There is no doubting that he went an awful long way in a very short time at the start of a managerial career which is certainly making people sit up and take notice. The brand of football that he was producing in tandem with Eddie Gray in his early days at Leeds was not very far removed from the spellbinding fluency which saw Arsenal romp to the Premiership title in 2003–04 and another wise old saying – 'If it ain't broke don't fix it' – should have been adopted when he chose to shunt Gray aside and put Brian Kidd in charge of training and coaching. From that day forward, it was never the same. Out went the freeflow and in came the caution. Where Gray's philosophy was that 1–0 should become 2–0 and 2–0 should become 3–0 as quickly as possible, Kidd's approach seemed to be that 1–0 should be defended to the last. Both are flawed, but there is simply no argument about which was the better to watch.

O'Leary left himself open to question in other areas. From the stands, his use of substitutes was poor, he should never have associated himself with a book called *Leeds United on Trial* when he was the manager and his media-savvy was very shallow. Irritatingly, he would use flippant asides like, 'I've been lighting a few candles for our trip to Rome' and 'Nice place such and such . . . I like the restaurants and the hotels,' when the many assembled hacks wanted his views on the football match in question. Clearly, though, he is learning. He did well in his first season at Aston Villa and, whichever way you look at it, Leeds United have fallen into disarray only since his departure. Who knows what might have happened had he stayed?

Maybe the last word should go to club stalwart Lucas 'The Chief' Radebe, the brilliant South African central defender who has spent a decade at Elland Road:

> There have been a lot of question marks over some of the players at the club. This season, I have seen a change in the attitude of some of the players during training. The players did not enjoy it as much, and some of them were just coming in to pass the time. I feel that most of the players just gave up and accepted the situation, and some of them knew that they would be going somewhere else at the end of the season. It is disappointing when people have that attitude. We have responsibilities, we are not just here to take the money and it is hard to respect those players who were not trying.

Radebe absolved Alan Smith and Dominic Matteo from blame and added:

> You would try hard to get the spirit back during the week, only to find that during the game it would go again. But Dominic, Smithy and a few others always worked hard for the club and it is sad to see them end up in this situation. Division One is a tough League; you only have to look at what happened to Bradford City, who were relegated from the Premiership in 2001 and have now gone into Division Two, to realise that. What you need to come back up is to have quality and fighting spirit in the team and, while I realise that some players will go, the people who stay at the club must fight to come straight back up.

In the summer of 2004, as yet another manager, Kevin Blackwell, was appointed, more players left. As the hunt for new bargain-basement players began in earnest, the words of that old Michael Holliday number, 'The runaway train went over the hill and she blew' sprang to mind. Only, on the Leeds United runaway express, what 'blew' wasn't just steam; it was the club itself – which blew right up.

DAVID O'LEARY'S BUYS AND SALES AS MANAGER OF LEEDS, FROM OCTOBER 1998 TO JUNE 2002

IN

1998: December: David Batty, Newcastle £4.4 million

1999: May: Eirik Bakke, Sogndal £1.75 million; June: Danny Mills, Charlton £4 million; July: Michael Duberry, Chelsea £4.5 million, Michael Bridges, Sunderland £5 million; August: Danny Hay, Perth Glory £200,000; September: Darren Huckerby, Coventry £5.5 million; December: Jason Wilcox, Blackburn £3 million

2000: January: Danny Milosevic, Perth Glory £100,000; March: Shaun Allaway, Reading £200,000; May: Olivier Dacourt, Lens £7.2 million; July: Mark Viduka, Celtic £6 million; August: Dominic Matteo, Liverpool £4.25 million; September: Jacob Burns, Paramatta Power £200,000; November: Rio Ferdinand, West Ham £18 million; December: Robbie Keane, Inter Milan £11 million

2001: October: Seth Johnson, Derby £9 million; November: Robbie Fowler, Liverpool £11 million

Total outlay: £95.3 million.

OUT

1999: June: Gunnar Halle, Bradford £250,000, Lee Sharpe, Bradford £200,000, David Wetherall, Bradford £1.4 million; July: Clyde Wijnhard, Huddersfield £750,000; August: JF Hasselbaink, Atletico Madrid £12 million, Derek Lilley, Oxford £50,000; October: Danny Granville, Man City £1 million, Bruno Ribeiro, Sheffield United £500,000

2000: May: Martin Hiden, SV Salzburg £500,000; June: Alf-Inge Haaland, Man City £2.8 million; July: David Hopkin, Bradford £2.5 million; December: Robert Molenaar, Bradford £500,000, Matthew Jones, Leicester £3.25 million, Darren Huckerby, Man City £3 million

2001: March: Lee Matthews, Bristol City £100,000; July: Anthony Hackworth, Notts County £120,000; October: Alan Maybury, Hearts £100,000

2002: Warren Feeney, Bournemouth (free), Kevin Dixon, Barnsley (free), Gareth Evans, Huddersfield Town (free).

Total income: £29.02 million.

Deficit on dealings: £66.28 million (approx).

LEEDS UNITED